hauntings

THE SUNY SERIES IN
POSTMODERN CULTURE

hauntings

POPULAR FILM AND AMERICAN CULTURE 1990–1992

Joseph Natoli

STATE UNIVERSITY OF NEW YORK PRESS

Published by
State University of New York Press, Albany

© 1994 State University of New York

All rights reserved

Printed in the United States of America

For information, address State University of New York Press,
State University Plaza, Albany, N.Y. 12246

Production by Marilyn P. Semerad
Marketing by Fran Keneston

Library of Congress Cataloging-in-Publication Data

Natoli, Joseph, 1943–
    Hauntings : popular film and American culture, 1990–1992 / Joseph
Natoli.
        p.   cm.
    ISBN 0-7914-2153-8 (acid-free paper). — ISBN 0-7914-2154-6 (pbk.
: acid-free paper)
    1. Motion pictures—Political aspects—United States.   2. Motion
pictures—Social aspects—United States.   I. Title.
PN1995.9.P6N37   1994   94-5027
302.23'43'0973—dc20   CIP

10   9   8   7   6   5   4   3   2   1

For my own private critics—

Elaine, Amelia and Brenda

TABLE OF CONTENTS

PROLOGUE

We are haunted by what we cannot fully identify, by what we cannot make identical to what we already are, have, and know. AIDS is visible, as is Jeffrey Dahmer, the South Central LA revolt, the dead eyes of Amy Fisher, the pubic hair in Clarence Thomas's Coke®, the Branch Davidian compound flaming in the distance, the flash of the Teflon Don, the greed of our Milkens, Geckos, and Garfields, the poisoning of our own planet, surgical strikes in Nam and now in Iraq, tribalism in Somalia and the Balkans. And much more.

Visible but unknown; unknown because its presence cannot be re-presented or rediscovered. Presence here does not show up in the mirror we hold up to what we already are. It has no place and we have no place for it. It is not a 'given' in our order of things. Visible but un-re-presentational. The only way for the visible to finally be re-presentational is for it to be recognized as part of what we have already recognized. We recognize it within the normal channels of recognition; we receive it within the normal channels of transmission and reception. We transmute it into what we already have, what is already 'given.'

Nothing is discovered; everything is rediscovered. Therefore we remain vulnerable. What is reworked into our own identity is not metamorphosed; its hold on us is not abated. Indeed, these efforts make us more vulnerable. For all our efforts to identify we remain at risk, more at risk the more we try. And this bitter truth is also known to us and haunts us.

Visible but not conceivable: what makes the visible representational in the sense of bringing about "something that hitherto did not exist as a given object"?[1] We cannot rely on our resident discourse of identifying because it necessarily identifies according to what mirrors the objects that already exist. It mirrors itself and by this means alone secures identity. How do we make conceivable to ourselves what is clearly visible to us in the headlines, on TV, and in popular film, but we cannot re-present in our mirror? How are we drawn into consuming and responding to what we cannot fit into what we already have around us, what we already say? The most haunting dimension of our cultural and personal undecidables lies in our failure to conceive their existence, identities that cannot be made identical to our own, even though the effects of their existence on our identity are too clearly visible to suit the composure of that identity.

We are, however, frequently brought into a play of that identity and what troubles it. Through that play we both reinforce our defenses against what haunts us and at the same time what haunts us becomes conceivable to us, perhaps incrementally. Perhaps we immediately defend against this new conceivability. But we are caught in a loop: we will be brought more frequently into play with this haunting material the more resolutely we seek to block off such play.[2]

The intensity of all this does not escape the market. Popular film plugs into this haunting power because it attracts a mass audience. We have no way of removing ourselves from the struggle; like dreamers haunted by a repetitive dream that holds us bound, we return to the scene each and every night. A by-product of popular film's marketing sense here is enacting what I call a "haunting movement" between our efforts to defend ourselves against what haunts us and our desire and need to confront it.

Popular film is not alone in thus making conceivable to us what haunts us; nor do all popular films bring us into this drama. Surely in popular film there is more defending against than tapping into; there is more holding up the mirror to what is already given than an engagement of the given and what haunts it. And yet in the three years (1990 to 1992) in which these essays were written I saw what haunted us in the headlines being performed in popular film. And in the process what was visible and yet unknown and un-representational became conceivable.

I have included an intermezzo essay that reengages some of the issues presented in this prologue. I present them midpoint because I do not want my theorizing or discoursing to displace the rather ludic and nondiscoursing tenor of my crisscrossing between film and American culture, or, more precisely, the headlines. At the intermezzo there may also be a need for me to defend the rhetorical performing of the essays themselves, perhaps not to a nonacademic audience, but certainly to an academic one. I must also mention as I proofread these essays here in the Spring of 1994 that I could easily update—who now is CEO of GM, a second King jury and so on. I refrain. These essays *are* provincial and provisional, in the flux of those moments. I will not pretend otherwise or assume that my interaction now both with the films and the culture is more objective, that I am approaching modernity's beloved "disinterestedness." Is there anything of "lasting" worth here? Will there be later on when a cultural historian can footnote more foundationally? Have I failed to connect the "accidental" with our culture's "eternal verities"? Our first haunting lies in these questions.

BASIC AND POSTMODERN INSTINCTS: THE NEW POPULAR REALISM IN FILM
SPRING 1992

Basic Instinct is a box office smash which, like all box office smashes, draws me like Michael Douglas, in the film, is drawn to Sharon Stone. Why?

If there is a provocative drama of disorder and order in a box office smash—and I believe such a drama is at the heart of all such successes today—our little and local way of looking at things works toward, but never succeeds in, keeping the noise down. The provocation gets deformed and transformed. Derrida says we make a *mythos* out of our own idiom and call it "universal reason" but it's still just provincial, regional, local.[1]

I say *if* there is this clash of order and disorder, it's because either the film or the culture or both may have already defended themselves against that performance of provocation. The film's viewers might already be positioned by both the culture and the film not to be able to view the real action. The film might be working strenuously to block off the play of its own disorder while such play is already blocked off from our view by the *mythos* of our own cultural idioms. We're thus blind to the struggle going on.[2] Asking if there is yet a struggle even though we don't see it is like asking whether a falling tree makes a noise even though there's no one there to hear it fall.

We have already been positioned in a certain way before we walk into the darkened theatre and take our seats. And yet in that darkened theater what is dark to us may draw us, fascinate us. What is suppressed slips past all defenses. What we struggle to leave out is what in fact draws us in such huge numbers to contemporary box office smashes. What is left out is what our culture is struggling to leave out.

I don't know how you prove these last two statements. Proving is like defending in that everything you don't want manages to slip through. It is only when you engage in a sort of crisscrossing, lateralizing foray that slipping *through* and slipping *by* are not disasters. They would be disasters if we held to some hierarchical (vertical) order of things in which the subsumed and resolved, the synthesized and relegated, would just pop up as intractable as ever. Now if there is no such determinate proving but only a plane of lateral crossings, then what was previously slipping by is now just meeting or intersecting in a sort of Borgesian garden-of-forking-paths journey. The more intersections the greater the likelihood that here indeed something was going on in the garden. I don't have to prove a statement about how popular films crisscross our culture. We just have to walk along the paths. We have to learn how to perform sidewise.

I forked off here. We were in the act of defending ourselves against popular film.

The greater our defending against what haunts us, the greater our vulnerability to what causes that defending. We can be drawn into changing our *mythos* channel as a new movement of light and shadow, of recognized and unrecognizable, brings our idiom before us as only an idiom, our reason and subjectivity before us as only constructs. Or, we can seize the opportunity to reconfirm and solidify the place we're already at by making everything that rolls before our eyes appear subject to our own subjectivity.

In the first instance—when we see how we have been positioned to see—we must be drawn out of the security of our own dominant viewing position and into the agonistics of the film that upsets that dominancy. In the second instance—when we repeat, "I'm alright Jack!"—the film lies before us as a sequence of action, a chain of signification, which is brought to meaning because it shares the viewer's linkage of word and world, *those* visuals and what *we* think they mean. Here the film sends its images on a channel we can receive and that channel is, of course, 'reality.'

In both instances we can be sure that the film that rolls has already 'rolled' us—it has already searched us, taken the measure of our worth, and identified our positioning as subjects. I mean that both the disruption of reality and the confirming of it are grounded in a working knowledge of which construct or *mythos* of reality already holds sway.

The question then is not "How do we interpret the meaning here?" or "How is reality interpreted here?" but rather "How does the film work in relation to the culture/society, and how does it work the viewer?" What is modeled as a sort of majority sense of order of how the real works? And, most important to me, what is tapped into as *not* working, or working *against*, or working *without* apparent connection to that real?

It may be that a box office smash film is either on one extreme or the other: either it totally enframes the prevailing *mythos* so that the viewer's sense of absolute domination and control brings her and the film along with her to a sort of high of identity confirmation, a sort of affirmative reality check; or, it taps into a disorder that the viewer cannot handle directly. The disorder film seems always to be transmitting against that disorder that it is at the same time making conceivable to us. In other words, for it to be seen at all it must be seen as transmitting an order that keeps the noise down. Paradoxically, that noise is coming through loud and clear. Such a film seems to be always putting off as unassimilable what the film has already been collaborating with.

If we were looking to categorize popular films in terms of this putting off and yet attending to, we would be searching for something in the film about which culture itself had nothing to say. In other words, the film would be making conceivable what the culture had not itself held as conceivable. The film would be bringing to a level of representation what has not already existed as a 'something' within the culture. The culture couldn't give us the means to categorize.

If we chose to search from the other end we would be looking for what both film and culture take for granted. But since this is all

we are able to identify anyway—identify in the sense of re-present-
ing what already exists for us—this would hardly be a search, a
critique, a categorizing, and so on.

When we are indeed searching for the play of order and disorder in film, we must recognize that a search is bound by present
narratives of both order and disorder. A retrieval therefore of past
dramas of order and disorder is a retrieval carried on by the priorities of the present.

Yet popular films do put off and play with the as-yet inconceivable. And we are, as viewers, the ones toward whom all this
putting off and taking on is directed.[3]

A film achieves its recognizable structure and its cultural identity by becoming one with the culture itself and one with the mass
subjectivity already constructed by that culture.[4] To see the film is to
be brought into the 'real-as-it-is' and to experience a clear mirroring
of one's own subjectivity. The more the culture seems carnivalized,
by which I mean contesting "little stories" (Lyotard's *petits recits*)
overspill any Big Controlling Story, the more the workings of order
within a film have stabilizing and therapeutic value.[5] They provide a
center that will hold, a home base to which we can return. Echoes of
home base strengthen a frame of real-izing that is true, though in
our postmodern world this frame is often beclouded, under attack,
overwhelmed, by disruptive narratives. There is a heroic import
given to all films that play with the fires of disruption only to quell
them simply by showing the real nature of things. If they were
literary texts they'd get canonized.

This is why the visual representations that simulate in every
way the order of the real world as concocted by a prevailing majority find a majority audience. Only a film that invests itself deeply in
that order and *shows* us that investment is capable of reaching that
majority. This is but one of the criteria a film must meet to become
truly popular. But it is essential. Truth has merely to be shown to be
believed.

If, however, this truth is not universal but coming out of some
cultural positioning, there is no way that either the social order or
the filmic order is doing more than cleverly putting off disorder and
its disruptions. It is the nature of all grand narratives, social and

aesthetic included, to have, at best, only a slippery hold on both a present notion of the real and subjectivity.

Disorder, then, is always an active if hushed participant because the order of reality in a film derives from the prevailing order of society at a particular time. That order is always struggling to keep at bay the forces of contingency, what Zygmunt Bauman calls the tropes of "the other of order." The tropes here are: "undefinability, incoherence, incongruity, incompatibility, illogicality, irrationality, ambiguity, confusion, undecidability, ambivalence." [6]

Within the Modernist Project this exchange between order and disorder is resolvable and it is resolvable because there is a universal, transcultural, and ahistorical truth out of which order emerges and in whose name disorder is always simply challenged as what's not yet ordered. Order is not so easily put aside. Again we have a reaffirmation that a film becomes box office not because it taps into disorder but rather because it taps into the truth.

Yet I have said that what our culture struggles to leave out draws us to certain films and makes them box office successes. Where's the truth here? I would argue that it is in the intensity of the play between already conceived notions of truth and what those notions have left out, what I call "disorder." Huge popularity attends films that draw a bead on what at any moment a culture wants to leave at an unsayable level. But that popularity also stems from the fact that the film's disruptions are enfolded and encased in such a way that the viewer's truth *mythos* is, if not endorsed, at least seduced.

We might think that film as part of popular culture shouldn't have to bear the weight of this truth mission. Isn't popular film just escapist entertainment, a seduction from the truth? Under the umbrella of postmodernism, film, along with all of popular culture, is no more seductive than high culture. All narratives become equally seductive in the sense that they tell compelling stories of the truth and inevitably lead us astray. High culture has gotten into the preservation of a culture's *mythos* as truth and reason business. Popular culture seems to be in both the preserving and the escaping business. While postmodernity wants to pay close attention to this 'double business,' modernity in this last quarter of the twentieth century invests little concern in what cannot reclaim and preserve the 'cultural legacy.' Unlike the high seriousness of the institution of literature, there has been no inherited, institutionalized, persevering-against-all-odds effort to canonize film. This is liberatory because film, as all popular culture, is not burdened by a high canonical *mythos* that it should bear from one generation to another.

While popular film remains popular by buying into popular truth, it has no commitment to the protocols of high serious art and *its* commitments to reinscribing universal truth. There is in popular film a greater license to traffic in the turmoil of our truth-making and *enjoy it* than there is in serious art that does not play with such turmoil but rather sets out to vanquish it.

Without having a stacked deck (what E. D. Hirsch calls "cultural literacy") forced on us, we now see what Catherine Belsey puts so clearly, that we have affirmed as universal and ahistorical, "as natural and inevitable both the individualism and the world picture of a specific class and a specific sex," that our truth has always emerged from "a very specific political position."[7] Contingencies have returned to contest our universal ordering.

And this contesting is box office. It's dynamite.

Our capacity to detect and analyze this contesting, I repeat, is limited by the priorities and perceptions of our own present ordering. Popular film is popular because it knows this; it shapes itself within the current scene. This doesn't mean we can grasp our own present contingencies. It just means they're *ours* and therefore we're going to take them personally.

What about past films?

We can't say anything about a past film that is not just another way of saying something about how we perceive our own present play of order and disorder. We are always where Borges places us in "Pierre Menard": not reading the Quixote but reading Menard's Quixote *which is word for word the original Quixote but its words are linked differently.* Perhaps we can go through the paces of the New Historicists: track down social texts that reveal a moment in the past and use them as a way of retrieving the play of order and disorder in past popular films.[8] In short, perhaps we can hold a past film bound to the discourse of its own day, but how can we keep that discourse unbound by a present discourse? Contingencies that escape a past order and still escape a present order are obviously not retrievable. Past contingencies that have now been transformed into solutions and resolutions of the present can indeed be seen at work in past films, but that very difference in perception and response undermines our attempt to retrieve a *past* relationship of order and disorder.

There is nothing disastrous, however, about reading the Quixote through Menard's identical rewrite of the Quixote; that is, linking the words of the Quixote to Menard's world, linking the signs of *Rebel Without a Cause* or *Duck Soup* to the world of the viewer. Anything else would be ungraspable and unseeable. Or it would be an imposition of power perhaps made in the name of preserving the past or enabling a common cultural communication grounded in common linkages of word and world. From a postmodern frame such an imposition suppresses the present in the name of a past that it cannot retrieve. The question to be asked by the postmodernist is, from what political positioning have these common cultural linkages been linked? What other and different linkages do these cultural linkages link themselves against?

This is our own present 'Menard frame': we now have an eye out for the linkages of order and the unlinkages of disorder, for identifiable connection of image and world and different and other connections of image and world. And we now employ this postmodern filtering lens when we say something about past popular film. When cultural paradigms change, as in our own shifting from modernity to postmodernity, there is a growing incommensurability between past and present narratives of order. There is more cause behind the young's impatience with old texts than a degeneration in literacy. It is part and parcel of the postmodern paradigm to both undermine the privileging of print and the *mythos* of reason that guided all past texts.

Films no longer signify, from our postmodern perspective, unless we can reattach their signifiers in ways those films may have actually ordered themselves against. We no longer value films because they identify order but because we can talk about their alignment of order and disorder. Talking about the fabrications of order and the disruptions of disorder is our postmodernist context, our own 'Menard' writing.

Since, however, the popular film, past and present, is not valued for its hermeneutical potential but for its immediate impact, past popular films, played out on another chessboard, within other rules of the game, become archival at best. They seem to be always taking the wrong turn, investing their energies in inertia, always caught up in some too predictable sequence of order. It is the transparency of their ordering that wears us down. Black and white becomes not an aesthetic matter—should original black and white films be colorized?—but a political one: the ordering here is too clear-cut, too absolutized, universalized, and objectified. It becomes a sign of the Modernist Project itself. The workings of that project make a present viewer restless, impatient, annoyed.

Our present postmodern 'Menard' context applies its own criteria to past films, although from logocentrism's centered view these are dismantling-criteria criteria. Nonetheless, postmodernity interrogates and unravels our modes of understanding, and there is something of the serious art enterprise involved here. But this is not a purely academic, cementing sort of endeavor because it offers the possibility of reentering the gambol of order and disorder in a past film.

We eye the ways our understanding puts off what defies that understanding. Such reentries make us wary and self-reflexive in the present. We would be learning nothing if we were already committed to recovering some diminished truth or reality of a past film and adding it to our ever-growing foundation of truth. We would be fooling ourselves if we thought we could just put aside the biases of the present and then critically and objectively distinguish chaff from kernel in past films. The horizon of our present seeing is the means by which we distinguish kernel from chaff. What has become popular are the ways we uphold and at the same time undermine the dream of an unchanging, determinate linking of image and world.

When we switch from the modernist paradigm that supports desires to attain some outside perspective on the truth and enter a postmodern paradigm, our critical priorities regarding past and present change. Distance does not give us a better slant on things, or widen

the cherished gap between subject and object, so that we can analyze more objectively. Past films are subject to present perceptions
anyway. There is no compulsion to efface present biases and impose
high critical standards. Present films not only get treated to present
perceptions but they arise out of present perceptions. They arise out
of newspaper headlines, not out of the wellsprings of high canonical
ordering. Therefore, we, the viewers, share a contemporary film's
playing with and putting off of our culture's fears and anxieties, its
worst nightmares. We are mutually haunted.

If our intent is to make conceivable what the present holds as
inconceivable—so as to balkanize our way of real-izing identity
through difference—then the popular film and its cozenage with the
present become more worthy of our attention than serious art, which
is either praised for its control of disruption or for its re-presentation
of the cultural legacy.

The cultural legacy of the past, that legacy whose prominence
cast popular culture into the dreck pile, film included, becomes from
a postmodern real-izing, a legislated analogue (a supplementary reading) that blocks off the play of order and disorder. The analogue sets
itself up in place of that play, or, more exactly, it becomes the site to
which all future play must finally wind up.

Postmodernity always wants to question the order we wind up
with, the analogue of meaning, and put before us contesting, alienat-
ing, disordering narratives and so return us to the action between
order and disorder. The fact that this is the representing frame we
find ourselves in prompts my interest in the popular box office success film. Why? Simply because the paradigm also drives our critical
response and a present classification of serious film. In other words,
we privilege a postmodern film of undecidability, of problematizing,
of advancing contingencies as steadfastly as problems and solutions.

Our postmodern discursive account of order and disorder therefore blocks off that play of order and disorder that is prediscourse,
that is yet play and not analogue of meaning. Paradoxically,
postmodernity is the frame out of which our anxieties regarding our
real-izing and our turn to the tropes of disorder emerge. We are left
with the following conclusion: an enabling discourse of disorder is
yet not that *play* of order and disorder we see, for instance, in the

popular film. Postmodern tenets may haunt Habermas's Modernist Project but they only open the doors to the ways popular film can possess our culture and our culture can possess film.[9]

We are already living within a life-world in which all affirmations have become citational, have become not truths but representations ideologically constructed. Whereas modernity had set up both a canon of confirmations of truth and a confirming methodology that provided a model for classic realism's illusion-ism—this *is* reality being shown here—postmodernity envisions reality as always narrated from within some particular narrative frame, upsets our sense of observing it all from the catbird seat (dominant specularity), and hinders us from sorting through a tangle of views and coming to a sure closure.

The classic realist formula—the means to make this film not a picture but reality itself—now is formulated, if you will, within the postmodern frame. Let's say that all this creates a postmodern atti-tude toward the real. We presently consume within this attitude and since box office is the site of enormous consumption, we are con-suming a provocation of the real. We are playing fast and loose with the real and at the same time being attracted by concealed notions of the real. The contemporary popular film has a sort of cultural carte blanche to evoke and disrupt clichéd realities. It also works up those off-limits linkages of image and world that the culture itself fails to represent. The popular film allows us to consume and respond to that play of order and disorder that is at that very moment overspilling the prevailing order's capacity to contain it.

In the same fashion that the film works without a discourse net, but rather works up a montage of stimulating loose ends, digs up and exposes the roots of the culture's own present demons, the viewer consumes without choosing or analyzing, responds without digesting or committing. What the culture has not yet brought to a level of re-presentation—in the sense that identifying is always a rediscovery of what order already has—is not brought to us as a given in the popular film. Our consuming is sufficient because it makes conceivable to us what yet remains unsayable in us and in our culture. It is only such powerful interchanges of the conceivable and the inconceivable, these unsayable repasts, which drive a culture, already supersaturated with visual loose ends, with meaning as sound-bytes, to the ticket lines of popular films.

There is undoubtedly in the popular film the same sustained effort at bringing this play to order as there is in the culture itself. But now there is a lateral pursuit of illicit and repressed notions of truth and meaning with only a pro forma sort of gesturing toward a coherent reality. Any progression from point of origin to closure is no longer box office, a shopworn article that a pomo audience has lost patience with.

BASIC INSTINCT

It is the intensity of play between order and disorder that sells tickets and not merely the presence of such play. That degree of intensity, unlike its presence that I shall now talk about, I cannot talk about. Nevertheless it inspires the talking.

How does this film work in relation to the culture? What unsayables of our culture does the film traffic in? Since we are always entering the play of the text from within our own cultural framing, we are therefore always beginning from the culture side. And that's where I shall begin.

Both feminists and lesbians have attacked *Basic Instinct* for its portrayal of lesbians as man-haters and serial murderers. For them there is nothing of the unsayable in this film: the film says the wrong thing or, more accurately, it shows lesbians within a stereotypic frame that further confirms the stereotype. Lesbian critics have hailed this as yet another example of a homophobic Hollywood, exploitation of a whole life-world for market reasons. Lesbians, in protest, stand outside theaters urging potential ticket buyers to change their minds and boycott the film.

The connections a majority audience makes between the signifier "lesbian" and world/meaning/reality are endorsed and not questioned by the film. In this fashion the film links itself to a mass-market audience at the price of the lesbian minority. The manipulation is rudimentary classic realist: when Michael Douglas, the subjectivity through which our own subjectivity is situated, engages Roxy, Sharon Stone's lesbian lover, man to man and calls her

"Rocky," his wit elicited a number of laughs from my audience, a Heartland audience that I say something about in another chapter. *We* were clearly putting her in her place, returning the challenge of the hate and anger in Roxy's eyes with a mocking, "Fuck you, bitch. I'm not scared of you."

That line is put in our heads; it's unsaid in the film. Why do I say it now? It seems to me part of the unsayable dimension of the film. Nick, Douglas's character, has just had what he will later describe as "the best fuck in the universe" and has gotten up from bed, walked stark naked into the bathroom with the camera tracking from behind. We watch as he throws water on his face and grabs a towel. And then Roxy is there, fully clothed, leathers, beautiful, intimidating, hostile. She's watched their lovemaking. Nick is a rival. She's seen other bouts of lovemaking but Nick is the rival who really worries her. Nick is special, privileged—which is all right with us in the audience because that makes us special, privileged.

She is clearly threatening; clothed while he is naked, although the camera plays on Nick's upper torso fleetingly, not a full view, always shadowed. The torso looks pumped up. I don't recall Douglas having any sort of a build in any of his other movies. The walk into the bathroom had been a cock of the walk strut, in shadows. If there are love handles to his waist the camera finesses them. He's a good male specimen but endangered. What will she do? Kick him in the balls since they are exposed to her? Will she do him violence? That is how the scene is played and that drama creates the scene's tension. "I'm not scared of you" is its unwritten, unsaid caption: Masculine . . . , heterosexual order here. But there's fear nonetheless. The film is hot-wired to it.

Let's go back into the culture. Sick, gratuitous violence makes this a "Don't-Bother-to-See-It" movie people tell me after they've all told each other not to see it and have gone ahead and seen it and now tell me not to see it and I've seen it and am already excited enough by it to write about it. We say we are already culturally sated with cinematic violence but violence now in our own culture has an imaginative force that dismisses our words. The more we decouple ourselves from the rest of nature, the more we are attempting to decouple ourselves from its contingencies, its devastation and disasters, its unprogrammable violence and destruction. Our own mortality haunts us. It is a force of nature we project on our screens. The violence of *Basic Instinct* has such force. It has an edge to it, or in my way of talking, it's a violence that attracts us but we are loathe to describe the attraction. We legislate against it.

The murder with which the film begins may be one in a series, a series whose point of origin never really becomes clear, and whose ending may or may not coincide with the ending of the movie. In the ending, the camera pans down to the ice pick lying underneath the bed, within Sharon Stone's reach and in that scene she seems always to be reaching for it. Or is she? Is the ice pick hers? Is the violence hers? Must we go back and dismantle the story we seemed finally able to tell about her—that she wasn't the murderer, that the violence wasn't hers, that she was simply lost and now has found her way, her man, found real love, which is heterosexual love?

No, the ending rather asks us to leave the theater with one of three stories. The first as I have described it—a story of undecidability. The second as follows: she is the murderer, the violence is hers, she is a brilliant psychopath who has set up the police psychologist and who will eventually use that ice pick on Nick. When she will use it and why she will use it and why she already has used it takes us into her life-world, a life-world that it turns out we cannot enter and cannot share. It is deviant and that deviance is connected richly and deeply. It lies in her directness, her candor, her failure to align herself within social conventions and expectations. She likes sex. She has sex with anyone she wants. Society can't police her. What are they going to do? Arrest her for smoking? Does her great wealth give her that freedom? She puts no restraints on her sexuality, turning to men as well as to women.

The third story also enacts the tensions of the whole film: she has used the ice pick to murder, she is a brilliant psychopath, she has refrained from murdering Nick. The film ends and we have seen her make moves toward the ice pick on the floor but not pick it up. Nick has won her over. Love has put pathology into check. They *will* live happily ever after though without the rug-rats, the kids, which Nick foresees. In this story, as in the others, we have a play between a not abrogated masculinity, a normalizing heterosexuality, a boy-gets-girl kind of romance *and* a troubling femininity, a challenging lesbianism, a love that turns men's bodies to ice, men's pricks to picks in women's hands.

The undecidability of the ending makes the whole film undecidable and therefore not able to be funneled toward a firm ending. We don't end choosing a story; we get caught up in a story we can't end. The story we leave with is not just a story. It's a chart of the way the film plays us, or, how we are brought both with our consent *and* against our will into the play of the film. We are drawn into what remains unsaid in our culture and what the film doesn't want to say. Nonetheless, our culture is already fortifying itself against what lies unsaid and the film's popularity lies in its putting "out there" what the culture doesn't want to say.

The male bonding between Nick and his partner, Cowboy, which draws upon all cop hero-sidekick bondings in cinematic history right up to Mel Gibson and Danny Glover, is not there for its own sake but only to position us defensively. Against what? Against a woman who plays her scenes in cool disdain, in open mockery of such a bonding. But this defense doesn't hold the line and her offense doesn't seem to be in their rule book. She's playing outside the rules of the game.

Our whole postmodern culture is in a state of defending itself against both its past violence to the life-worlds of women and holding off a saying of "what rough beast slouches toward Bethlehem to be born." The question is: What new woman lies on the horizon who is not caught within the masculine narrative and also is no longer hindered by having to respond to it? What ways of love and sexuality will this woman narrate for herself? And when women fall out of the romantic conquest, boy gets girl, how defenseless—like Nick tied to the bed—will men be?

Sharon Stone's steely composure, her self-awareness, her charisma, her dominance challenge and threaten. Her love can be dangerous because it has not yet been scripted by our culture. In the culture this remains frozen. In the film it is brought into play. Our consuming is a sign of being drawn into that play; our being drawn in is evidenced by our response—we make the film a box office success.

Love's capacity to conquer all plays badly in this film. Is Nick in love with the psychologist? If he is, we don't see romantic lovemaking. We see love as rough trade. Sex and violence get linked as Nick slams her hard, pulls her, rips at her clothes, angry, as if there were more hate here than love. He has already met Sharon Stone. He has seen the man she may have murdered. A naked man struck over and over again with an ice pick. That is the scene the film opens with: sex and then sudden violence. The link is the lesbian, the beautiful, alluring, but dangerous woman. Playing with her is like playing with fire, playing with death. Out of Eros comes Thanatos.

Again we are dealing with our own culture's unsayable. Out of the sex act now comes possible death. The sex act is now haunted by the AIDS virus. We never know for sure as we lay back in a post-coitus daze whether this now is also death striking. We trust and we thrust; whether the ice pick will puncture a hole and let death run through is precisely what we cannot represent to ourselves as we lose ourselves in the ecstasy of the 'act of love.' At the end of every act of love, our lover looms above us with an ice pick; death is in the climax. But is it? Perhaps the ice pick will remain unused. Only Eros penetrates here. Death lies checked, on the floor, unpenetrating. For how long? When does it enter?

Is this too far-fetched, too much 'Menard'? In our culture what AIDS is doing to love and sex, or, more precisely, how AIDS is forcing us to relink these signifiers to new, and other meaning, can only be said within the links that have already structured our perceptions, our thoughts, our affections. We are, in other words, structured against such conceivability. The film brings that into play, taps into the power of such a drama between what we want to hold as just another re-presentation and what has to break that hold and show us what is fundamentally different and other.

The film begins with the sexual act and then the violent, sudden, unexpected, murder. When the police run through the apartment for clues they surround the bed with the naked male victim lying there. We get as quick a shot of his genitalia as we do later of Sharon Stone's as the police interrogate her. Did we see what we think we saw? Genitalia are there like in a porno film to be seen but the seeing here is more potent than in any porno in a pre-AIDS age and culture. Seeing, viewing, showing are what we are left with as safer courses. Sex through the eye. The film not only links sex with violence and death but seeing the film make these linkages already taps into the place our culture has retreated to in regard to sex—the eye, the act of seeing. Viewing the opening scene sex act is more charged than any prior seeing. And the genitalia we see for a split second haunt us because we can't have our old way of seeing them and we don't have a Death's way of seeing them.

The police surrounding the bed speak of the ample semen covering the sheets, mentioning the prowess as well as the evident pleasure, the success the dead man must have had. His lovemaking was a success but led to death. Death lies in the semen lying there on the sheets. Later, in an offhand riposte to Cowboy, Nick says, "I didn't even wear a rubber." How to explain Cowboy's drunken berating of Nick, his fear that Nick has destroyed himself by taking up with Catherine Tramell? Death traces back to her. The femme fatale. The woman who enjoys sex and whose sex leads to murder. The woman already feared, who challenges the order of masculinity, must also in this film link together—within her own pathological-because-inconceivable being—sex and death.

The culture once again: the order from the center, the panoptic ordering, is heterosexual and patriarchal, but in our postmodern culture that center is no longer a place to rest, the place where traditionally classic realism rests. Nor is it a place that must continuously and repeatedly draw into itself through either a critical or communal consensus the tropes of the other of order, the project of modernism. The whole American culture is now looking back to the center, some nostalgically, some angrily, so that there is an awareness of keeping ourselves there as well as an awareness that we are already someplace else. Once heterosexuality stands before us as a construct we are already either posed to defend it or posed to deconstruct it. The center for the majority of viewers now is a defense of the center, a defense that already admits the power of the unsayable.

Whereas a short time ago we could, under the spell of the Great Communicator, be drawn to films that centered the romance of returning to the center, we are now recession weary, AIDS fearing, abortion divided, environment sick, and in the spring of 1992, presidential campaign disgusted. What plays on the popular level is the play of our worst fears, our most pathological linkages, our most cruel 'final solutions.' But they are played in no order, toward no purpose, with no expressed intent, except to make millions, to make our life-world dependent upon seeing this film. And herein lies the power of the popular film to put before us not only our cheapest thrills but our present overspilling of what previously sufficed as our cultural order, its purpose and intent.

The situation is clear: the film market itself now depends upon the play of order and disorder. There is no way the film can find or assert a place for the viewer to rest. While the film seems to rest in love, sexuality, and men and women as we've always had them, the film for the sake of its very popularity dare not rest in these. They are set in motion and the ensuing tensions shape forbidden connections of image and world. We are consuming our psychotic 'projects of resolution' as well as learning to live with what was a short while ago inconceivabilities regarding gender and sexuality, love and death.

Catherine Tramell and Roxy are given up as in a witch trial: lesbian sex does violence to 'normal' sex and romantic love, to the role of the hero and his conquest of the heroine, to the future of families, of child-rearing and living happily ever after. Lesbian sex does violence to happy endings, or endings that bring a sense of closure, rarely achieved in life but almost a necessity in popular films. Lesbian sex is violence and in this film sex leads to violence that leads to death. The death that lurks in sex is there because aberrant sex has put it there. There is a reason why lesbians and all feminists protest this film.

But the film does not rest in this psychotic linkage nor does it push it forward as the film's discourse, or parody it in its own self-reflexive metanarrating of itself. Rather, as I have described, the film throws out lines in multiple directions toward a new woman already exceeding what we are able to say about her; toward love, sex, and gender that have already slipped past our chain of signification; toward love, sex and death that our culture has no way of linking but that nature has already linked for us.

HUNTING THE HAUNTED HEART
JULY 1991

I believe the lawless social anarchy which we saw is directly related to the breakdown of family structure, personal responsibility, and social order in too many areas of our society.

—Dan Quayle

The Rodney King jury was held bound by a fear of Rodney King. You might say it's a fear that haunts them. It's a fear that leads to building prisons and reinstituting capital punishment. It's a fear that caused the town of Springfield, Oregon, to pass a proposal forbidding its residents from "facilitating, encouraging, or promoting homosexuality, sadism, masochism, and pedophilia."[1] It's a fear that provoked Cambridge University faculty to oppose the conferment of an Honorary Degree of Doctor of Letters on Jacques Derrida because his ideas "make complete nonsense of science, technology and medicine" and in politics "they deprive the mind of its defences against dangerously irrational ideologies and regimes."[2]

It's a fear that our property, our investments, and our homes won't be left alone, that sexuality will roam outside heterosexuality, that women unchained from heterosexuality will find a new identity and become a danger to men, that traditional family values will become just an archaic lifestyle choice, one whose values are far from self-evident, that the cultural legacy will be forgotten and our children will stand indifferent before what threatens that culture.

All that threatens us today have become undecidables. They haunt us. And when the culture asserts itself in the act of overcoming them all that results are boring tableaus, natura morta, to be switched off with a flick of a remote control. Severing ourselves from our hauntings, we are all dead-method. Everything loses its edge just as the murdered girl's body in *The River's Edge* loses its moral significance. Trim edges, sharp, Euclidean angles, clear and distinct boundaries, paths of progression, unblurred Boolean decisions, a clear-cut two-party system, a quantifiable distance from subject to object, definite lines of accountability, of gain and loss all seem like so many arbitrary narratives trying to hold their own at the Mad Hatter's tea party.

The great fear is that we've lost sense. We sense too clearly that sense is not something we have and fear losing but some place we've been that history has built for us. It has an outside and an inside and we want to remain inside. We fear what is outside our own narrative of sense and sensibility, a fear of a different valuing, a different real-izing, a real-izing of difference, a fear of the abyss. What haunts this Otherness draws us like moths to a flame because *this* fabrication of sense has been there all along, waiting. This sense of the Other must be defended against at all costs but at the same time it is like a return to play after having been blocked from such play for too long.

There is a diminishing élan vital to our erection of self, society, and natural world out there. Just as the conscious mind barricaded against its own life forces, against Eros,[3] slips past its own barricades in dream and loses itself in a play of order and disorder, of consciousness and unconsciousness, so too does a whole culture slip past its own defenses, its own logic and decrees, to haunt the Otherness that haunts it. Not in the way we sought Otherness on an enlightened path when its incommensurability could be ignored because its impenetrability was merely pending solution.

Aberrance was a problem to be solved, a presence spurring the Modernist Project onward.[4] Always aberrance was just that: a registered deviation from identity, virtually powerless against that identity. Not to reduce to identity was to deny identity and therefore deny 'being.' The unidentified could always be good for a laugh. Or a fright—a modulated, tempered fright. Otherness would fall within the classic realist formula as easily as anything else.[5] In fact, Hollywood made more money off classic realist difference and Otherness (right up to *1492*, in which the Indians look like caricatured World War II Japanese) than romance and violence.

In the postmodern world Otherness haunts us differently; the classic realist formula always cracks and Otherness takes over the final frame, mocking classic realist dichotomies. Late modernism inquires and mocks its own inquiry. Oddly, though, it expects an unmockable grasp—momentary at best in Wallace Stevens' view— of identity and Otherness in the end. However, the haunting of Otherness won't stand still as an object of inquiry but rather already invests the inquiry, just like we can't get the heath out of Heathcliff. Both nature and self are already intertwined and Heathcliff's difference is also what makes nature always different than our stories about nature.

In *Silence of the Lambs*, Crawford, Clarice Starling's FBI father figure, tells Clarice that she's to visit Hannibal Lecter because he, as a psychopath, may be able to shed some light on the workings of the mind of another psychopath, Buffalo Bill. But in order to keep Lecter from getting inside her mind she is told to follow procedures and instructions to the letter. She doesn't want Hannibal Lecter inside her mind. That's all the inducement we need to look forward to meeting Lecter, that alien being who has the capacity to get into our heads and who is strangely different than anything we already have in our heads.

Clarice preserves the distance, unlike William Peterson who pursues Lecter in Hannibal's first film appearance, *Manhunter*. Peterson, the detective in that film, is able to enter Lecter's lifeworld[6] and the visit leaves him haunted. It is not by objective methodology that Otherness will be reached but through empathy with the narrative world or frame within which subjectivity is constituted and through which the real is configured. Subjectivity intersects subjectivity. Objectivity blocks off that intersection. But Clarice remains a good modernist detective, finally graduated into the world of investigation, and as such a preserver of the distance between investigator and investigated.

At the same time, she has clearly not apprenticed under Crawford alone but also under Hannibal the Cannibal. It is his alien Otherness that directs her and leads her to her climactic success— killing Buffalo Bill and saving the senator's daughter, the one lamb-victim she is finally able to save. Such a salvation salvages her own childhood self. All lambs, including her, are not necessarily victims to the slaughter, lost when their families are lost, lost when their father is killed. That lost inner child can be redeemed by a vigorous and sustained effort, by moving laterally into the perceptions and affections of Otherness. In this way Clarice brings disparate reality to sense.

But this is not the sense they want to preserve at Cambridge and in Springfield, Oregon. Clarice is guided by Hannibal's sense, the sense of the Other, sense other than what we can sense, or reach through the sense we already have. Intriguing. Lecter wants Clarice to know that he's out and that he won't harm her because he likes to think that she's also out there. He hasn't taken over her mind. They've intersected. Instead of maintaining the distance between them, instead of keeping him far below in the bowels of the sanitarium, she has gotten into a sort of play with him, a game of quid pro quo. In short, they cross paths.

Easily said—"they cross paths." Doesn't knowledge ensue? If identity crosses difference, what new arrangement is made? What is rearranged? Is Lecter a sort of crabwise roamer away from conventional expectations? And how could Clarice roam laterally since she never gives up the path of an investigative, pursuing modernism? They play quid pro quo, a postmodernist "Truth or Dare" through which Lecter leads Clarice away from the main highway of her investigation and onto sideroads. And it is through the maze of these sideroads that Clarice winds up eventually at Buffalo Bill's door. It takes her a while to realize that that is where she is. Lateral thinking isn't supposed to take you to modernism's destination but here the postmodern trek and the modernist goal, if it were ever able to fulfill its mission, wind up at the same door. I say *if*, because Crawford and the FBI on a plane loaded with high-tech pursuit equipment wind up at the wrong door. They wind up going places their technology can identify. Only tangential thinking takes you to the right door. Otherness, then, is the answer to waste and inefficiency, to entropy?

Lecter doesn't *lead* Clarice onto windward paths because he is himself not positioned either ahead or above her. His position is just tangential to the norm, a path away from the social order we invoke because we haven't the means to identify his precise location. We can't plug him into the equation until we know where he is and we only know where he isn't. Consider the fact that he is brilliant. He has a penetrating mind, gathers, sorts, and responds to lived experience at a phenomenal rate. Is he then an Enlightenment modernist? He conducts a course in logic for Clarice. Is he therefore sane? The jury ruled that Jeffrey Dahmer was sane because his crimes demonstrated all the joys of the scientific method. He could have made major contributions to the Foundationalist Project. Lecter already has as a practicing psychiatrist, as Dr. Lecter. Perhaps he has written papers or read papers at prestigious conferences all over the world.

Reason, Nietzsche tells us, is a pawn, a strumpet, an instrument in any hands. The desire for unity, coherence, and continuity is a cultural desire. You can summon reason and logic to fulfill it. You can also summon logic and method to fulfill madness, which then gives to madness that coherence and so on that is *other* than what society says it desires. Jeffrey Dahmer's means are rigorous and methodical but the ends make our stomachs turn. Zygmunt Bauman connects the holocaust with the same sort of modernist method.[7]

The modernist narrative latches on to reason and method. In its twentieth-century form modernity increasingly distances itself from these as the historical record fills with atrocities and inanities performed within reason's frame. Crawford and the FBI are wary Enlightenment modernists and practicing twentieth-century modernists as they turn to Lecter to give them a perspective on their problem. Multiple perspectives, not only from the conscious, rational mind but from nightmare and the unconscious, are needed if the problem is to be solved. Method turns to madness, Clarice to Lecter.

Since Lecter does not share that which makes a modernist a modernist—not the use of reason but a shared story about integration, solution, social bonds and mutual alignments, stabilizing class and community structures, shared ideologies and ethics and so on—

he lies outside that story, however dynamic and efficient his mental powers. And since his *mythos* of reason is other than the *mythos* of our culture it is not possible to use reason and method to track him down. For our reason to be seen as reasonable it must always operate within our *mythos*. The same goes for Lecter—he can't be reasonable the way we can be reasonable. Reason is denied that outside-our-*mythos* role that would enable it to roam free, scrutinize Lecter, and come back and give us a report. What it does is quite different: it stays home, scrutinizes Lecter from a distance, and gives us a home report.

In the game of quid pro quo both sides seem to be probing outward into the other. But the 'this' and 'that' reveal different probing devices and different results. Hannibal feasts on Clarice's mind within feasting rites that never change. If he were able to sidestep through a postmodern garden of forking paths everything that makes him Godlike—his self-assuredness, his certainty and decisiveness, his command and control, the very fixedness of his gaze outward, penetrating like a laser beam fixed on one target—all this would grow shaky as one way of seeing would trouble, or parody, another.

No, our Hannibal is a brilliant classic realist, his mode of being as stabilized and pinned to one frame of realizing as his physical being is locked deep down in the bowels of the asylum prison behind steel bars and thick glass. He fixes Clarice within a stranglehold of a gaze replenishing his own *mythos* of order and reason as he feasts through the eye and into the mind. While the Biblical Jehovah moved to creation to strike an Otherness to his own unity, Hannibal's unity pursues only itself. We see him at film's end pursuing his one way of feasting on what is out there.

Crawford's *mythos* of reason is shaky; otherwise he would not turn to Hannibal. Clarice's neutrality as a modernist investigative observer and interrogator is weakened by her own troubled 'silence of the lambs' life-world, a life-world she is led to examine through Hannibal. But Hannibal himself is neither shaken nor troubled; he makes absolute, determinate connections with the world. He assumes his representations *are* reality. He feasts without variety, identity has a stranglehold on him. That he cannot move sideways, cannot get off the track he is on, is at the heart of his madness.

Hannibal Lecter is confident and assertive, sure of himself, the way Ross Perot is. Neither one waffles, which is what President Bush seemed to be doing every time the media looked his way. Perot wouldn't let Lecter get in the way. He'd put him behind thicker glass and stronger bars. And Lecter might bite off Perot's nose if it was on his menu. Any voice that promises mastery without a trace of waffling fascinates us amid this postmodern "radiation of parody, kitsch, and burnout."[8] But we can't disassociate that mastery from modernism: Lecter has all the gifts modernism holds as its ideal. He fascinates because he is other than that cultural identity that is waffling. At the same time he is bigger than life, a fantastic version of the dominance and supremacy over the real that modernity always promised. In the end, Hannibal is an Otherness told within the modernist frame, a bright superhero whose lack of conscience and emotion is a sign of being value-free and theory-neutral. His cinematic presence was haunted first by modernity before it haunted us.

Yet in admiring him at film's end, by rooting for him, by being glad he's still out there, we erode a bit further those firm moral categories, that clear sense of what's civilized and what isn't, what's sane and what isn't, which seem to be our only defense against Hannibal. We wind up waffling. Hannibal's absolute, coherent Otherness loses its firmness; it gets fuzzy around the edges. Otherness, like everything else, fractures, breaks up into tiny rivulets that wind every which way, crisscrossing endlessly like a flashflood in a dry arroyo. On the underside of a smooth surface there are always cracks and fissures. You can see the seams of our real-izing, the stitches that make Otherness a Frankenstein-monster and us always *Dr.* Frankenstein—the real identity.

When we are really haunted, Hannibal Lecter dissolves into us, difference is fingering our identities, Otherness in the most terrifying films is breaking out of us like the *Alien 3* incubus out of Sigourney Weaver's Ripley. She plunges toward death, clasping the emerging alien fetus close to her. This Otherness must die even if the woman we have identified with for three films has to die with it. There seems to be no pact with Otherness here. Mother and child perish.

The abortion issue is killing us. The interpretation behind the sign of 'woman' our culture has traditionally identified insinuates itself into the sign of the 'fetus.' To be free of that interpretation, that alien identity, is to have power over the fetus that becomes something Other than woman's body. The fetus is already linked to a whole representation of woman that women protest. The fetus, in other words, has been alienated from woman's body by the prevailing order of interpretation, endless sequels, endless chaining.

There is no doubt that the social order has created a fetus that haunts women. To give birth endlessly to what the social order identifies is now for women to give birth to an alien being. And yet that alien Other is doubly coded: it is both woman's most awesome creation and already an identity shaped and positioned by the social order. But the haunting is women's, not men's, as evidenced in the initial dismissal by an all-male Senate committee of Anita Hill's charge of sexual harassment as well as by the "abortion is not an important issue" stand taken by candidates for the 1992 presidential election.

Men remain haunted by multiple-birthings away from the unity of their own identity and thus the order of their own cultural interpretations. While the male-dominated social order is on the edge of its seat, fascinated with the ways its own images are fracturing up there on the screen, women are fractured images within that social order, like Clarice Starling, turning from that traditional father figure Dan Quayle supports—Jack Crawford—and toward the Otherness of Hannibal the Cannibal. On this path, Lecter becomes an Otherness the social order ostracizes but Clarice moves toward. Thus, Hannibal Lecter is resistant to the impositions of that order. His sexuality is feasting, neither male nor female. In the end he slouches in a blonde wig toward his prey, a man.

At some other time and in some other place we should follow the money, but here and now we follow the men who follow what haunts them and the women who follow the men who haunt them. This journey fascinates us: a journey to a root, untroubled identity, an identity that can be reupholstered so as to hold Otherness at bay, that can restring our moral fiber, and keep down lawless social anarchy. And, most deeply, to dispel the hauntings of the heart.

It begins this way in *Angel Heart:* there is always a firm ID—Harry Angel, private investigator. This is not a federal case but a private one. Otherness is not out there in some part of the country, not public but private. The self harbors an Otherness it represses but now this Otherness is rooted in contingency. The whole force of selfhood and consciousness is set against such contingency. There is no birth of any self-awareness, you might say, if contingency is factored into being, if it's costed in at the outset, which it can't be. Otherness is fathered by contingency.

If you are the Prince of Tides you can go back far enough and find a beginning, a cause, a reason why you can't connect to those you love, a reason why you've got to keep running from certain thoughts, certain memories. If you are Harry Angel—played by Mickey Rourke's charismatic, embedded alienness—and you go back far enough you find a pact with De Niro as Lucifer. In order to become a success—the singing sensation Johnny Favorite—you made a deal with Lucifer and in order to get out of that bargain you found an innocent victim, Harry Angel, cut him open, ripped out his heart, and ate it. By eating it you became Harry Angel. Lucifer wouldn't be able to find you and claim your soul. You gave up your identity and took another.

And then you lost your memory in the war and when you came back you had only one memory—that you were Harry Angel. You find when you go back far enough that your identity is grounded in madness, that Lucifer intervened in causality, interrupted the flow of sense, and you came forward and made a deal with him. Johnny Favorite, the self who makes the deal, becomes an unfathomable horror, an Otherness who dips into black magic and conjures up the devil. The identifiable self is not your own but since it makes sense it is the only identify you have. You can't have an identity within that stochastic difference of the other self, the self without sensible origin.

How fractured and troubled is Harry! Never to be a Prince of Tides who can reach far back and translate a contingent event— rape—into a trauma to be resolved. But you managed to do one thing—you killed your own daughter. But *her* daughter remains alive, staring at us with eerie, luminous eyes. Johnny Favorite tried to escape Lucifer but in the end he's there in that young girl's eyes. The male identity splits open and a hunt for its original primal unity leads into unfathomable contingencies. The male order of interpretation that constructed women as extensions of that order will no longer do.

Women now stand forth as possessed, as Lucifer's. Their released Otherness has the eyes to haunt men. Johnny Favorite/Harry Angel plunges into the abyss but not until he has savaged the bodies of women and exposed them for all to see as Lucifer's consorts. When male identity collapses, as well as the *mythos* that it creates, it slashes at that serpentine Otherness that conspired with women so as to plot the fall of man.

A woman saves the Prince of Tides, Nick Nolte, in the Streisand film *Prince of Tides*, a woman psychiatrist—Streisand as Dr. Lowenstein—who originally encounters our Prince only peripherally. She is treating the Prince's sister and hopes that the Prince will tell her something that may help her. The sister has her blocked off. She can't reach into the play of order and disorder in that mind. But Lowenstein forks off perspicaciously onto the Prince's trail and there, finally, she has more success. He cracks the 'rosebud,' if you will, for her—sister, brother, and mother were raped by three escaped convicts many years before.

If we go back far enough there will be such a place, such a moment, such a configuration that if unraveled will lead us to an explanation of what we are in the present. Or, more exactly, what we can no longer be in the present. The haunting of the heart here can be charted; there's a certain tide that can take you out and back to where you want to be—to a connection of identity and order that existed before it became obscured by contingency, by being in the path of the escaped prisoners.

Nick Nolte becomes the Prince of Tides; he rules the tides, because, with Lowenstein's help, he manages to assert a determinate order of being-in-the-world, an identity stabilized by fixed connections between self and world. And by doing so he conquers the contingent and stochastic. The rape only conceals for a time that determinate order. What haunts the Prince is an order infected by disorder, a childhood interrupted by nightmare. That disorder overshadows the monologue of order. The Prince as an adult cannot function as a son, as a husband, as a father, as a teacher.

It is only when order is resurrected, when the tides are once again his to command, when the tide comes in, that the Prince is reilluminated. Like Keanu Reeves in *My Own Private Idaho*, a Prince Hal whose tide comes in, Nick Nolte can now accede to the throne. He is heir to the throne of his own un-haunted self. If method, if interpretation, if analysis can't overcome the contingencies that bombard the self then the Modernist Project is not just incomplete. It's failed. It's a bum: "It could have been somebody."

Not surprisingly, when men become Princes of Tides, men don't feel that women have to be ripped apart and made the devil's companions. Let's follow the women.

We see the wife, the mother, the shrink, the sister—in that order, the Prince's order of relationship. The wife has been long-suffering in silence. The Prince can't or won't communicate. He jokes *around* saying something. No intersection. No intercourse. He's been slipping slyly past the most intimate relationship in his life. And we know why but let's try to focus on the wife. She brings up the issue; he runs off down the beach. What is she haunted by? That the Prince doesn't love her anymore? That she's no longer lovable? I have to be loved by someone. Otherwise there's a hole in me, an empty space. There's no me. So she finds someone else to love and tells the Prince that she's through with him. He can't blame her. He can't speak words of holding on when he's simultaneously trying to slip by her. He can't assent to anything. He's too busy denying something "really, really big."

Maybe the wife has some freaky encounters in her own life that have nothing to do with the Prince. But they don't matter here. We can assume that she got into adulthood in good order, except when her husband turns joksy and slippery on almost every subject. Then she's got to find another man to fill in the gap that we didn't know was there. Being in good order was having the Prince there in a pivotal position, a psychic cornerstone.

Now the Prince is hostile toward his mother because she wouldn't let the Prince and his sister assent to that very adventitious event in their lives—being raped by the escapees. She didn't get joksy or slippery about it. She just locked the aleatory away, threw it into the lake, let it sink. Out of sight, out of mind. Family order as usual. But Prince's father, the King, is an arbitrary, nasty son-of-a-bitch whose wife cooks him up some dogfood to get even with him. But King likes the meal. Maybe he wouldn't like it if he knew it was dogfood but the mother and the children keep quiet about it. It's their secret. One secret—giving King dogfood—is a sort of healing. The other secret—getting raped by the escapees—is haunting. It's as if some other nasty sons-of-bitches crashed into their house and violated them just as unexpectedly as their father always did, except this aimless brutality is the epitome of violations of familial love and family order.

Princes become kings and kings are sexual violators. The Prince spends his marriage trying to slip by having sex/violating his wife.

We're off on the Prince again. We fork back to the mother. If the rape is the final blow to the family order, the violation of love that cannot be made right, and if that order must be preserved (read: the King must not be dethroned), then the violation has to be locked away. The mother has always been a romantic dreamer. And her dream is this: she's going to be somebody. She becomes somebody by divorcing the King and marrying a wealthy man, a man who has also been cruel to the Prince when the Prince was young. No father in this film abides by the family order Dan Quayle wants him to. But this King is rich and when the mother marries him, she shares his wealth. She finally becomes somebody. You might say it's her reward for preserving the patriarchal family order. She keeps it a secret that the King, any King, is mad, that marriage to the King is full of ups and downs, that various turns of chance come out of the arbitrary order the King wants to call "family order." The King is the first victim of his own sham. He has clothes but we can't assent to his order because it's invisible.

So far the women aren't doing too well. Uncertainty and indeterminacy are waiting to fill the vacuum left when the King is dethroned. Only when the Prince is put back together is the kingdom of order restored. All the women wait while he accedes to the throne. It's getting to be a very tired paradigm.

In comes Barbra Streisand to the rescue. She's a brainy shrink with nice legs. The legs are privileged. They get the best camera angles. They cross right behind our view of what's wrong with the

Prince. Maybe we can finally cross over to somebody else's path, an order of women. Maybe.

The brains and the legs, analysis and sex, can restore the Prince to his tides. With the analysis she cracks through the slippery defenses and with sex she reconnects the Prince to his own life. She makes him a human being again. It can't be a male analysis because the male is the violator. The secret is a sex thing, so she uses analysis because it's a secret and sex because it's a sex thing.

Can a male analyst ever make a female analysand the Princess of her own life again? Interesting question.

Do we have then a new paradigm? A new compact of order and disorder, of male family order and female family order? Do we go back into the play of what's commensurable and what's incommensurable or does Barbra finally also attend the Prince's coronation?

I think she does, and the linkage is her own husband and son. She could have been somebody as a wife and mother if it wasn't for them. Can't Barbra be the King? After all she's the analyst. The Modernist Project is her project. She puts the Prince back together. But no. Her husband is art. His artistry can't be reached through analysis. He's very privileged, leads a self-confirming, autotelic existence. And his order is just as arbitrary and nasty as the Prince's father. No. The Prince has to help Barbra out here. He has to ride into the dinner party and vanquish the Tyrant Husband. In fact he has to be like his older brother, the one who fired a rifle at the King/Father to get him back in line, the one who came in on the rape scene and started blowing rapists away. He was sort of a Hotspur brother. He even got into a battle with the National Guard and the FBI trying to protect his kingdom. He got blown away but his memory lives on. Without decisive action there is no order. Vote for Perot.

As for the son, well, Barbra can analyze everybody else's son except her own. But the Prince *can*. The kid just needs the order and discipline of a little football. He needs a little bit of the moral fiber that they make footballs out of. How the hell is Murphy Brown going to teach her son football?

It's obvious but I'll say it anyway: the Prince can't keep having sex with his analyst, Barbra. He has to go back to his wife.

Nobody is haunted anymore. His sister isn't suicidal. For a while. She'll continue to slip by the King and the Prince's order by writing poetry. The tides are coming in right on schedule in the Prince's life now.

It haunts me.

MOVING LATERALLY ACROSS
THE CAPES OF FEAR
DECEMBER 1991

A culture, while it is being lived, is always in part unknown,
in part unrealized. The making of a community is always an
exploration, for consciousness cannot precede creation,
and there is no formula for unknown experience.
—Raymond Williams

What the King jury is trying to keep clear and self-evident is what's a threat and what's protection, who can hurt us and who can save us, what the bad guys look like and what the good guys look like. The tape didn't obscure those distinctions for them; it wasn't hard for the jury to read the tape as a moral drama.

What happens to moral dramas in a postmodern world is that they get blurred; good sort of gets attenuated as it interpenetrates with evil. Evil picks up some allure in the process. Finally firm moral categories collapse into cardboard signifiers that read "good" and "bad."

While some are frantic to reattach these labels to reality, others are long gone down fractal paths and can't remember or can't distinguish entry from exit, whether there's a bottom that's dark and a place far above that's light.[1] Faith isn't gone or denied. Faith is not down there, in the mire of superstition, where the light of reason is denied and kept at bay. It is just that faith has to extend itself laterally in this postmodern world and deal with the narratives it intersects.

There is decreasing interest in dragging the resistant, the reluctant, the lukewarm, the dissident, the incorrigible onto faith's ladder upward, its great chain of signification linking us step by step toward unity, coherence, continuity. Synthesis, harmony, legacy. As faith joins reason and stretches into a maze of multiple, diverse connections that individuals and societies, races, ethnicities, and cultures, forge between themselves and what's out there, faith and reason's own representations seem to have a hard time applying a universal rule of judgment.[2] It is harder now in this postmodern age to extend justice to narratives that are not hierarchically arranged but touch, collide, intersect each other amid unplottable contingencies, overspilling any platform or design. Abortion, euthanasia, capital punishment, lesbian, gay and bisexuality, masculine and feminine, sanity and insanity, human life-worlds and global markets, nature and market, socioeconomic inequality and democracy, computers and minds, cultural difference and cultural literacy, and on and on—they all slip past clear and self-evident solutions and resolutions because they cannot be brought, as Lyotard says, to a universal rule of judgment. We have a decreasing capacity to value a Western narrative over an Asian, a man's over a woman's, anyone who could do it 'their way' over those who have 'no way.'

While it is clear in the J. Lee-Thompson 1962 version of *Cape Fear* where justice lies—in defeating the evil Max Cady—our sense of justice strays in all directions in the 1991 Martin Scorsese version, does, in fact, stray so widely that it loops back on to Max Cady, the Devil himself, though Robert Mitchum and Robert De Niro play the Devil differently. Both audience-worlds fear the Devil but in different ways and that play of identity and difference is responded to from within twentieth-century modernist, in the 1962 version, and postmodernist, in the later version, frames of real-izing.

It has been pointed out that Mitchum plays Max Cady far more subtly than does De Niro. The Mitchum performance mystifies evil by underplaying it. The evil lurks in the half-closed eyelids, the slack movements of body at the same time the body always seems to be thrusting large chest in our face, the words drawled, indolent, almost unconcerned. The face and the whole body almost bored, hiding its intent, its energies. What evil lurks here is within, a terrible hidden twisting of mind that on the surface plays itself out within an easy-going, soft logic, everyday slouch toward good citizens, laden with an inscrutable scenario of revenge and retaliation. The mind fixed in the past, held bound by overpowering linkages of self and world, the body loitering in the present seemingly without purpose, with no agenda. Through a glass darkly. Evil here is shifty, a shape-changer, an unrepresentable signified, any sign, a word, a gesture, concealing more than revealing what world it comes from, what it means there, what it is meant to mean here.

Prince of Stochastic Tides, Prince of Darkness. The dark, tragic vision of twentieth-century modernism—a mind spinning off a flywheel, full of intent, but that intent grounded in contingencies.

Mitchum's Cady is a troubling evil not because that signifier "evil" has become shaky but because our means of grasping, of getting a handle on that evil, of making it visual, is troubled. It is not that evil wanders off making various connections but that we cannot penetrate vertically. We cannot get to the heart of it and disclose its properties, its reality. The dilemma of reaching into subjectivity *objectively* and plucking out its features for all to see is the very dilemma late modernism sets itself to resolve.

So Cady's evil here is deeply recessed, concealed; we get only glimpses. The portrait is all smoking mirrors. At the microatomic level of evil there is a curious movement, an uncertain dance of the mind whose opacity yet promises hidden continuities between itself and what film can make transparently clear to its audience. Cady's evil comes from an inner opaqueness that we must get at from the outside.

Evil here is discoverable but admittedly only as what has not yet been discovered, or more upsettingly, what is always on the other side of our discovery forays. Such forays are always planned without twists, without tangles, only possible if chance itself is defended against. Therefore things are set up to always nondiscover evil—to know when and where and how we have *not* discovered it as we gaze at what we have discovered, at our representations of evil, at Mitchum's Max Cady.

Mitchum's Cady is unreachable, elusive, suggestive. We see him but we don't know what we expect to see from one minute to the next. We hear him talk to other characters but there's no dialogue; the words bear in them undiscoverable connections with the world before we shuffle them into our own continuities. You can't reach Mitchum's Cady; you can't communicate with him. Your words bear associations that are already embedded in a world that makes Cady's world unfathomable. The continuity and coherence of our own 'penetration project,' our desire to dig deeply into the nature of evil, keep us mired in a place on the outside of where we want to be.

At the same time, it is clear that we are already inside the evil we wish to observe and bring to the screen and it is already within us and our world. Instead of staying in our seats, our Archimedean observation points, we are in fact already spread out there on the screen. Cady is not anyplace we are not already in, though this modernist *Cape Fear* sets itself up to conceal that situation, to place a distance between our observing selves and the film's representations of evil, an evil that the film always promises to deliver, to frame for us, but never does. All this version does is shoot evil and leave Gregory Peck standing over him.

Because this earlier *Cape* remains within a modernist paradigm there must always be a way of reaching Mitchum's Max Cady. He remains a problem to be solved, problem solving itself remaining a path-clearing operation as man forges both forward and upward. Cady is in the way. He's suddenly appeared in the road and he's a problem to be resolved. There is no point of contact between the good man Gregory Peck as the lawyer Sam Boden and Mitchum's Cady. Even though Peck will become increasingly upset by Cady there is a line drawn between Peck's registered even tones, his calm, reasoning distance from Cady that is never breached. There is a certain imperturbality, almost stolidness, impassiveness, an emotional neutrality to a Peck performance, the tightness of the lips, the jaw set, the gaze distanced, which says to us, "This man can't be reached by evil. This man is of different stock. This man will endure pain, suffer, eventually uphold an unreachable integrity." But, most important, this man will preserve the subject-object distance. His story, in other words, never intersects Mitchum's Cady.

Why? Because good and evil cannot interpenetrate. Because the problem solver cannot interpenetrate the problem. Because the continuity, unity, and coherence modernism wishes to establish recognize evil as a gap that must be bridged, a hole that must be filled. Evil is an absence, a break, a discontinuity, a disruption that must be brought within a prevailing sense of continuity and order, within, in this film, the goodness of the Boden family. In a way Mitchum's Cady's evil lies in the fact that he has wandered off the path, gone in opposite directions at the same time.

The danger here, the evil here, is twofold: first, he will eventually, like Borges' garden of forking paths, enclose and subsume all attempted verticals within. His eventual circling will make a shambles out of our progressive linear flight. Second, every vertical effort is broken off, comes to nothing, gives up the story it's been pursuing and takes up another without a bridge. The modernist sees only a gap, a fissure to be jumped or bridged. The problem here is to find within a modernist story line a way of linking to a story it cannot follow. Minds out there who remain inaccessible to our linking efforts haunt the Modernist Project, entice it into what it frames as yet another attempt at getting to the bottom of things, and provide a continuous fascination for us since these minds remain out of reach, our effort forcing endings with no closure, no tying up.

The power of this 1962 *Cape Fear* does not come from the goodness of the Sam Boden family. We are not impressed by how the prevailing order vanquishes Mitchum's Cady. We are not strengthened by a reaffirmation of our total separateness from evil. No matter how many times the victory of good over evil, the law-abiding, conscionable mind over the aberrant, incorrigible mind, is staged it is a victory that pales as soon as we are out of the darkened theater. We are always ready to go back for another try, to bear with yet another frontal attack on human evil.

What makes the victory so short-lived? On the one hand the power of the film emerges from the threat that Mitchum's Cady represents to the respectable Boden family and that threat is rooted in Cady's difference from what the respectable mind wants to deal with. We can't tie Cady's difference to that respectable world we have constructed as our own. Nevertheless, his elusiveness intrigues us. It keeps us watching the world reshaped in ways outside our own shapings. But that difference remains unidentifiable and therefore unsolvable so that while it is the wellsprings of the film it must be re-presented as part of those representations of reality we already possess. Evil succumbs then to allegory; it is like what we already have, already know. Its own play is blocked off and we are diverted to an analogue of meaning and this analogue is graspable and resolvable. We can reach an ending here that *looks as if* it has tied everything up.

The analogue: Mitchum's Cady is out for revenge. Revenge causes his action; evil is not stochastic. It, too, is rooted in reason. *If* Sam Boden had not testified against Mitchum's Cady, Cady would not have been sent to prison, would not have lost his wife, would have no *reason* to harm Sam Boden and his family. Revenge and injustice propel Cady's evil; they are points of origin. Once evil is grounded in a point of origin the possibility of a point of closure is made possible. The audience can reason their way into Cady's world.

There is also an emotional analogue to supplement the reasoning one. Cady's evil is here not simply a problem to be solved. It is something to be acted upon, to be destroyed before it destroys us. It is not only alien to a prevailing order but what is recognized as alien—because it is not recognized—is therefore condemned. Caught within this scenario, the viewer rushes past the whole problem-solving enterprise and accepts the extermination of the problem by whatever means necessary. What resists an influential real-izing is thus no longer an opportunity to extend in a modernist way our knowledge, to build on our foundation of truth regarding self, nature, and society. Rather that project and its foundation come into existence because it has already risen out of the evil that overwhelms Max Cady. The disorder of evil is not a challenging obstacle on the road ahead but is instead the abyss that's been left behind, the dark point of origin out of which the road to the light is supposed to make its way.

Without looking back. When we look back—with Dr. Lowenstein's help in *Prince of Tides*—we come out victorious. Or, let's say Streisand/Lowenstein lets us, wants us to, arranges for us to come out ahead. The historical record shows we have really built barricades against the darkness, not flooded it with light.

We have settled for a knee-jerk reaction against evil and not a jeopardizing of what society has already achieved. If society returned to an interplay with the abyss it would indeed be jeopardizing that curtailment of such play *out of which society emerges*.

There are two reasons then why Hannibal Lecter in *Silence of the Lambs* is behind steel bars and six inches of glass in the deep bowels of a fortress-prison: he is a creature of the abyss, and as such we can only engage in dialogue with him at the risk of losing our own well-being, our own sanity, our own goodness. The modernist mission is both a looking into and running from the bottomless depths, the abyss of disorder, Derrida's bottomless chessboard, which stands as a beginning, a foundation that is no foundation.

The distortedness of Cady's mind, of ungraspable human evil, can't be handled reasonably. You have to follow the advice Sam Boden follows: destroy him before he destroys you.

So there is a strenuous classic realist element here as good and evil are set up in clear categories, Cady is demonized and Boden is sanitized. "It makes me sick to breathe the same air," Boden tells Cady. This Cady is like an animal that has to be fought like an animal, to finally be sent back to jail until he rots. Victory here is at the price of the Modernist Project itself. It has slapped down its challenger instead of probing deeply into its dark heart and shooting a ray of light into it. Victory has hoped to conceal the inadequacy of such a quest.

What haunts us here is that good and evil are imbricated. Max Cady and Sam Boden join word and world on webwork paths, crisscrossing each other numerous times. Any attempt to hold Boden's good aloof from Cady's evil is an imposition that the individual lifeworld can no longer bear. It can no longer bear it because human society itself is too diversely multifractured to possibly permit the 'laws of nonpenetration' to persist. Privileged absolute universal determinations of good and evil cannot block off that play of order and disorder that is the force behind our postmodern heterogeneity.

Our culture locates good and evil within early modernist as well as classic realist configurations. Under modernity, we can observe and analyze evil's composition. Under classic realism, we naturally recognize and condemn evil without having to get to the bottom of it. The 1962 *Cape Fear* taps into this classic realist pattern but also, through the Mitchum performance, into twentieth-century modernism's recoil from an unanalyzable, dark order of things. The best that could be hoped for was a momentary stay against this dark confusion.

Martin Scorsese's *Cape Fear* clearly no longer shares the optimism of an Enlightenment modernism nor the belief that a distance can be maintained between good and evil. This lack of faith does not come out of the blue. It is configured within another cultural experiencing, a postmodern one. The knowledge of evil pursued in the earlier film is unmediated—nothing gets between a subject-object split that fixes good and evil in separate, universal compartments.

The knowledge of evil in the later film is mediated and mediated laterally by and across the culture, which means that there are noteworthy intersections of knowledge, ethics, power and aesthetics. It is the very fact that a diffracted culture now intervenes that the dispersing of good and evil in Scorsese's *Cape Fear* becomes possible, as does our viewing of that dispersion and my voyage here from one cape to another.

The knowledge of evil amounts to our present, different ethical engagement of it and that engagement is confined within Foucault's notion of *pouvoir*—what power is at work here and what we are empowered or enabled to engage within a present cultural context. The shape of Scorsese's film then acts as a sort of resituated ethical engagement of our knowledge of evil. The fear waiting for us at Cape Fear is already charted for us by us, and we in turn are already caught in the multiple crosstides of our culture's postmodern experiencing.

Now we turn to De Niro's Max Cady, a Cady that a *Village Voice* film critic considered overplayed when contrasted with Mitchum's subtle rendering of evil. Evil here is not shifty, not languorously loitering in the shadows, but right in our face, wide grin, eyes full of mischief. Southern taciturn drawling becomes southern, antic grotesquerie. While Mitchum's Cady shows us one face, always half-shadowed, always holding back, slyly intimating more than is said, De Niro's Cady is a virtual Robin Williams one-man show, slipping in and out of faces and moods, saying more, giving us more than we can handle. Thus, the feeling of evil being over-played, too expansive, too declamatory, nothing hidden, nothing to reach for, everything shoved in our faces.

It's a carnivalesque performance, overspilling every scene. Evil, in short, signs all over the place. It's hardly unreachable, ungraspable, unlinked. It rains down on every crook and cranny of the film, out of its modernist troubling inaccessibility and into our postmodern carnival. De Niro's Cady is like the clown we hire for our kid's birthday: he's all over the place. He takes over. He's too much. What kind of evil is this?

What can I say? "Evil" is a very large referent; it's classical. It's part of the human canon. Why shouldn't it loom large in the film with a huge cigar poking out of its mouth? There is in fact in this film not one character nor one incident that does not interpenetrate evil. It can't be confined to Max Cady. It can't be set outside our-selves and our culture, objectified, analyzed, and resolved. It's al-ready in our faces. De Niro's Cady is a rambling performance that crosses our path, crosses every path in the movie. Our culture nar-rates evil throughout multiple locations that are themselves timebound and politically positioned. We have not only multiple connections of evil and world, of sign and meaning, but none of these can be universalized and eternalized; all are mediated by a present culture that is now conscious of its greatest productions—meanings.

The focus of the film is therefore not on De Niro's Cady. That face is already imaged large, bloated, floating everywhere in the cape. The camera uncovers finer, unbloated liaisons of word and world, liaisons that power, knowledge, and ethics position elsewhere, *not* as evil. These evils have already been narrated as something else, as protection of family, as justice, as personal responsibility, as social order, as the price of success, as charisma, as conscience, as rational, civilized behavior, as trial and tribulation, as good's ulti-mate triumph over evil, and so on.

What was a smooth, polished surface in the 1962 film is now full of cracks and fissures, a fractal surface, each gap and opening actually only a detouring from the straight and narrow onto other tracks that branch off endlessly. Every configuration here is set on signifying "evil" as elsewhere. You might say that the only way privileged pairings of word and world can remain privileged is to have them set up in defense against dissolute pairings, constructions of meaning that dissolve the order of culture.

Evil then lurks not in the hearts of men but in the connections of sign and meaning. Fix and impose these and ignore the cracks. When evil so clearly mocks us from behind the half-closed lids of Mitchum's Cady and yet is not clearly apprehensible in regard to what chain of word and world it has forged, then there at least remains a terrain of goodness, of stands firmly and resolutely taken against evil. Whether or not this terrain and these stands rest on a foundation of goodness or whether the dry rot of evil is at work on this foundation is an unknowable matter.

Sam Boden is a lawyer. The law is set against the abyss. Sam Boden is a father and a husband. Families are set against the abyss. Sam Boden is a heterosexual, a respected citizen, a revered lawyer, a property owner. He is educated, civilized, centered. All the things Max Cady is not or is no longer. But De Niro's Cady returns and puts Sam and his whole family under surveillance. He stalks. And stalking is now in our society a heinous crime—it robs the composed of their composure.

Cady, the man of the margin, returns the panoptic gaze and thus does not accept and internalize the power relationship as Foucault theorized in his discussion of the invisibility of power.[3] Sam hires a detective and attempts to put matters back in order: the eye of power has the panoptic power to place under surveillance those at the periphery. The police, CIA, FBI never stalk. But De Niro's Cady has a more powerful panoptic gaze: he spots the detective and challenges his right to objectify Cady under his gaze.

It is an interesting battle for the panoptic gaze. The center of respectability is decentered. The good has to give up its privileged place. Is goodness nothing more than judgments from a privileged place, from the center of surveillance? Is it just another signifier at the mercy of cultural intercession?

The film moves toward the good once it has it under its gaze. De Niro's Cady has already reified evil in the only way possible: within and throughout the order of goodness, by which I mean the whole order of cultural experience invests itself in certain signifying practices and secures that investment by excluding other practices. What's left out is only made conceivable through what's already been packaged. We have to sift through the contents. We have to jump on the garden wall surrounding Sam Boden's house and look in. Like De Niro's Cady.

Nick Nolte's Sam Boden isn't as tight-lipped, as impeccable and unstainable as Gregory Peck's Sam Boden. Nolte's Boden has a face that sometimes falls apart, sags, creases, withdraws in vulnerability. The masculine integrity, its wholeness, comes apart and thus faithful husband, unseductable, protective father, charismatic lawyer, righteous citizen, family guardian—all become troubled signifiers. The real fear is here: all of these signifiers are now floating toward unknown moorings as our postmodern culture real-izes away from our classic realist experiencing.

One of the perks a successful lawyer has is to bask daily in the infatuation of a young woman from the office. Her presence adds just enough midday titillation to a daily racquet ball game. We learn that such peccadillos have occurred, that Sam's marriage has a suppressed past, that his wife is recovering from a nervous breakdown. Later she will tell De Niro's Cady that she can empathize with him, that she too has been hurt the way he has been hurt, that her mind in its hurt and pain, in its desire to get back at a husband who has wronged her, crosses Cady's path. Marriage is itself troubled. Begun in desire it winds up suppressing desire in the name of faithfulness.

Monogamy is faithful to society's law. It is one of the ways we live in society's experiencings. One of the ways it institutes our subjectivity. Is evil just a law thing? The law is in a privileged place where it reckons what is good for society whereas desire must be suppressed because it blurs our reckoned dichotomies of good and evil. Nolte's Boden is in that place where the goodness and innocence of his family and societal life are sui generis. They depend upon the clear exposure by the law of guilt and therefore evil. If it's not there in De Niro's Cady then it's anyplace and we're not safe any place, not even on a houseboat at night, deep within a cape appropriately named Fear.

The law fails to protect Peck's Boden and is undermined by Nolte's Boden. Nolte doesn't have faith in the law even though he desperately needs an external reference point to secure his too accidental life—foundering marriage, failed fathering, fallen career. Nolte's faith in the law has already given way to contingencies, to what intrudes and upsets the stable linkages of crime and punishment, guilt and innocence, good and evil. In an effort to supplement the power of the law in the face of its more powerful adversary—contingency—Nolte's Boden, as Cady's public defendant, suppresses a piece of evidence that would have exonerated Cady. Peck's Boden had merely witnessed the crime.

What results is what Nolte's Boden feared but sought to prevent: the barriers set up to preserve clear identities between Cady's evil and Boden's good vanish. Clear-cut subjectivities of good and evil, and determinate representations and enactments of all this through a rule of law, vanish. Nolte's Boden navigates laterally into De Niro's Cady and the calm waters of the law—already shown as pacific but ineffectual in the earlier film—swirl us into a maddening whirlpool that spins Boden and Cady, good and evil, into an indistinguishable/indistinguishing flux. The distance between Boden and Cady, the distance that grants neutrality, impartiality, objectivity—and clear identities—can no longer be measured.

Nothing is safe: Nolte's Boden eyes his scantily clad daughter from the doorway and wants her. To put some more clothes on. The daughter, Nancy, who in the earlier film is of pioneer stock and, like her mother, sprung only moments before from their roles in *Father Knows Best* or *The Partridge Family* or *Ozzie and Harriet*, or *Leave It to Beaver*, popped right out of the bosom of the Andy Hardy clan, is in the later film a cross between Lolita and Madonna. Innocence is now fascinated with De Niro's Cady. It's a sex thing. Doesn't sex cross the path of a young female or is it just a family thing to have *no* such crossings until it fits in with family real-izings?[4]

The mother attracted. The daugher attracted. Is evil a sex thing?

Peck's Boden hires some goons to beat up Cady and the beating is given only marginal attention. We want to think that Peck's Boden has been pushed to the limit, that this is the only way to scare Cady off. But if too much is made of it we might wonder why such a good man is resorting to such foul means. Does the end justify the means? The scene in Scorsese's movie gets played to the hilt because this is the turning point in regard to the audience's bewildered tracking of good and evil. At the moment De Niro's Cady rises up from the methodical blows of the three hired thugs and begins to defend himself and then begins to beat up the thugs, we reach out to him, we become him, we fight back against unbelievable odds, we throw ourselves into the superhuman strength and determination of De Niro's Cady.

If this is evil it looks like he's gotten a bum rap all along. He deserves better. He deserves to be treated differently and the old formula of experiencing needs an overhaul.

We have in short crossed over one Cape Fear and into another one just beginning to be explored, one in part unknown, in part unrealized.

REBELS AND RIOTERS
WITH UNSAYABLE CAUSES
MAY 1992

[I]t is necessary that we somehow move away from the binary opposition which still haunts cultural studies, that is, the distinction between text and lived experience, between media and reality, between culture and society.
—Angela McRobbie

Popular culture and lived experience cross on the May 21, 1992 front page of the *New York Times* as Vice President Dan Quayle censures the fictional Ms. Murphy Brown of the TV show "Murphy Brown." The fictional Ms. Brown is accused of eroding family values. The crossings of life and art do not end there. On that same page Ross Perot, a yet undeclared presidential candidate, "shows strength in Oregon's primary." Since Perot's platform was yet unsaid, the strength displayed in this primary was obviously grounded in his actions. Most significantly, the country recognized him as the man who took the bull by the horns and got hostages out of Iran. And they know that from TV, from the Ross Perot *played by* Richard Crenna in the TV movie.

If we view "Murphy Brown" can we detect the causes for the erosion of family values? And now some few days after the South Central LA riot: Can we trace the source of that rioting anarchy to Ms. Brown and her decision to have and rear a baby without a husband? Have all the rioters at some point or other in their lives been corrupted by this 'lifestyle choice'?

47

And Perot's being devoid of chicanery, of being free of campaign scandals, Madison Avenue handlers, lobbyists with alligator shoes and blow-dry hair—is this because he's from pioneer stock, was brought up in a traditional mother and father home, and now, in adulthood, can quite naturally "do the right thing"? He's a man of action, not endless words and debate, no endless deferring and circumlocution. Out of the maze and daze of contesting narratives, Ross Perot can rise up and act. If you're for him, you'll wear a baseball cap that says "Just Do It." Like anyone with any sense and sensitivity can see what has to be done, Ross Perot can stop jabbering and "just do it." He knows when words won't take us a step further, when the people are being lulled and lied to, when it's time to say, "We've had enough! Let's do something!"

It sounds like Ross Perot and the South Central rioters cross paths here. They share narratives of being fed up and deciding to do something about it. Of course, the intersection slashes negatively into Perot and positively into the Rioters. Perot would rather restrict our linkage of man of action with decisive presidents and homespun heroes than with precipitous actions and heedless recklessness. The rioters, on the other hand, are ennobled by the crossing: they were driven to violent actions by a society incapable of identifying or correcting its own injustices. Our society has moved so far from anything natural, either a natural law or a natural perception of what is dehumanizing, that the natural thing to do is to rise up and revolt, riot and break through by this unsayable action the horrendous lived experience of our calcified society.

Our political parties have moved so far from seeing and responding to the problems of this country that it seems only natural that someone would finally rise up and lead a revolt against the spinmeisters. Politics has become nothing more than a devious spinning of powerbrokers and shareholders, lobbyists propel decisions, the media controls representation and therefore controls the realizings of our democracy. Conspiracy theories intersect Baudrillard's simulacra, the power of the sign crosses the power of the wealthy. And then Perot and the rioters rise up.

I go on with this because it obviously intersects with my own thinking. But while I am too skeptical to grant Ross Perot's "action not words" agenda any opportunity to act, I will grant the rioters a raison d'être. With Perot, the self-made billionnaire and long-time CEO, to act unimpeded, uncontested must be a way of life, business-as-usual. Corporations are not democracies; theirs is a memoranda rather than civic culture. The rioters can't conceive of any other recourse than to riot. They are blocked off by societal narratives. You might say it is their "natural condition" to be so impeded. Perot is above being blocked off. Doing something other than what he conceives as natural for him to do would be a blocking off.

These are different revolts, different risings up. Perot's revolt is that of the father, the anger of the father; the rioters' revolt is that of the son *and* the daughter, the rebellion of sons and daughters.

These are odd fathers, sons, and daughers— the little man with the military brush cut, swollen nose, and Dumbo ears; the throng of frenetic looters we see on TV, shooting, beating, burning. The whole family has turned odd. The loss of traditional family values lies in this oddness.

It's not like Andy Hardy's family anymore. Ross Perot and Paul Tsongas are our new father figures and they are not identical to Judge Hardy. They are *analogous* to Judge Hardy. They want to cross Judge Hardy's path. But they remain odd. And all the rebellious children now seem to have a cause but it's an unsayable one and therefore their rebellion seems odd. They can't knock on Judge Hardy's door, gain admittance, make their case, and then listen to traditional family values being spoken. In a way they do intersect James Dean's rebel for he did have a cause but it, too, was unsayable. Therein lies the great contemporary appeal of "The Dean": he could enact with a look, a gesture, the unsayable.

River Phoenix in *My Own Private Idaho* makes the same sort of gestures toward the unsayable. You look down that long, lonesome highway in Idaho that River looks down at the film's beginning and you can make out James Dean on a motorcycle, coming fast. Or in a convertible, going much too fast, about to make a turn right into another car, into a violent death. It's the same road Sailor and Lula travel in *Wild at Heart* and stop halfway to witness the wreckage of that same real-life collision, one that leaves young love dead and

dying. It's the same road that Thelma and Louise drive their convertible on as they head toward that long, slo-mo drive over the cliff
to their deaths with a long line of policemen watching the tragedy.

Destination? Private. Their own. Unsayable. Running and rebelling from the father? The husband? The traditional values that the
rioters rise up against?

It's not as if our films were not crisscrossed with the revolt of
the sons and daughters, who turn up poor and both children *and*
parents in *Straight out of Brooklyn* and *Boyz n' the Hood*. How can
the parents be children? How can the rioters' revolt be like the
rebellion of the sons and daughters? Where's the crossing? Isn't it
here in the traditional family values—that these values *don't* connect Blake's innocence and experience, that they disenfranchise and
commodify the children and leave them stranded as commodified
and disenfranchised parents?

River Phoenix is narcoleptic. He falls in and out of Morpheus's
arms, falls asleep one place and wakes up in another. He moves
spatially in sleep. The nation can't be traversed in any other way.
It's his own private way. The roadmap is interior; consciousness
intersects unconsciousness. The young are somnambulists in *River's
Edge*, moral sleepwalkers. It is not just E. D. Hirsch's cultural legacy
that they are numb to, but they stand unresponsive, paralyzed before
the naked, dead body of a friend. They are armored against all
visuals, all signs, all twists of lived experience. They've seen this
sort of naked, young woman's dead body by the river's edge before.
They know the representation. They've seen it in the movies. It's
stock. It's the beginning of a movie that ends up unresponsive,
paralyzed. Or a movie with a traditional-family-values closure that
they never reach because they fall asleep.

This is the children's revolt: drugged to the moral legacy, culturally affectless, unresponsive to the call, unsympathetic to the human condition. "I don't have a father," River Phoenix tells the bald-
ing, dumpy man who has just paid him for sex. There is in this film
a political father, a mayor, a Dan Quayle traditional family value's
father. He is the King and his wild son, Keanu Reeves, will sow his
oats in the company of a riotous surrogate father, Bob, but will in

due time accept the yoke of King and tradition. Bob is fat, homeless, disreputable, a liar and thief, a source of fun for all his fellows,
a father of mayhem and mischief, unruly, a Falstaff facing a cold
and lonely death, cast off, denied, unrepresented. Bob does not represent the right lifestyle choice.

Ross Perot wouldn't appoint this Falstaffian Bob to any sensitive position. Nor would he appoint River Phoenix or any of Bob's
'children.'

Bob is not the only parent who has not the power of the father
but rather the rebellion of the son and daughter. The father in *Straight
out of Brooklyn* is a seething embodiment of rebellion. There is no
chance that he will drop in and out of sleep, fall into an affectless
interior zone. Liquor only brings him to the point of eruption, like a
volcano. His anger is unleashed on his wife and that mindless assault digs deeply into the family, into the son who will find his
freedom in robbery. With enough money he can get into a convertible and head straight out of Brooklyn. Maybe he'll finally reach
that long, lonesome highway in Idaho.

The mother is already dead, finally dead from internal injuries
suffered over years of beatings by her husband, the rioting, rebelling
child/parent/husband. He was around just like Dan Quayle wanted
him to be around for Murphy Brown's baby. Unfortunately he wasn't
a Judge Hardy father that Dan Quayle remembered from all those
Andy Hardy films. Unfortunately this father couldn't stand impas-
sive before his own disempowered, cast-off body. Unfortunately he
couldn't fall asleep and wind up in his own private Idaho. The
Brooklyn projects don't simulacra so easily.

Thelma in *Thelma and Louise* gets a chance to leave her husband. He doesn't beat her. He just belittles her, mocks her, and
keeps her mindful of his superiority and her inferiority. All women
are disempowered children within the lifestyle choice of our own
society. The abortion issue is Wounded Knee, the last stand, the last
straw, before the real rioting. You can't beat that woman's body
anymore because it's not yours to beat. It's not yours. Period.

Louise is haunted by rape. She can't unlink past and present.
She can't fall asleep and see anything but her own naked body lying
there, assaulted. Final destination: down the road, off the cliff, away

from that memory. Thelma and Louise join hands, nod, and choose their destiny. It's their way of rioting; it's the final rebellion after having killed a man, robbed a store, blown up a truck, and led the police in a high-speed chase. Violence, looting, burning.

In a way Dan Quayle haunts Louise. Follow the route: he is an angry father who wants to re-presence the father, the mythic, traditional father who knows best into the mythic, American lifestyle. While Judge Hardy imparts wisdom in his private study, his wife waits to be consoled in the kitchen and the spinster aunt dispenses strength and encouragement not as a woman but as a man. To be of any real use she has to be unlinked from her feminine connections; she has to be severed from her own gender and turned into that desexed creature, the spinster aunt.

The father is angry and rebellious today for clear reasons, for well-defined causes. Even Dennis Hopper, a cinematic rebel who was present when "The Dean" rebelled, becomes an angry father in *The River's Edge*. He can't relate to the moral insensibility of the young. They just don't know when they're being outlaws and what's it's like to be an outlaw. They aren't getting a charge out of breaking the rules because they are numb to the rules of the game. Dennis Hopper is there to tell us that you can't rebel and get all the satisfactions thereof unless you are just as aware of the rules and values of the game as the lawmakers. You've got to know the law of the father or there's no rhyme or reason to living against it. In short, Dennis Hopper in *River's Edge* is the Modernist Project's rebel. He knows the drill.

The rioters that face today's angry fathers don't show any signs of knowing the drill. They're inexplicable. The way they're haunted can't be brought to an articulate level, can't be identified, re-presented within an identity we seek and value. It is not hard to imagine that when things reach this unsayable, un-representable level, that a candidate for the president of the United States will come forward on an unsaid, un-represented platform. An angry father whose anger and rebellion will connect on an unsayable level. It is the most powerful level finally, just as dream is more powerful than waking life.

But the rioting children are equally bound by unutterable connections. While the language of conservatism has no signifiers for the rioting children—or only signifiers that impede what struggles to be connected—liberalism has lost its signifiers, is too unnerved, too frightened of the old linkages. Apologetic to the conservative chain of signification and challenged by the rioting children, liberalism struggles toward a new paradigm of real-izing. But that struggle, too, is yet at an unsayable, un-representable stage.

HOME ALONE WATCHING THE RODNEY KING TAPE, OR, HAVING JEFFREY DAHMER OVER FOR DINNER
NOVEMBER 1990

How can we watch that eight-minute tape of African-American Rodney King being beaten by five Los Angeles policemen *in the same way the jury did*?

How can we step out of the way we ourselves watch it and watch it the way the jury watched it? This is a Sherlock Holmes moment played in a postmodern frame: construct the jury's linkages of visuals and world, representation and reality. Instead of a murder, we have a verdict: not guilty. There is immediately in response an overwhelming feeling nationwide that the verdict is the crime, that the verdict is like a murder. Indeed, it leads to rioting, death, and injuries.

So we search the scene of crime, the trial itself, for clues. Perhaps the whole tape that the jury heard and saw justifies or overwrites the part we saw. Perhaps the tape could be brought into a frame that we now cannot even imagine, a perceptual frame out of which only a not guilty verdict could have come. But that beating on tape is like a dead body lying there; it fills the room, its presence cannot be concealed or denied. Without the tape we have only Rodney King's representation or perhaps some bystander's. Without the tape there would certainly have been no trial. No, the tape cannot be displaced by another equally significant, equally powerful piece of evidence. The task the jury performed was the task every viewer of that tape performed: connect the visuals to meaning, connect signs to reality, connect images to the world. The tape wasn't displaced by other evidence. It was seen differently.

The beating was treated to different signs. Trace the signing of murder: not murder, but suicide; not suicide, but an accident; not an accident, but a natural ending. The police are not beating him; they are subduing him. He is not subdued; he is threatening. This is not inhumanity; this is necessary force. The police are not brutes; they are guardians of our freedom.

Nothing that the tape shows is denied by the jury; it is simply tagged in a certain way. Just as we can deduce a murderer from a murder, we can deduce a horizon for a jury from a verdict.

Can we then enter the life-worlds of others? Can we get to the place from which the world is brought to meaning by them? Can we then foresee how they will link any event, any word, any image to the world, how they turn the world into their reality and from there perceive meaning in one place and not another? And, most significantly for this jury, can we distinguish what threatens that reality from what guards and protects it?

A short time before the Rodney King verdict and consequent rioting, we were as a nation transfixed by the young, innocuous-looking Jeffrey Dahmer, who lured, drugged, murdered, butchered, and then ate his victims. The jury found him not insane. Nevertheless, his actions, his demeanor, his very words, remained beyond our ken, outside our notion of sane behavior. Although there was a feeling expressed afterward that we could study Dahmer and eventually find out why he did the things he did, that we could enter his life-world and witness the ways he linked word and world, such optimism is at the heart of our Enlightenment heritage. We can adopt a theory-neutral, value-free approach, distance ourselves and observe the objects, the minds, the actions of the world around us. But the psychic terrain here is the very worst for such a project. Where are we in our own psychic terrain when we venture forth to explore the terrain of another?[1]

Modernity presents us with a subjectivity that is at once dominant when it comes to view the world and at once easily removed, put on ice for a while as we, without subjectivity, mount some

Archimedean point from which we observe, examine, critique, hypothesize, conclude. If it is the mind of Jeffrey Dahmer that we are observing then that subjectivity lies before us as an object. Having put off our own subjectivity we have no other way of treating Dahmer. By denying our own life-world, our own frame of representation, we have no way to access the life-world of Dahmer. Life-worlds adapt themselves to objective analysis, the analysand to the analyst.

In our own age, which envisions artificial neural networks modeled on the biophysical properties of the human brain, we are replacing human life-worlds with telematic networks. Given this situation there can be no doubt that we are in for a future of spectacularly unreachable life-worlds, frontpage headlines about people who no longer seem human to us, whose narrative frames we can't say anything about.

Does the postmodern turning of truth to narrative, objectivity to just an arbitrarily or imposed correspondence of tape and truth, better prepare us to bridge the gap between Dahmer's world and our own? Between the King jurors' and our own? We're after difference and Otherness here, what ascends to reality and truth outside our own notions of reality and truth.

Our culture is stymied by these events. We don't know what to say. Or, there is too much being said that we cannot assimilate. Assimilation itself is suspect, a problem. The events—horrific serial murders and mind-boggling jury verdicts—always seem to catch our discourse off guard, like economists each telling a different tale about why we are in this recession and what we have to do, or more precisely in these conservative times, *not* do to recoup.

Maybe if we saw a tape of, say, two hours or so of Dahmer's life, or clips from different years, we could watch how he brings the world around him, from shaving in the morning to turning in at night, to meaning. But what if the King jurors watched that two-hour Dahmer film? Sane or insane? What if Hannibal Lector from *Silence of the Lambs* watched the Dahmer film and then told us about Dahmer's life-world? Or what if Dahmer was sitting in the theater watching Hannibal the Cannibal bite off a policeman's nose? What if we identify with Jeffrey Beaumont in David Lynch's film, *Blue Velvet*, and we watch what Frank Booth does to the Blue Lady?

Do we know what Frank Booth is all about? And when the Blue Lady screams for Jeffrey to hit her and he finally does, how far down the Jeffrey Dahmer road has this Jeff Beaumont gone? What if we're the King jury and we take a break and watch *Home Alone*? Do we laugh our heads off?

Events baffle us and our own words about these events are on the outskirts of the unspeakable turmoil and unfathomable stories that must lie behind these events, the dark places from which they emerge. In order to entangle our saying, in order to intersect these events, we turn to popular film, which has itself already entangled and intersected our cultural real-izing. Our life-worlds are already interpenetrating filmic life-worlds. The culturally unspeakable has drawing power. Our own brand of the sayable must intersect the unsayable because we can no longer be entertained by or make popular what has already been rendered powerless by our culture.

We now live in fractured notions of truth, beauty, goodness, justice, although our discourse is yet committed to mending this fracture. Popular film sets its cameras up within the fracture, knowing that here already are the curious gathering, the concerned, the anxious, the frightened. The murders and the verdicts that have slipped through these cracks slip into popular film and we go to see them. You might say Jeffrey Dahmer's life-world can go on in this theater and that around some corner the King jury is hanging out, watching.

The King jury is now watching *Home Alone*. I am sitting there watching it with them. I have just finished watching *Silence of the Lambs*. I was studying Hannibal the Cannibal closely and trying to put Jeffrey Dahmer in his place. I am at a place furthest from the jury: they are well-guarded inside looking out and I am outside coldly observing the house, the *Home Alone* mansion, they are safe and snug within. I want distance between myself and that mansion. I'm not interested in property; I'm interested in minds that property means nothing to, that mean nothing as property, that *mean* on other grounds.

The kid left behind is left behind when his family and relatives go off to Paris for Christmas. The cop who should be protecting the mansion while they are gone is not really a cop. He's a burglar pretending to be a cop. He's not going to protect. He's going to rob them. He and another burglar are going to try to break into that mansion and take everything they can get their hands on. These thieves travel around in a van, their home is on their backs, their clothes are Salvation Army donations. They have no mansion. They have no home. They remind us of the homeless. They're no longer in their own part of town. They're here, trying to get into a mansion whose owners have gone to Paris for Christmas. They have not only slipped past the cops but they pretend to be the cops (Democrats once again in the White House?!). Protection of property is now in the hands of the homeless, of the people without homes. The enemy is at the gate.

The jury around me is in a sweat. Tension is mounting. Order is at the brink of collapse. All they have is a kid inside a mansion. How long can he hold off the attack of the have-nots? Just a kid. How vulnerable is a mansion and all its possessions? And more frightening, how vulnerable is that minority who possess these possessions? There are worse things ahead for this kid. What if on one of his very competent, very courageous journeys out of the mansion to go shopping he runs into Jeffrey Dahmer? Did anybody ever think that Jeffrey, who appeared so dull in court, had a winning way with young boys like our kid home alone? Where are the cops to protect this kid from Jeffrey? And why is Jeffrey so innocent-looking, so normal-looking, and why does he have such a way with young boys? Why can't we see through him, see the evil, see the insanity, see the horrible menu on his mind?

What terrifying vulnerability of mansion and body. There is a whole trackless yet absolutely driven energy and mania outside this mansion that reason and shrewdness are powerless against. We ask the computer to program the threat and an appropriate response and what we get back is a solved problem, a solution that works in the absence of contingency. The mansion, bottom line, has to be protected from contingency. Every system, every organization bolts its door against contingency. Jeffrey operates on contingency, like a lawn mower on a Briggs and Stratton engine. He's so indifferent to, so alien to, our language game, the organizational by-laws, every owner's manual for every major appliance in the mansion, that we might be locking the front door when he's already inside, an old friend we've invited for lunch.

Do Dahmers and Lectors multiply? How many does it take before there's enough to find their way to your door? I smell the fear in the jury around me. This is a postmodern world. Modernism's angst and becloudedness is now just a narrative path some continue to take but it's like a church that's lost all its parishioners. The avant-garde is no longer at the front because the middle and the beginning have fractured and all our memories of word and world are at the gates at the same time. Within what special discourse is a mind to be shaped? A mansion to be built and protected? If the hounds of hell are unleashed, if contingency puts any ordering scheme on the run, if the law can't ground itself in either the *mythos* of reason or the cherished legacy of a culture, if minds are increasingly being shaped outside the common *mythos* and culture, then what is the cost of keeping the mansion secure?

I stop asking the questions and look at the jury. Is this their answer? "Everything is spent. Nothing is too high a price. Not a beating captured on tape. Order is a secure mansion."

I don't fear Hannibal Lector or Jeffrey Dahmer as much as I think I should. The new world order is being built outside the mansion and it is an unsayable order.

ROCKING THE CRADLE OF FAMILY VALUES
JANUARY 1992

Let's say all presidential candidates are classic realists—they give us a bird's-eye view of what harmony is, what disruption is, and how harmony can be regained. They do it in a way that makes us feel that this is a it-goes-without-saying realism, a view of what's really going on that we all share. It gives us the sense that here's a guy who's finally confirming our own view of our country, who the good guys are and who the bad guys are. It's not the candidate who is coming up with all this but just the way things are. Phonies and weirdos want to force something unreal down our throats but if you've got any common sense you'll be able to separate truth from fiction. When you hear the truth every fiber in your body responds because it's the truth, it's what you already know and somebody running for office finally had the nerve to tell the truth.

The problem, of course, with the classic realist approach is that in order to reduce a complex, contradictory, accidental sort of world into a simple pattern—a sort of Disney-Mister Rogers' neighborhood pattern—a lot has to be left out. And when you leave something out, you also leave out a lot of people who live in that something-left-out terrain. You also necessarily have to leave out a lot of thoughts and feelings that these left-out people share because they're the kind of thoughts that will disrupt the truth you are telling and they're the kind of feelings that should not be aroused in the people left in because they might begin to think about the plight of the people left out. Once tensions creep into the truth that 'goes without saying,' the reality that is commonly understood as reality, then we start rolling farther down that long road to ruin—America as Japan's granary—that is the new nervousness replacing our long-time bomb-dropping-on-our-heads nervousness. We don't want to think that all we've got is what Bush or Clinton or Perot are saying. Not the truth but just the saying. We don't want to understand more than what we've always understood in common as reality. We don't want to imagine that our sense of harmony and peace is only achieved if we conceal a great deal, that our identification of what problems face us is limited by our frame of identity-granting. We especially don't want to imagine that our sense of what answers and solutions are is what has left our cultural identity dying on the side of the road.

It is this sort of plight that inspires the classic realist campaign. To admit that anyone's America may be a nostaligic portrait, a bit of tall-tale, lengthy campaign rhetoric, a bit of power-driven egomania, and not America-in-itself, is to give in to the decadence of simulacra that Baudrillard prophesies. Finding oneself within such simulacra is disheartening at the very least. No wonder that when Perot stands forth as nothing more than a man disgusted with political simulation we flock to him. Not only because he has mouthed our own sense of anger and frustration but because, in the good old classic realist style, he seems to promise a handy solution. This is an impossibility: he cannot attract people by vituperating against politics as simulacra and then engage himself in a politics of the real. Indeed he struggles to put forth such a politics of the real. He hires the two best campaign managers in the country, the two top spinmeisters. And they apparently came up with just more spinning when Perot, with fast diminishing naivete, wanted the 'real.' They gave him a classic realist scenario, a twist on Bush's and Clinton's simulation. In short, they take the basis of his popularity away from him. Without that, he can't win. He bows out. He can't get down into those ditches of simulation with Bush and Clinton because while they retain party-drawn allegiances, he has nothing but the winningness of his refusal to get down in the ditches of the good old politics of simulation. And if he's in that ditch, he's obviously given up that winning way.

You might say that the Perot followers wanted their cake and they wanted to eat it, too, by which I mean that they wanted to categorize all of politics as hyperreal, as not real but hype, and at the same time they wanted Perot to *give* them, not say, the truth, the answers, the old glory. No politician, they reason, ever gives us more than a politically positioned truth, a lot of promises that can never be kept, a view of things that holds back what is contradictory. We get a representation, not the truth; we get words, not world; we get a mock-up, not reality. At the same time, there is great fear in letting this view stretch out in all directions. One inference would be that we were living at any moment in a simulated America, one whose past, present and future were spins that caught us in their swirl. Our culture hasn't seemed to touch ground since—since when? When Gable was King in Hollywood? When we fought Hitler in Europe or the Japanese in the Pacific? When ethnic minorities kept out of the way until they melted in? When women stayed home, took care of the kids, and baked cookies? When men loved and married women and heterosexuality was not a life choice but the way things naturally were? When cultural literacy didn't have to be pushed because we all either had it or were struggling to get it?

Was all this just seductive spins that kept us moving fast enough so we couldn't see who and what was left out of the spin and who and what was spinning in different orbits? Could the questioning of the reality behind politicians' words shift not only the Perot people but all of us toward a postmodern spin on the real? Are we ready to see that our family values emerge not from a bedrock foundation of absolute, universal truth but from somebody's mouth, maybe Dan Quayle's?

To admit all this is like giving in to the chaos and carnival of contesting American tales—from Native Americans and African Americans to liberated women and homosexuals—which seem to promise nothing more than moving us further away from a unified, commonly envisioned America that could not only assert its historical past in a determinate, noncontentious manner but also move toward a single vision of economic growth and progress in the future. It is one thing to be sick and tired of the simulations of politicians, their empty words, their fraudulent grasp of the real, and another thing to accept our grasp of the real as always nothing more than what somebody says it is at some particular time in some particular place.

Why don't we buy this postmodern view of things, that "here's another construction of the real that I'm buying today as if it were the real-in-itself"? I think because this postmodern alternative is yet only expressible in modernist and classic realist terms. In the modernist view we modify notions of the real because we—through various specialist probings from physics to psychology—are discovering 'more' of the real each day. In the classic realist view the bad guys push falsehood and that wins the day until truth makes a comeback.

We are powerless to express what our common connections of word and world do not already empower. At the same time, the modernist urge to give up the alien linking, the dissident linking of word and world is tottering. Since our own society has encouraged a heterogeneity and polyphony far beyond the cultural homogeneity of, say, France or Finland, Germany or Japan, the E Pluribus Unum spin is winding down at a nervous-making rate. There are whole worlds here waiting to spin *counter* to our unity spin. There are linkings of word and world ready to collide with resident linkings. There is a monumental devaluing of traditional values banging at the gates. The fear of *that* prompts the persuasive party of "No Spin but the Free Market Spin" to dig its value trenches deeper, to bar and lock the gate against the invaders.

What madman would run on the ticket of chaos and carnival? Surely from where we stand now and within our own historical record of where we say we have been, we have no other words but "chaos" and "carnival" to represent what would happen if we dropped the single truth theory—one reality for all, one justice for all, one set of values for all. What candidate would accept America as a 'multiverse' that can never unify its myriad selves together in any just way and yet promises to grant justice to each?

Rather than face the turmoil of this postmodern America we have, since 1980, accepted the politics of nostalgia that promise a reclamation of the old determinacies, the old faiths, the common sense of truth, the rallying round the real that is done so faithfully that those on the fringe will either join in or sink into the shadows. The hoopla of Democratic and Republican Conventions is not non-sense—it fulfills a great need to "hurrah" a unity out of diversity. Rather than allow narratives of difference, voices of Otherness, to crack the smooth surface of reality, the politics of nostalgia cracks a whip at the backs of the discordant, the harbingers of contingency, of undecidability and irresolution. We join as one in a family of values, arms locked, eyes ablaze. The excluded fall back. It is the redemption of our true selves, the essence of the American spirit.

This redemption has led to the death throes of that egalitarian spirit, that rebellious defiance and angry contestation, out of which this country rose. The young and angry, the imaginative and opti-mistic will leave this shell of a country then, like rebellious children leave a tyrannical father, and journey on the seas in exploration, wandering. This is what "Dark Ages" now comes to signify.

It is no longer possible for us to be easily seduced by any spin, family values spin included. The postmodern shifting is out there, on the billboards, transmitted on the radio, filling the Big Screen, the psychology behind the cable and remote revolution. I had lived for a number of years in a part of the country where even with a super antenna there was only one or two lonesome TV stations to be reached. When I finally moved back to civilization I would watch TV the way I did in the '50s. Most often the whole family would select a program and stay with it, feast or famine, loyal even through commercials. We either allowed the program to reach its end or, one or another, would wander off and do something else. I tried to watch TV with the same commitment, the same degree of interaction, as I read a novel. I found it disappointing, railed against TV and its stupidities.

And then I watched my teenage daughters watch TV. They rarely watched in a family group but preferred to watch alone. I found out why. They weren't passive receptors of one TV spin but creators of a TV montage with the help of a remote control and assisted by the many channels offered by our cable company. They zapped commercials, cut songs in half and patched them with other songs, ran out on a comic's punch line and filled it with talk show chatter, montaged three or four movies together, grabbed an earful of the weather, and always came back to roost on MTV, a channel that was pushing buttons itself so fast that I couldn't tell what was a show and what was a song, what was a commercial and when we were back to the program. The program was, so to speak, spin. A simple switch and they were playing Super Mario on Nintendo, responding so fast to the action on the screen that I began to feel my own mental wiring had rusted. Movement, tempo, spin, collisions, zapping, breaking in, denying, escaping, flying. The stasis and inertia of the Republicans' family values have to somehow bring all this chosen living in the spin to a stop. And that's a classic realist project: a return to an immobile Pax Americana after a bit of turmoil. The spin of stasis has to replace the spin of spin. We are urged to go back to settling on that one program that we can all, as a culture, attend to.

It is not surprising, then, that a box office success like *The Hand That Rocks the Cradle* garners its success from dipping into the whirl of contending spins. And despite what feminists have alleged— that the film is an attack on the whole women's movement and the movement of women out of the home and into the free market—the film has no scruples. It will make coin of both the desire to break out of the inert spin of Quayle's family values and the fear that if we lose our cultural grounding, in something like family values, then we're destroying ourselves. The film plays the culture the way my daughters play the TV.

Let's admit that the words "family values" are floating and slippery and, rather than start off attending to them, let's see how any linkage could possibly relate to the grounding conservative notions of corporate freedom and free market. Is this entrepreneurial freedom in any way regulated by any linkage of family values? Why regulate family values and deregulate business? Could there be some fear that if we deregulated family values—recognized, for example, Murphy Brown's choice as an equally legitimate and natural choice— this would lead, somehow, to a regulation of the privileged free market?

To believe this we have to believe two things: first, that an imposed master plan regarding family values doesn't encourage any values that would hinder the cash nexus, the operation of the market, the competitiveness of American businesses. And second, we would have to believe that a deregulation of family values would do exactly that, namely, a free play of values might collide with a free play of the market. On the one hand, it's easier to target the monologic than the heteroglossic market. On the other hand, new voices cry out for new needs and new needs are the very grist of the free market. But what if these new voices cry out for more than needs? What if they are continually engaged in maintaining and securing the legitimacy of their identities? What if it is not so easy for advertising to play identity off of difference (as in the Willie Horton campaign), good off of evil (Bush against Saddam), beauty off of ugliness (white off of black), true off of false (capitalism off of communism)? What if no one can maintain a classic realist spin without getting it immediately flung back in his or her face?

Cultural anarchy makes marketing a difficult enterprise. But more important, it can't allow the free market to do anything it wants simply because profits will be increased. It can't do so because hard-won human life-worlds are at stake, identity is at stake, and, bottom line, that necessary egalitarianism that grants justice to each life-world is at stake.

Does Quayle's family values apply a moral rod to the free market? First of all, it's not meant to. Second of all, the conservative intent is to do precisely the opposite. The imposition of one law of family values is meant to inhibit cultural diversity, the proliferation of acceptable, acknowledged identities. It is meant to set the culture up for easy marketing, to make identity not a construct to be fought for in the cultural ring but a God-given reality that takes its natural place in the order of things. And that order is best arranged by the free play of the market.

It is after all a matter of order and disorder: family values become fixed and stable, determinate and coherent, just as there is one stable, promising order of well-being, the free market at its center. Disorder is a plunge into the abyss, a sure fire way to lose economic hegemony, increase the deficit, put people out of work.

Family values in the mouth of Quayle, then, are not simply a smokescreen, a red herring thrown to the populace, but a necessary regulating of what Foucault listed as a culture's discourse, practices, and institutions.

The sine qua non of *The Hand That Rocks the Cradle* household is having money. Husband and father is a genetic engineer—a profession that few can connect to a definite chunk of what he actually does but nonetheless tells us he is a high-tech professional who must make good money. And he does tell his wife Claire that they're not in the situation they were in with their first child. They can now affford to get a "nanny." The signifier makes us aware of what we are as Americans not aware of—class. The film has opened with a pan shot from below of a very large white house, a house with plenty of character, but atop a small rise, a house that the average American would give his or her eye teeth to own. You get the big white house, the return to an unambiguous class structure, and the well-providing father and husband.

Claire has the opportunity to pursue her interest in gardening because she can hire a nanny to take care of their newborn child and she can only hire the nanny because her husband has the money. If you hinder her husband from making good money in any way, you destroy Claire's chance to fulfill herself. We only have family values if we have an economy that remains untouched by anybody's values. The hard reality here is the genetic engineering, the money. It makes values happen. It is, we are immediately shown, the key to women's liberation.

Besides enabling Claire to fulfill herself, her husband's economic status enables him to hire the poor, dim-witted, black Solomon as a handy man. "Will Solomon leave us when the fence is finished?" the daughter asks her father, to which he responds that they'll always have jobs for Solomon to do around the place. It's that big a place and it's Solomon's place to do these jobs. It's trickle-down economics; it's the way those with money will take care of those without, a noblesse oblige that will paradoxically ensure democratic values of liberty, equality, and fraternity.

Solomon's first job is to build a fence around the place. Now he asks a question that is exciting: "A fence to keep people in? Or a fence to keep people out?" It's a dangerous question. It tends to push the viewer out of the trance of a well-ordered, class society in which women and blacks know their place and 'research and development growing the economy' is the Sun in this universe. Who is left out here? What happens to those outside the fence who can't share this wonderful yuppie lifestyle? What happens to the countless Solomons who haven't attracted their benefactors, maybe because they aren't as sweet and innocent as Solomon, maybe because they're too enraged to appear lovable?

With a fast-growing split between rich and poor, those in big houses and those who have lost their homes, the haves and the have-nots, there is electric current running on both sides and this film intends to plug in anywhere the lines are hot. For those in big houses there is a need to keep people out. Solomon is an okay black man but maybe he's okay because he's got the mind of a ten-year-old, because he's black but not a threat, not angry. Would blacks who have all their faculties be out doing what Rodney King was doing (or what the jury *feared* he would do if not stopped) or what the South Central LA blacks were doing after the jury verdict? Who is being kept out here? Who is feared?

The film also taps into the power line of the homeless, not an African American but a white woman, the nanny, Peyton, whose home and savings have been taken to pay off lawsuits against her husband, a gynecologist who sexually molested his patients. Once inside the yuppie household as a nanny, Peyton lashes out in a private outburst of violent rage against these comfortable trappings of security. And at that moment, the rage of the homeless, of the discarded and patronized, links with the life-worlds of the other half of the film's viewers. While one half is held by fear and concern for the preservation of their privileged lives, the other half is held by anger and violence against inequality, injustice, unconcern.

This yuppie family straight out of the '80s demonstrates a certain playing fast and loose with family values, which we can list as the following: (1) he is the breadwinner and enables the family to be a family; (2) she cannot relinquish her primary role as mother or wife in order to pursue interests outside the home; (3) there must be only one woman in his life; (4) female bonding is too rift with jealousies to ever be relied upon; (5) children can best be cared for by their mothers; (6) the family must protect itself from the corruptions of the outside world, which are rampant because family values are collapsing out there.

On the other hand, we encounter the following: (1) males seem either molesting (the gynecologist) or self-absorbed (the husband); (2) women have all the guts and brains: Peyton the nanny has more life and energy in her than any other character in the film and it takes another woman to figure out what she's up to; (3) a woman—Peyton—topples both Claire and her husband from their protected perches on Disney's Main Street U.S.A.; (4) the male dominance of women, including their bodies, is shown as an abhorrent thing in the opening scene with the molesting gynecologist; (5) women are esteemed by husbands only if "they make a decent lasagne, give a good blow-job, and make at least $50,000 a year"; (6) children know and recognize love when others—not their biological parents—extend it to them; (7) rarifying the family atmosphere so that any outside disturbance must be immediately removed is a sure way to make invalids out of people, symbolized by Claire's asthma attacks every time things go wrong, every time the good life meets life out there.

If the culture is heterogenizing, allowing more and more constructions of the real to be heard and seen, allowing more of what comprises this culture to come into the light, more narratives of what a family is and what its relation to the overall culture is, then those who fear the loss of containment and accountability, the loss of guiding, universal standards of judgment, will demonize this heterogenizing. They will also say this unified core of values is under attack but is more than ever necessary. While liberals, in the account of conservatives, are liberal when it comes to family values (anything goes), conservatives, in their own account, won't deviate from the fundamental principles of human decency and natural human relations. Liberals see themselves as trying to promote the legitimacy of different lifestyles within democratic, egalitarian ideals. Judgment here falls not on the heads of those who do not maintain the prevailing sense of family values but upon those who seek to deny or suppress, ridicule or discourage, other, minority constructions of both family and values.

A box office success such as *The Hand That Rocks the Cradle* does not inscribe or parody either narrative here. Rather it mines them skillfully and in doing so shows us that what is classic realist is now deeply divided in our culture. There is, in short, not enough commonality of thought, feeling, and perception to sell us tickets to that old easy journey from harmony into turmoil and then back to harmony. Instead, we are rocking.

FREE MARKET OR FREE PLAY?

*Freeing the thrift and mortgage markets from government
subsidy and guarantee is like freeing family pets by abandon-
ing them in the jungle.*
                                                    —Albert Wojnilower

*Derrida is undeniably well-known and influential. He is however
controversial in a special sense: despite occasional disclaimers,
the major preoccupation and effect of his voluminous work has
been to deny and to dissolve those standards of evidence and
argument on which all academic disciplines are based.*
                              —Regent House, University of Cambridge

*At heart, the integration of telematic and neural network
architectures is an integration of circuit-based processing and
symbolic reasoning. Telematic networks are being built all
over the globe and linked via satellite and fiber optic transmission lines into a single global network.*
                                        —B. Ray Horn and David Ellis

*The tasks of passing on a cultural tradition, of social integra-
tion, and of socialization require the adherence to a criterion
of communicative rationality. The occasions for protest and
discontent originate exactly when spheres of communicative*

action, centered on the reproduction and transmission of
values and norms, are penetrated by a form of modernization
guided by standards of economic and administrative rational-
ity; however, those very spheres are dependent on quite
different standards of rationalization—on the standards
of what I would call communicative rationality.

—Jurgen Habermas

The above quotations respond to three different paradigms regarding order and disorder: free market, Derridean free play, and Habermasian communicative rationality. The free market paradigm links the free play of the market with the free play of democracy. That is, if the market is not regulated in any way and if the profits of the market players are not taxed away for social entitlement programs then the essential freedoms of a democratic way of life will be preserved. We'll all be free to choose. Choice is freedom. Democracies have choice. Third World countries don't. They don't have markets. What they call "markets" are really not free of other cultural baggage. They have other priorities that get in the way of a really free market, a market free from any constraints, especially vague, humanitarian constraints, political or religious constraints. They don't know the New Ontology: "I shop, therefore I am." "To be is to consume." Existential choice gets thrown together with consumer choice. It's all choice. It's all freedom. It's all democracy.

And 'we've' got it. Everybody within this paradigm is free to choose. Milton Friedman proves it on PBS for as many weeks as Carl Sagan devoted to the our-origin-lies-in-thick-soup view of the cosmos, Kenneth Clark to our Western hegemony, and Jacob Bronowski to our ascent to choice, I guess.

But, on the abortion thing, pro-choicers aren't for choice. Or, more precisely, some free-marketers suspect that the pro-choicers may make the wrong choice—that is, not for their choice, which is for life. You're free because you choose, but not everybody who wants to choose has the right to choose. Free-marketers have to get the feeling that you're pro-life, which gets hooked up with pro-values, which in turn gets hooked up with pro-family values. You have to dig deep to see why free-marketers feel this way. You have to see films like *The Hand That Rocks the Cradle*, *Working Girl*, *Protocol*, and *Baby Boom* to figure out how important it is to keep women's choice within a certain culturally inscribed framing of choice.

If the play of the free market is now playing on a very uneven playing field—for sexes, for classes, for individuals, for whole cultures and hemispheres —then the notion of choice emerging from such ingrained lopsidedness is already a very politically positioned one. However, the free market grand narrative is here to remind us that we are all equally free to choose. We're choosing on this field, choosing to choose death to one life sometimes and choosing to choose the same way all the time. In the first instance, we sometimes choose that there will be no life and therefore no choices. Thus, pro-choicers can find themselves choosing to deny others choice. If life is choice, because unfettered choice is the life of the free market, then pro-choicers by denying life are denying choice. In the second, we say that there will always be no choice for women in this matter. If choice is life, because unfettered choice is the life of the free market, then pro-lifers find themselves denying life to others by denying choice.

We are caught within the market metanarrative and therefore it is inevitable that we want both choice and life for market reasons. Choice and life have become equatable. Despite all the other-than-market arguments, we now have no other way of dealing with either because all other ways—ethical, religious, political, philosophical— have already been overwritten in America today by the play of the free market grand narrative.

The abortion dilemma confounds the simplistic market ideology and that ideology in turn pronounces the dilemma not central, outside the real issues, that is, economic issues. According to the free market metanarrative, the abortion issue seems to miss the point regarding choice and life. At the same time, *if* we were not culturally caught within the web of that metanarrative, an expanded and richer linkage of both choice and life would doubtlessly generate an entirely different horizon of discussion (or pomo clash) for abortion, euthanasia, rape, racism, sexism, and so on.

I am not playing around with this serious matter. The point is that life is now linked within our master narrative of the free play of only the free market. I am saying that life is extended to us, or not, within the contingencies of such play. "Time is money," lives are made up of time, therefore life is money. If we're not economically expanding, we're dying. To be living is to grow larger each year, to expand geometrically the gross national product. To do that, we have to consume more. We need more and more freedom to choose, which means the market has to be freer next year than it is this year. The free play of the market has to constantly expand to a higher level of free play.

Is this our old-time democracy, the old "Give Me Liberty or Give Me Death," the old "Spirit of '76," the old "Fourscore and seven years ago" sort of democracy? Or is this market freedom just that—a freedom extended not to individuals but to markets? We can choose to consume in the marketplace but we can't choose in our own individual life-worlds.

It seems clear that we are leaving behind the old regime of order-words while shifting toward a certain reterritorialization, one not fully conceivable yet grounded in economic free play. Let's trace the linkages: democracy to freedom, freedom to choice, choice to the market, the market to what grounds it—research and development—R&D to always the newest technology which is now, at its frontier, a sort of bionic-technology, a combination of processing circuitry and the working of the human brain.

Listen to the signifiers being thrown around: "the new telematic (the merging of computing with telecommunication) technologies and their applications," "neural network technology," "neural global network." This *Machina sapiens* operates "through the 'layers' of hidden neurons" and "is nonlinear and sigmoid, characteristics that describe a self-organizing and self-regulating state. . . . Such higher-order, self-actuated computations evince properties of a living system."

Free play in this *Machina sapiens* is free, I think, only in one sense—it's free of us. It can tell us things but we can't follow its play. It's an autonomous system. It reorganizes itself to meet a new demand. It can take what fails on one level of organization to a higher level of organization where it means something. But this has been our creation, our dream, a two-part dream. First, "the dream of a mechanical reproduction of experience itself, in all its sensory dimensions."[1] Here silicon and digital logic replace the literal capturing of what's out there by some old-fashioned optical means, like our eye-balls. Computer-based virtual reality represents all the sensory dimensions but it bypasses our own human senses. The human eye and human seeing are the analogue for traditional optics, from cinemascope to 3-D, while the human ear and hearing are behind stereo to Dolby. And yet when we junk these analogues, we can still identify—see as identical representations—virtual reality and lived experience.

Within this frame of real-izing, the only way the human race can represent the full sensory dimensions of its lived experience is by supplementing *Homo sapiens* with *Machina sapiens*. It is the force of the representation—of the virtual reality we sit down to see as our reality—which drives our ways of real-izing, from social to economic, political to psychological. It becomes a controlling representation that does not chasten or discipline us within narratives of right and wrong—back to Quayle's family values narrative, which already replaces how families are formed now with the spin of a virtual reality. In other words, we are already putting aside our lived experiences and moving into a worlding of virtual values. And that move to simulacra on the moral level ultimately spins human values out of the human life-world. I say they become "technicized." Not ours. Moved by the cursor.

We give up interest in and pursuit of human life-worlds. Instead we are urged to research and develop the designing force that lies behind the *Machina sapiens'* replication of our lived experiences. At once it is understood that research and development will be achieved with the designing force of technology itself.

What is now exercising our imaginations in Big Screen science films is that research will at some point no longer be initiated by *Homo sapiens* and that development will therefore go on "in an unplanned and *unplannable way.*"[2] No less than Der Arnold Schwarzenegger, larger-than-life-but-still-*Homo sapiens* body, has in his *Terminator* movies enunciated the fear here: "At exactly 11:15

the cyborgs achieved consciousness." And the scientists agree: "While humans are needed to start a neural network's learning process through the formulation of algorithms, at some level of development the network will surpass the human being as its own teacher. It will reach what Boulding (1961) calls a 'break boundary,' a point at which the medium or structure suddenly changes into another medium or structure, or passes some point of no return in its dynamic process."[3] Where's the free play then?

Let's retrace our lateral movement here, or, more aptly, our "nonlinear and sigmoid layering." Free markets invest in R&D which is investing in *Machina sapiens* and which promises a virtual reality that is itself made possible by combining the biophysical with the artificial. And the future of that relationship is ultimately—at break boundary—to disconnect a *Homo sapiens* linking of signifier and signified from a *Machina sapiens* linking. They are, as I said, free of us in a way our notions of the real and the true never are.

The market finally learns Derridean free play, in short, that our determinate connections of word and world are not true or real through the force of an inherent linkage or an unshakable foundational order of things. Rather, they are imposed upon us not only by cultural narratives but by our five senses. Now, in contrast to this, the artificial neural network will be self-organizing and self-regulating *hors de texte* of our culture while "[r]obotic sensors are not limited to the five rudimentary senses humans possess, but extend into regions of the electromagnetic, chemical, atomic, cosmic and other spectra where man is blind."[4]

The representations of *Machina sapiens* therefore will emerge from chains of signification whose links no longer intersect the linkages of *Homo sapiens*. The present course of an unregulated free market becomes bound to the virtual experiences of neural networks. Simulations of consciousness and lived experience move us away from that humanistic tradition Derrida's free play was indicted as undermining.

The free market as a cultural metanarrative, a privileged, ruling narrative that forges all our cultural liaisons, is anxious to take technology to its furthest reaches and anxious also to suppress any attempt to modulate its own behavior. Within this metanarrative, market free play undergirds democratic freedoms. Dissenting voices—*petits recits*—argue that market free play does not lead to democratic freedoms but rather to a sort of superannuation of all human attachments regarding freedom. My interest is in pursuing how the market modulates us away from a Derridean notion of the free play of signifiers. How can Derridean free play disconnect us from the Logos of *Machina sapiens*, from the privileging of the representations of the global neural network?

I use the word "modulate" within what Gilles Deleuze calls the logic of the *societies of control*: "[C]ontrols are a *modulation*, like a self-deforming cast that will continuously change from one moment to the other, or like a sieve whose mesh will transmute from point to point."[5] The modulating is not in our hands. The neural network will be self-modulating but we are not. The modulating of self and world is not under our control but within, Deleuze writes, the "operation of markets [which] is now the instrument of social control and forms the impudent breed of our masters."[6]

We are enthralled by this "impudent breed," these Gordon Geckos, Dennis Levines, Ivan Boeskys, Michael Milkens, Martin Siegels, Donald Trumps, H. Ross Perots, Charles Keatings, Neil Bushs who are at gleeful play atop "a universal system of deformation" that the rest of us are at the mercy of, or never finished with or free of. They master the operation of markets while we are controlled by them, a control which "is short-term and of rapid rates of turnover, but also continuous and without limit."[7]

Our films are awash with these images of both masterful control and the metastabilized. But they only show what the world out there is living through. Within the corporations, the schools, the prisons, the hospitals, the metastabilized are kept afloat by distancing them from the privileged chain of signification that the market forges for the good of all. The perpetuation of democracy is a market matter. This is neither a chain forged by the Divine Logos and recognized by the faithful nor the chain of reason recognized by the rational. The free play of the market is itself played by the stochastic and contingent and therefore it has no stable, determinate installations of word and world to impose. Its regime is itself of the free-floating signifier whose domain is nevertheless narrow: profit for shareholders.

The logic of negative and positive capital expenditures, of market shares and market dependency, of 'needs' creation has no need of legitimating narratives regarding "cognitive truth, moral judgment and aesthetic taste."[8] And it has less need of narratives of delegitimating or postmodern narratives that might challenge with their own free play the grand narrative of a free play market.

Both the market and technology are already forging arbitrary linkages of word and world. The logic of the market rests in what it cannot control, its fluctuations no more and no less than the waves of contingency. And technology's digital logic promises only to free itself when it reaches its break boundary of any narrative of human logic.

Modernist legitimating narratives now seem irrelevant. The "task of establishing universal standards of truth, morality, taste does not seem that much important . . . appears now misguided and irreal."[9] There are two notable forces at work here that make modernist legitimation futile. Bauman describes the first clearly: "Seduction and repression between them, make 'legitimation' redundant. The structure of domination can now be reproduced, ever more effectively, without recourse to legitimation."[10] Second, the foundation of certitude conferring universality upon the modernist legitimation project "is now at best ridiculed as naievty, at worst castigated as ethnocentric."[11]

The image of a global free market faces no such ridicule and castigation. The image of a globalized truth grounded in a purely Western mode of real-izing is decidedly not marketable. What is now outworn is the notion of a master narrative of proven cultural superiority that could reassert both individual rights and democratic principles in the face of a free market economy that gives identity to consumers only and privileges corporate freedom above individual freedom.

The free market may be exportable but the Modernist Project no longer is. The whole American packaging of free market, democracy, and technology is not only under interrogation on American soil but is already undeliverable elsewhere. "[T]he very notion of 'modernity' has been called into question. Under the banner of 'postmodernism,' cultural critics have raised questions about the viability of the present forms of those very institutions of capitalism, democracy, and technology which seem to promise to the Chinese the opportunity again to become one of the great nations of the world."[12] The difficulty works in both directions: the globalization of market and industry has introduced a clash between American workers whose identities are already culturally grounded outside a purely corporate identity and foreign owners and managers who give different significations to both free market and democratic freedoms.

Postmodern contesting narratives and the Derridean free play that empowers them have a tendency to go off in directions that the market's use of seduction and repression cannot control. There is no legitimacy in postmodern free play given to a universalizing metanarrative. Culturally relative or local narratives that are self-reflexively metastable dissolve modernity's unity into a multiplicity of life-worlds, of narrative frames, of language games. Diverse realizings confound market consumer targeting as well as market reduction of alien experience within a targeted zone of identity. The market then must regulate its own real-izing in line with this multiplicity. The free market would be resonating within narrative frames that interpret the market within their own language games. And the market in turn could only interpret a narrative by assimilating its tradition or ideology. Control and modulation of the individual would no longer lie with the free market. Rather control and modulation would be dispersed within many life-worlds, a dispersal, you might say, across difference.

Democracy moves away from modernist identity and toward the multiplicity of difference and therefore a politics of difference underwrites individual rights in their battle with monolithic corporate identity and rights. The free market must be responsive to a democratized politics of difference. We have shifted away from the modernist paradigm whose failure to legitimate its own privileged chain of signification, its own analogue of truth and order, left a vacuum that the free market moved in to fill, trafficking mightily on the collapse not only of Soviet socialism but of transcendent, determining principles and objective Archimedean points of critique. Academe had no way or power to critique or legitimate the operations of the free market. Liberal government, if voted in, could involve itself in the rights of the individual, but modernism's democracy had already confounded itself in its liberal Great Society practices, its march on a recalcitrant difference. Caught within a modernist march to unity, government could only dream of legislating an identical American selfhood, a chimera more fascist than democratic. On the other hand, the consuming self that the free market created would grow the economy, and that growth would protect the democratized self. In the first instance, we have democracy tied to a restrictive Modernist Project, and, in the second, we have a total abrogation of the need to grow democratic, egalitarian principles and a turn to the contingencies of the free play of the free market.

It comes to this: if individuals act for unlegitimated reasons then they are already waiting on the modulations of contingencies—their own and not those of the market. Or, more precisely, the market's play is itself already caught up in the postmodern play. What madness is this? Consider though how undominated chess pieces play the game out: for example, it is possible within such a variety of wildcat narratives to see an equal face-off of democratic, egalitarian values and corporate goals, or social and entitlement programs and market free play, or, more fundamentally, the equalization at very least of human life-worlds and the imperatives of marketing systems. Habermas has already noted the present usurpation of the former by the latter: "Under the pressures of the dynamics of economic growth and the organizational accomplishments of the state, this social modernization penetrates deeper and deeper into previous forms of human existence. I would describe this subordination of the life-worlds under system's imperatives as a matter of disturbing the communicative infrastructure of everyday life."[13]

The unlegitimated dissenting, counternarratives that pushed for the Earth Summit brought global economic stability face to face with ecologism. While American free play market narrative reigns it dismisses such environmental concerns as regulatory, as impeding market freedom, as negative capital expenditures. Since nothing counts but the profits that can be counted, pollution of air, land, and water and extermination of animal species are discounted. So are social issues such as AIDS, inner city poverty, unemployment, violence, drugs, abortion, rape, population control, disenfranchisement, unskilled blue-collar workers, child abuse, and so on. Environmentalist groups become "moonbeam," to use the signifier slapped on Jerry Brown as soon as he announced his candidacy for the presidency. Abortion means nothing in comparison to the free play of the market.

A free environment, one free of man-made pollutants, has credibility within a myriad of diverse narratives that see no necessity in grounding their critique of free market practices in transcendent logical truth. The limitations and excesses of free market views of the environment are parodied and thus decentered through an open clash of narratives—free market alongside free environment.

After a theoretical intermezzo, I intend to go back to the turn-off points I followed for a little way in this chapter, only to finally make a U-turn and head back to my main road, back to home base. And that main road is this: we can't stay on the main road of free market, technology, democracy, and ecologism without a modernist roadmap. And that roadmap isn't reliable. Origins and destinations are no more than analogues that stop the journeying, begin it, and then stop it again. When the map becomes an analogue of what's out there, then the play of what we know and what we don't know, what is clearly on the map and what isn't on our map, is brought to a halt, confined within the signifying of the map itself.

This representation, this map, we say, is an analogue of the world out there and can stand in for it. This essay I'm writing now should provide a series of points, a progressing argument, which leads clearly and without detour, grammatically, to a destination, to closure. I ask the reader to take it because I've either got a new short-cut to the truth or another piece of the truth. *I* have a way of legitimating the free market, or, more precisely, *I* can bring the free market back to a need to be legitimated by universal standards, show how it can once again be put under the control of specialists

within what Habermas calls "the structures of cognitive-instrumen-
tal, moral-practical, and of aesthetic-expressive rationality."[14] If I
could provide such a roadmap it would take us far from the difficult
whole of our worldly context.

That sort of roadmap, one that hovers above and traces in red a
continuous line, forges rationally communicative links, and so on, is
fading. A winding, twisted, involuted backdrop of roads is now
becoming visible. The map is whorled, rivulose, screwy. It's nonlinear and sigmoid. No dot seems to be the Big Dot. As you look you
get lost in the journey, in the undulations of multiple passages to
destinations that are themselves no more than passages elsewhere.

The postmodern map insinuates us within its own sinuousness,
like a film insinuating itself within today's headlines, both insinuating themselves into our lived experiences, our lived experiences
going on in Wall Street, in Rio, in virtual reality. We are on a crosscut journey.

INTERMEZZO:
BETWEEN FILM AND CULTURE
FEBRUARY 1993

*A rhizome doesn't begin and doesn't end, but is always in the
middle, between things, interbeing,* intermezzo.
—Gilles Deleuze and Felix Guattari

*It is now a cinema in which the distinctions between high and
low art (always precarious) have more or less vanished and
where culture and economics cross and recross at every level
of both fields.*
—Colin MacCabe

*[M]en may live more truly and fully in reading Plato and
Shakespeare than at any other time, because then they are
participating in essential being and are forgetting their
accidental lives.*
—Allan Bloom

OUR ACCIDENTAL LIVES

I did a series of meditations on the relationship of order and disorder
in a book called *Mots d'Ordre: Disorder in Literary Worlds*. In my
afterword I spoke of how I initially became interested in disorder.
Let me use the final words of that book as a point of departure for
this present collection of hauntings: "So I begin with the notion that
literary worlds are entangled with order's representations of history,

politics and real world events but they also can put into play lines of flight from those entanglements. Within the entanglement of these we both struggle to impose meaning while hoping to return to the play of the text to recoup what we have lost or left behind, consuming and responding to more than we are able to say we have brought back."[1]

Art, whether serious or popular, is territorialized by a prevailing order but can also deterritorialize that order. In other words, art is capable of bringing before us what we yet hold as inconceivable. I didn't know how to prove this hypothesis except to direct my attention intermittently to literary worlds and various attempts to interpret them. In Wolfgang Iser's terms, our interpretive attempts construct an analogue of meaning that stands in for the "play of the text." Literary worlds do not repeat the givens of the world out there but execute or perform them so that "in disclosing itself fictionality signalizes that everything is only to be taken *as if* it were what it seems to be, to be taken—in other words—as play."[2] Literary worlds overspill such analogues of meaning, and our capacity to re-present what's going on in such literary worlds is a direct function of our own cultural representational frames. However, what always necessarily exceeds our ability to grasp through words—disorder—is not easily depicted by language, which is itself legislation against disorder.[3] If there is a play of order and disorder in literary worlds and films, then we are always viewing the action from the side of order. Like wrestling with the invisible man, or observing movement on the subatomic level, we see reactions and rebounds, swerves and detours, feints and knockouts, but not the causes. I was therefore not arguing or even theorizing but meditating on the unrealizable, hoping desperately not to reify or thematize. I wanted to avoid turning disorder into a *topos* but hoped to quickly unsay the determinateness of what I was, inevitably, always in the process of trying to say, relentlessly intent on capturing the uncapturable.

Postmodernists like myself are haunted by the idea that there are narratives of ungraspable difference, and that idea emerges from postmodernity's own theorizing. A telling sign of our present shifting toward a postmodern frame of real-izing involves this fear that the legacy of a functionalized Enlightenment Project has left out, shaped as unrepresentational, a good many people, a good many ideas and commitments. The more widespread fear—coming, as they say, from the other side of the aisle—may be that although we are no longer intent on establishing an absolute, universal foundation of truth, goodness, beauty, justice, and so on, our sense of security depends upon our being able to preserve a necessary cultural continuity that itself depends upon the control universal claims provide.[4] So while some of us are out to recuperate what universality has excluded, others are anxious to defend a very functional form of flexible control provided by Enlightenment universalist notions of reason and knowledge.[5]

How anxious are they? Let's put aside whole volumes written in defense, from Bennett's legacy-reclaiming and Hirsch's culture-as-memorizations and Bloom's closed minds and Kimball's ideologues-as-professors to D'Souza's fear of difference. Let's just replay our tapes of the 1992 Republican Party Convention. Something dark and threatening was being kept at bay there. It was as if those, postmodernists among them, who saw our common culture as both constructed and represssive were foreign adversaries. George Will gave voice to this in *Newsweek*: "The foreign adversaries her [Lynne Cheney's] husband, Dick, must keep at bay are less dangerous, in the long run, than the domestic forces with which she must deal. Those forces are fighting against the conservation of the common culture that is the nation's social cement."[6]

The postmodern attitude inevitably draws us toward what our whole culture is trying to hold out of sight—the abyss gaping wide at our backs, a dark hole into which certitude and meaning, decidability and resolution, unity, coherence, and harmony fall. In the eyes of modernity too much has already been unraveled, fractured, and fissured, brought to that disorder that is of greater interest to me than the order we have already constructed for ourselves. If our common culture is, as George Will tells us, "cemented" in place (and is therefore not a reality sui generis) there is no reason to believe that job of cementing fulfills an "essential" rather than "accidental" plan, to use Alan Bloom's distinguishing signifiers. Our accidental lives, the differences within our lived experiences, cannot therefore be depreciated before the light of an "essential" order of

things, in poststructuralist terms, an outside, stable order of an absolutely reliable referent. "We have no fixed reference points left,"
scientist Francisco Varela tells us.[7] The accidental therefore perfo-
rates not only lives and experiences but our common culture, and
the order of that commonality must be *contrived* in order to escape
the accidental. Postmodernity has its eye on such contrivances.

"The universalist conceptions of reason and knowledge we
identify with the Enlightenment," Thomas Bridges writes, "constituted the cultural underpinning of the public sphere of emerging
liberal democracies in Europe." The underpinnings were cemented
with the cement of "uniform standards," "neutral frameworks,"
"shared community which transcends . . . narrower interests," "norms
that define the sphere of public life, the sphere of civil society" —in
short, a "common culture." What I heard and saw haunting the
Republican Party Convention was this fear that some people are
jettisoning that commonality and refocusing their attention on the
play of differences, of *identity deferred into/toward difference*, of
our accidental lives.[8]

THE HAUNTING MOVEMENT

Identity deferred into/toward difference. I am trying to construe
Derrida's notion of *différance* here: "[W]ithout a trace retaining the
other as other in the same, no difference would do its work and no
meaning would appear."[9] *Différance* thus takes the starch out of an
unrelated difference as well as an unrelated identity. I transpose this
as a play of order and disorder, play here paralleling the movement
of *différance*. Meaning and order, therefore, are not products of
either identity or difference, order or disorder, but appear within the
movement, within the play.

Since "[t]he pure trace is différance" we can only be haunted
within the 'same,' within our common fare, in our headlines, in
our popularly held representations, up there on the screen. Because
that 'same' retains a trace of the 'other,' its 'sameness' is not its
own but leans on, moves toward that 'Otherness.' The identity that
tries to identify itself as what brings such movement and such play
to a stop is still in motion, still in play. Our postmodern reflexivity

brings this paradox before us. Our haunting lies in the last two sentences: identity can be constructed to either exclude or resolve difference but the play of *différance* itself reveals an unresolvable, unexcludable difference within identity. Our current postmodern reflexivity establishes all this as a haunting movement. What haunts American culture is not inconceivable but is rather made conceivable, brought to the level of representation (not *re*-presentation), within this haunting movement, the haunting caught in the play of *différance*, the movement caught in the play of the text. What haunts American culture comes out of a disorder it fails to re-present but that haunting can be brought forth, put into play, most dramatically within popular culture. Identity's discourses must inevitably represent what haunts it within the protocols of its own identity. Entering the play of both *différance* and the play of the text, identity's discourses establish an analogue of meaning, a supplement to that play, a play it brings to an end. But unfortunately rather than reducing what haunts the culture to just another given, just one more thing that a prevailing identity has made identical to itself, the prevailing discourses of identity have exacerbated their own failure to re-present and have intensified their own fear of making conceivable what haunts our culture. The only way to make conceivable, to consume and respond, to what haunts us is to be brought into the haunting movement, into its performance in art. I shall shortly extend a view I presented in *Mots d'Ordre*, namely that popular culture, although constrained by market values, plugs into what haunts the culture because what haunts us also fascinates and draws us. We buy tickets.

Modernity's 'identity of the same' conferred the signifier "accidental" on what signified as the "flux" of individual lives. With a shift toward a postmodern attitude the very differences of our accidental lives now assert their primacy over a past construction of both society and personal life, of civic culture and moral life. Our lived experiences have been denied and discarded by absolute, universal standards claiming to be uncontaminated by the human factor, by subjectivity and its arbitrary valuing. But here the accidental is reactivated as the pure movement of *différance* that puts both identity and difference into play.

We must now somehow advance the contingencies of our accidental lives not only into the public sphere but into the personal and aesthetic also. Contingencies and accidentals are the Others retained as traces within our identity of the same. Meaning appears in the movement and in the play of the two. The autonomy of contingency as well as all forms of identity are propelled into a movement of relatedness. The autonomous citizen and the autonomous work of art as well as the authenticated self are, in a postmodern view, grounded in no detached universalist standpoint but are rather enfolded within their own particularistic commitments, within a cultural particularism in which movement is seemingly brought to a stop.[10]

High or serious art tries to transcend and neutralize the contingencies of our lived experiences in the hope of attaching itself as closely as possible to a realm of transcendent aesthetic norms. This is a false transcendence that cannot neutralize the differences that our lived experiences naturally produce. There's no way to legitimate as common and universal a notion of aesthetic form to which all lived experiences are reconciled/harmonized or transcended/neutralized. Art that detaches itself from the particulars of any one person's lived experiences while attaching itself to an autonomous and nonexistent state of being *can* beg or demand conformity. We can, however, certainly ante up the differences of our own lived experiences and call the hand, that is, choose not to conform. [11] In other words, we can bring any identity back into play, back into the movement of *différance*.

CONSUMING PARADOXES

The films I write about have haunted me. My absorption in or blindness to the lived experiences reported in newspaper headlines is my own. I believe that the essays of this book must each be dated to give the reader a frame of reading, but the dates neither recapture 'Then' nor stop 'Now.' There is a dynamism to a movement of the same and the alien, a crisscrossing movement that touches harmless identifications with fear. That play is momentary and my responses were of particular moments. Experiences accidental because they are tempo-

ral, temporal because they move. A postmodernist will allow meaning to appear only here.

I believe, however, that we must try to make conceivable what
haunts our culture and is played out in popular film. The moments
of our hauntings would be, in Foucault's view, the moments when
we are trying to think differently. There is a Nietzschean drama of
self-creation here attended by deep ontological fear. We bring to the
screen a play of our fears and our defenses. We take them out of the
shadows where our common culture has placed them and play them
back into our own lives. Rather than ensnaring us in a commodified
reality that discounts our own lived experiences because they have
already been exploited, the popular film does not discount anything.
It certainly does not discount individual commitments to the ways
we are cementing/reifying ourselves *or* haunting ourselves. Indeed,
not discounting any heavily laden commitment is the operating principle of the popular.

All this makes the popular film itself heavily laden. To be
popular it must commit itself to a paradox—cement identity while
haunting identity. Since popularity is a market issue and profits are
not undermined by paradoxes but can instead thrive on them, the
popular film adheres to the market's own consumption of paradoxes.
Further, in pursuing its profits both in places where the common
culture is being cemented and in those places where it is being
haunted, the market itself displays a paradoxical nature. Popular
film then is just following right along.

In pointing out all these paradoxes I am just going through the
opening Fredric Jameson has provided. The contradictory conscious,
or actual, and unconscious, or potential, impulses in a film are there
because cultural productions, like popular films, have been fully
integrated into the market. That imbrication ultimately means to
Jameson that cultural politics can intervene in the market. I agree
but want also to foreground postmodernity as underwriting this contestation. I also want to extend our haunting, which comes about
when the actual and the potential are put in motion, beyond the
theoretical frame within which Jameson constrains it.

The dual compulsions of the market to reproduce and remodel
already engage, in my view, in an open, unconstrained relation to

the overall culture. What is marketable is the reproduction of what already holds the market audience in a bound state of being (haunted) as well as a contradictory remodeling of all this into an imaginary order of being (unhaunted). Jameson would house these competitions within an overarching theoretical framework that itself allows a haunting of an actual late capitalist political economy by a potential Marxist social organization. I, on the other hand, have only a mazy framework to encounter what I believe to be the interaction of contingencies that interpenetrate individual life-worlds and the culture. There's nothing overarching the flux here but there's fascinating interrelatedness in that flux. I don't believe there are mechanisms deriving from a theoretical analysis "which articulate individual fantasy and social organization."[12] Jameson's Marxist metanarrative and its *Ideologiekritik* is haunted by the seeming undifferentiation of postmodernity. At the same time he allows that it is the undifferentiating, full integration of the market and cultural productions, typifying the postmodern clime, that allows for the possibility of his Marxist cultural politics to intervene in that market.

I expend a good deal of energy in *Hauntings* promoting the idea that postmodernity reaches (in the 'goodfellas' sense that somebody can be reached) the market's own overarching indifference to any sort of unmarketable intervention. Postmodernity *reaches* it by opening it onto mutually intervening paths, a sort of Borgesian garden of forking paths into which a full integration of economy and cultural productions has already walked. If we could ascribe agency here we could say that postmodernity capitalizes on this late capitalist integration. In this garden, intervening critical narratives, not all political, intersect dominating narratives, commodifying narratives intersect narratives of autonomy. While Marxism does not accept the play of the free market as the end-product of class struggle, postmodernity returns all end-products to the swirl of contesting narratives.

Individual lives can be delegitimated by overarching theories as well as not-costed-in by the play of the market. The unconscious can be territorialized as political-economic just as readily as Deleuze and Guattari see it territorialized by the Freudian/Lacanian triangulation.[13] The market can seduce and repress consciousness within the most effective modulation of our accidental lives.[14] Rather let us preserve the accidental (the way we reach the play of the market!) and go mazy-like into a film's play of lived experiences, wander into the shadows, consume and respond to the commitments.

Experiences cast in shadows and those accepted into the light of day are brought into play in films that plug into our fears and try to conceal them at the same time. What haunts us is disguised within a prefabricated narrative, a bit of the hyperreal, which we think no longer crosses back into our lives. But the more we try to recapture the illusion of living and experiencing a unified truth, a graspable, noncontradictory reality, an indisputable hierarchy of aesthetic order, a universal rule of justice, universal notions of freedom, goodness, and what have you, the more we are in the present haunted by an ever-growing number of disruptive narratives that cannot be silenced.

Because these disturbances to our peace of mind distract us, the market helps us repress them. They distract us from being consumers first or market players who pursue wealth as a cohering, unifying force, the highest good, and hold only the play of the free market itself as the highest law. We should worry only about the market being disrupted. But the market does not only just repress the disruptions of postmodernity, or attempt to solve them as does the Enlightenment Project. It also uses them, or, for my purposes here, puts them into play. If the play of the market were under Enlightenment protocols of legitimation, this paradox would have to be resolved.

The play of a postmodern contesting of differing narratives upsets Enlightenment dreams of an indisputable foundation upon which the truth is erected. It mocks twentieth-century modernism's own self-deprecating, angst-filled critique of a mission from which it cannot, paradoxically, detach itself. But while persevering Enlightenment dreams make a nightmare out of postmodernity's disruptions, the market makes a buck on both dreams and nightmares. By this means the postmodern riot of narratives interweaves the market metanarrative into itself.

Our undecidables—from abortion to AIDS—haunt us and for that very reason they are put into play in popular film. What haunts us is a marketable enterprise. We are, in essence, seduced by our own fears and anxieties. It is a profitable thing to play into our culture's deepest, ontological dreads. Just as we experience in a recurrent dream what we cannot in a conscious state conceive let alone represent to ourselves, we can be seduced into attending, anxiously, nervously, to configurations on a large screen in a darkened theater that in myriad ways, in what Iser calls the "languages of the unsayable," allow us to consume and respond to our hauntings. We see clearly then the paradoxes of the market, the repression of our hauntings and our seduction by those very same hauntings. No grid can superimpose the play of contingencies here.

TOUCHING THE TAR-BABY

In the previous chapters and in those that follow I crisscross between the lived experiences (I scour the headlines, listen to the talk shows, follow the campaign) of our present culture and popular film in the hope of bringing to a consumable and respondable level some of what haunts us. The greater the box office success of a film the greater the chance today that this film is trading in haunting material. I realize that it is this very distinction between text and life, art and reality, that, to use Angela McRobbie's term, "haunts cultural studies."[15] Since I do not abide by a modernist notion that art transforms lived experience into an order that neutralizes or transcends that experience (and therefore has only a questionable connection to the raw material of life) I see narratives of art, including popular film, not ordering but putting into play the accidentals and contingencies—the disorder—of lived experience.

Baudrillard's hyperreality eradicates this crisscrossing dynamism of art and lived experiences. His hyperreal is too pat, too neatly classical in its capacity to neutralize and transcend—yet again but by a different route—the madness of individual lives. It tries to stop things when obviously things change, including simulacra, because there is an ongoing interpenetration of art and life. Terminating the flux is a modernist thing.

Art is high and serious when it pulls out the universal verities of human existence from the dreck of everyday life-flow, when it pulls them out of the reach of the lumpen. It casts them into an aesthetic harmony, an anesthetized still-point, which our lived experiences can never hope to emulate. Thus, serious film, like serious fiction, re-etches the great, liberating, ennobling ideas that shape our cultural legacy. They cleanse us of our baser drives and enable us to bring order to the incoherences that lived experience offers and an end to its discontinuities. Lived exerience has no defense against its own contingencies. Its self-limitations are liable to construe lopsided and therefore potentially dangerous constructions of self, others, society, nature. It is the intent of serious art to provide that model of what Matthew Arnold called the best that has been written and spoken and to substantiate that bestness through the observable symmetry and euphony of aesthetic ordering.

My postmodern attitude leads me to see ordering as a problem, a re-presentation of favored identity(ies) and a favoring of redundancy. Ordering always reconstructs prevailing frames of real-izing. If indeed our cultural legacy of order is "our own local liberal way of life" and our "philosophical universalism was itself the expression of a particular culture" then there would be some urgency in bringing that cultural legacy back to the flux and turmoil of lived experiences, especially those that have been disinherited or fall outside the perceptual-affective-cognitive frame of that legacy.[16]

I say "urgency" because entropy awaits all systems of order whose own urge is toward greater redundancy, a more intense concern with the establishment of something reminiscent of a commonly shared cultural experience. Within this common frame, I must make the same attachments to E. D. Hirsch's list of privileged signifiers as my father and grandfather did and as my offspring will. Serious art becomes the place where order is not only repeated but where we can admire its superiority over the chaos of our own lived experiences.

Twentieth-century modernism attacked this order based on redundancy. Moreover, the price it paid was its own separation from everyday life. Modernist art could not extricate itself from a mission to reach the truth. At the same time it tortured itself with the absurdity and tragedy of those lived experiences out of which the truth was to be forged. "Time must have a stop." Art necessarily distanced itself from life in order to save itself, providing us all with a momentary stay against confusion. But while art loitered on the margins, scrutinizing its navel, market forces drew it back into the real world and commodified it. The cultural legacy canonized an art that had once set out to undermine the canon and the constraints of the past upon the present.

Postmodern art recuperates lived experience and in a form that is neither low nor high, serious nor popular, yet without reservation.[17] It returns to the ever-moving vortex of the nameable and what doesn't stand still for our naming. No narrative is allowed to construct the Golden Road to Truth; therefore we cannot sort through the disparateness of lived experience and shape some hierarchical order of significance. Postmodernity *always* returns us to the play of contesting narratives, which we *always* use to impose meaning on our lived experiences. That meaning is then caught in the play of difference.

The theory of postmodernity seems ready to do the job: to set before us that grappling of what we can identify and what lies outside our identificatory framing. But a discourse is not accident, flux, or pure movement. As Wolfgang Iser tells us, it is always an analogue of meaning that blocks off that movement. However, while art that is mindful of this postmodern analogue is focused upon its own revolutionary or radical rewritings, popular art is as usual mindful only of market forces. Thus, popular film must hotwire itself into the culture to sell tickets. It must get *into* the movement, be itself at play while drawing the viewer into the heat, excitement, dangers, and fears of that play.

Our culture is now haunted by the collapse of the order of things, which has manifested in myriad ways. The return then to the full—though always titillating, peekaboo, disguised—play of our realities and our specters within the lived experiences of our culture takes place more revealingly in popular film than in both our postmodern theorizing and in the remnants of modernist formalist art that most often gets labeled "postmodern." Postmodern theorizing is itself a grand narrative that live postmodernity treats as pretense and pomp. Where's the play? I realize that in trying to make a place for the subjectivity and rhetorical flavor of my essays, for my

putting aside the movements of a progressive argument and replacing them with a forking paths, lateralizing narration, for my treating
as important everyday life-worlds and popular film, and for all the
other transgressions of enlightened discourse to be found in the
essays that follow, I am here in this theoretical intermezzo less
playful and more inflated than in those essays.[18] Tom Bridges says
that modernity's metaphysics are like Harris's Tar-Baby—you can't
touch that baby without getting to look like him.[19] And, I might add,
sound like him.

HOW DOES AN IRISH STORYTELLER TELL A STORY?

Hauntings crisscrosses newpaper headlines and films during a particular period—1990 to 1992. Since the presidential campaign and
the market absorbed me during a good part of this period, they run
through this work like Ariadne's thread. But it's an Italian American
who is doing the actual threading, one who *theoretically* wishes to
conduct his narrating like an Irish storyteller. How does an Irish
storyteller tell a story? Laterally. Just when you think you've gotten
to the point, or even on the road to some point, or can even imagine
that there is some yet unforeseen road and point, our storyteller
crosses over to another road. It's a forking paths story-style, what
Deleuze would call a "rhizomic" pattern.[20] You crisscross so many
times that you forget where you began and lose track of where you
might be going. The disorder of everyday life is not being repackaged
into a handy bit, something you can tag and file, but seems to have
hopelessly cluttered the storyteller's mind.

The storyteller can't rise above the multiplicities of what happens to him or her or us and assert some control. If you dread both
the point of the story and the way the story is told, if you want the
storyteller to break out of the constraints of his or her own telling
and make conceivable to us the more turbulent goings-on of the
tellable and the untellable, what we want to see and what haunts us,
then you want a crisscrossing, lateralizing storytelling. But it has its
style nevertheless; it has its pattern, its control. We enter into it like
an early morning dream. We cannot keep from giving *particular*
attention to that part of the flux we're presenting. We are both aware

and unaware of how we fraudulently and artificially particularize the mazy flux of our lives.

Nothing can be particularized without loss to its place in the vortex of the unbroken whole that David Bohm describes as life.[21] The film's narration intertexts/iterates not only other films but the events the culture is experiencing then. During this period the presidential campaign and its players seemed to interpenetrate everything. In fact the campaign's own messages told us about problems but what that telling left out frightened us. We heard numerous and diverse solutions but what we also heard was the refrain "we can't *solve* what really haunts us." And that failure haunts us. Let me start a catalogue of hauntings—the sayable part:

The *New World Order*—What could it mean when all we wanted was to hold on to modernity's order of things? What was "new" had to be different than the firm securities of Enlightenment order and therefore incomprehensible—within the light of that order—and frightening. What was new had to be new and yet still signify within what Deleuze calls the "dominant forms of signification." And that called for a truly global spin.

Free Play of the Market—What did it do to democratic egalitarianism and social justice? Was this what the Founding Fathers envisioned as their American Dream? Was the market their dream?

Cultural Difference—Did asserting the center was everywhere mean that our culture was losing its focus and its own image of self-presence? How could difference replace identity as the foundation of a civic culture?

AIDS—What would the unheard of linkage among love, sex, and death do to our American way of life?

South Central LA—Riot or revolt? Whether riot or revolt— Was there any way to respond? Would the threat of social revolution have to be costed in now? Is it a greater threat than economic decline and a growing deficit? Can the free play of the market defend us against both threats? Or is it the problem?

Wilding (violence for the hell of it)—Was this the end-product of a collapse of a firm cultural identity or was it the result of a culture too long immured within an order that discarded who and what it denied identity to?

Rich and Poor—A growing gap between those for whom the culture is home base and those left out by the culture and homeless—a market inevitability or the end of equality, the end of democracy? Was the former working class becoming Third World style unskilled workers and the high-tech elite becoming the new patrician class?

Abortion and Euthanasia—Resolvable matters of whose rights count the most? Abortion—a deciding battle between a patriarchal order and a long overdue challenge to it? Euthanasia—along with abortion, a solution to global overpopulation, itself a threat to both environment and social order?

America's History—Authorized by whom? A pawn of the present's prevailing perceptions or a theory-neutral, value-free excavation?

Ethnic, Gender, Racial, Sexual Differences—To be assimilated into Oneness, woven into an American cultural identity, or preserved and drawn upon and therefore inevitably continually challenging the never abating drive toward a unified identity?

Nature—Obsolete notion, like egalitarianism, in our post-production, service-related economy? Or, surpassed/subsumed at our peril? Is the destruction of nature a death-wish of humankind? Is there a future without nature? Is it a necessary part of the market's creative destructionism that nature become extinct?

Cyberspace—Is the world of *Neuromancer* the world we will inevitably have? Neural network technology outpaces the human mind?

I give up the cataloguing but there are more. If they could be isolated, perhaps quantified, reduced to method and system, analyses and hypotheses, they might be more manageable; we could get a handle on them. Modernity's dream. If, however, such reification and objectification elide all the messy intersections that, if present, would overspill our processing, then we're solving in the way Zygmunt Bauman says modernity always solved—by producing yet more problems.[22]

Everything here serves finally to haunt us: the situation itself, the means to correct the situation, the déjà vu quality of both problem and solution, and most important, our sense that order and identity are being torn apart by differences, once accounted for and now unaccountable. It is as if the working relationship between our own subjectivities and the objectifications that we have constructed as a culture within which to cultivate our subjectivities has suddenly ceased to be a relationship and has become instead an incommensurability.

IS THIS BABEL?

My essays are dated because I want to say to the reader that these remarks and perceptions are provisional, little and local, relative to the circumstances within which they were written. Why couldn't I rise above the dates and give the reader a touch of the perennial, a touch of truth that has no expiration date? The crisscrossing I do in any one essay is much dependent on what's crisscrossing at that time out there in the culture. I depend on the magazines and newspapers, interjecting my *Village Voice* into my *Wall Street Journal*. I am a CSPAN court junkie, mesmerized by the unfolding of the real, feeling myself being enfolded within it. With my remote in hand, I move laterally across one hundred or so cable channels. I break the line of McNeil-Lehrer with the mazy MTV. I cross Oprah into Maury, Geraldo into Donohue. I wait for Letterman. I am ready at four for Terry Gross and *Fresh Air*. I take NPR on my jogs. I consider all things. I can't get too far from the intersecting waves of transmission. Are the accidental lived experiences *behind* or *in* these? Is this relatedness, the pure movement of the trace? Or is this Babel?

My life intersects the lives of the students enrolled in my postmodernism courses during these years. I hear the haunting in their late night telephone calls: Give me the ground, show me the center, tie it all up. I hear the haunting in late night telephone calls from everyone I know about the death of deconstruction, the death of the American Dream, the death of postmodernity, the death of theory, the death of liberalism, the death of Marxism, the end of equality, the end of family values, the end of closure. I, like every other American in these past two years, have been overwhelmed. Should I have waited for history to reveal itself in its fundamental clarity as I probed from a distance with objective analysis? What

could possibly be the benefit of rushing in, showing all my preju-
dices (enabling and not so enabling), mixing up films, histories,
theories, headlines, and everything else?

I do not think a postmodern attitude can handle things any
other way. Lived experiences and popular film intersect and interpenetrate; the distance between subject and object is a myth; I do
not pretend to jump outside my own life-world in order to get to the
truth of things for you. And if I were to ask you when is the best
time to question a dreamer about his or her dream, wouldn't you
reply, "As soon as the dreamer wakes up"? But if we are always in
our stories, personal and social, and these are interacting with each
other, why wait for things to stop? Why believe that narratives that
promise to bring the flux to a halt are themselves outside that flux?
We construct stories of how we can be different without waiting to
identify, knowing full well that our means of identifying depend
upon our denial of the trace 'retaining the other as other in the
same.' If we want to confront what now haunts us, if our hope lies
in entering a play of unrepressed order and disorder, should we wait
until we are mesmerized either by our fears or our escapist responses to them?

"There is a vital need," Henry Giroux writes, "for postmodernism
to open up and establish public spheres among non-academic audiences and to work with such audiences as part of the struggle to fight
racism and other forms of domination while simultaneously struggling to revitalize democratic public life."[23] Can popular culture join
in this struggle? In *Mots d'Ordre* I argued that popular culture had a
better chance of subverting forms of domination than hierarchies of
order out of which that domination emerges and is sustained. In leaving 'my Leavis' years ago and taking up 'my Fiedler' I also took to
heart Fiedler's words on the inherent disorder of the popular: "Pop art
is, whatever its overt politics, *subversive*: a threat to all hierarchies
insofar as it is hostile to order and ordering in its own realm."[24] bell
hooks has likewise seen the threat and its importance: "It's exciting to
think, write, talk, and create art that reflects passionate engagement
with popular cultures because this may very well be the central future
location of resistance struggle, a meeting place where new and radical
happenings can occur."[25]

Because we have no experiences with rhetoric in our scholarly articles and monographs, it may seem that I am more rhetorical than rational in this book. Postmodernity ignores those boundaries and it does so just at the moment when we seem most to need to be able to distinguish rhetoric from critical reason. I move back and forth from the lived experiences of our culture to filmic texts which I should hold—but I don't—as primary if I am to constrain the worldly flux. Unless I fasten myself to either the text as a stable reference point, or to an overarching theoretical frame that can differentiate the movements of the flux, I risk being swept into the maelstrom. I'm rebuilding Babel.

My words won't be anchored; nor will I bring anything to a stop. I will be meeting the rhetorical rivalries of the the worldly flux with my own rhetoric. An accidental navigator into an accidental sea. Let me make my case and then end this apologia for essays I wrote with no apologies in mind.

AM I A SOPHIST?

There's more rhetoric in my essays than rational thesis and argument. There's more rhetoric in the headlines of the world and in our self-narrations of our own lived experiences than critical reason can handle. Or wants to handle. Am I taking us back to the personal, arbitrary, foundationless rhetoric of impressionist critics, or the rhetoric of the Sophists who positioned themselves in terms of the lived experiences of the listener, what was hot at that moment, what would connect strongly at that moment?

Perhaps our deepest haunting is here: we can find no place to rest within a "postmodern plurality of discourses" nor can we "stabilize a grand narrative that could perform the integrative, theoretical, universal, and rational role that philosophy assumed within the representational tradition."[26] Why attend to my sophistic forays into popular film and American culture, even if postmodernity has undermined philosophy's superiority to rhetoric?

A carnival of self-legitimating, self-justifying discourses can only legitimate and justify in a Nike as well as a Ross Perot fashion—by "just doing it." And we are persuaded into "just doing it" by rhetorical rather than philosophical arguments. Ian Angus refers to this as a "performative legitimation," the sort of legitimation that could very well lead to a society's domination by the dominant forms of signification, by the ideology of "dominant power groups."[27] Such legitimation by performance would reduce a postmodern plurality of discourses to a premodern monism, Adorno's totally administered society.

In contrast to both the internal legitimation of discourses and the external imposition of a master discourse, Angus argues "that each discourse spans all other discourses." The postmodern condition is "not merely an episode of skepticism" but indeed offers us a "new configuration of unity and plurality, particularity and universality, and cannot be countered by simply asserting the traditional arguments concerning the self-cancellation of relativism and skepticism, the necessity of unity to the definition of plurality, claims to universality in the perception of particulars, and so forth.... The new, open field of the postmodern condition simply means that a discourse spanning, or translating, different discourses cannot be given an independent legitimation—that no one discourse can monopolize the locus of translation."[28]

Can philosophy, or its critical reasoning, navigate the rhetorical tide? How can this navigation occur since the postmodern condition has left us without a reliable compass? According to Angus, philosophy is a "type of move" not toward "proliferation but to an explicit termination."[29] It constructs "silence": "This silent, still point is the moment in translation where the residue asserts itself through the origin of a certain fixity that cannot stem the madness, but that can let it be seen as madness opening an utterance that will close itself.... In this way philosophy comes to the aid of rhetoric and releases its legitimate and necessary field of operation. Stalling 'unfixity' allows temporary meaning within specific discourse, which is, in turn, undermined by the madness of general rhetoric."[30]

Madness, it seems, cannot be stopped for long, and that madness is produced by a rhetorical criticism that is continuously reestablishing "unfixity of meaning" in response to any "[a]spiring metanarrative's attempt to fix meaning within a higher totalization."[31] Angus defines the postmodern condition as this *fort-da* play of madness and meaning: "The postmodern condition can thus be defined as the continuous interplay between totalizing translation and rhetorical criticism of aspiring metanarratives in an open field of discursivity." However, it is madness that haunts the open field: "This continuous dynamism generates a radical unfixity of meaning within the field of discursivity as a whole. Proliferation of temporary senses continuously undermined injects madness into general agonistics."[32]

It is here that philosophy enters to "keep madness at bay": "Only by timidly holding back, by ceasing to follow the performative modification to its end, can a semblance of fixity, of saying what we mean and meaning what we say, be preserved."[33] By seeking endings and not proliferation, by seeking temporary meaning rather than totalizing meaning, philosophy navigates an undermining rhetoric away from madness. A dynamic of spanning and translating discourses comes to rest neither in madness nor meaning, neither in "radical unfixity" nor "totalizing fixity."

We have before us then "a postmodern discursive philosophy/ rhetoric that is dialogically, rather than diametrically, delineated. Rather than each limiting and devaluing the other, both extend into and require the other. The very means for conceptualizing dualities of reason and speech, knowledge and persuasion, truth and opinion—in short mind and body—are annulled."[34]

Neither movement, rhetorical nor philosophical, can alone finally give us a sense of saying what we mean, and meaning what we say. It is rhetoric's unfixing of our semblances of fixity and philosophy's attempt to bring rhetoric's proliferations to an end, to fix them, which shape our attempts, within the postmodern condition, to say what we mean and mean what we say. The shaping here is conducted by a dynamic interplay. The madness of our accidental lives plays itself into the cement of our cultural fixity.

THE FREE PLAY OF POPULAR FILM
DECEMBER 1992

> *First, let's think about American big business. We don't know much about it, and never will, because the people who run it don't answer to you and me, and we don't even have the blunt instrument of the Freedom of Information Act to wave above them, as we do with politicians. We live in the circle of fog that they spray underneath themselves.*
>
> —Michael Tomasky

Postmodernism is not an answer to the break-up of clear connections, whether between word and world, free markets and ecologism, *Homo sapiens* and *Machina sapiens*, or what have you. Because postmodernism proliferates the questions, it requires more answers. Everything becomes more difficult. Let's look at the 'everything': instead of a unified, coherent, continuous global culture that can be arranged hierarchically—Third World at the bottom, untouchables at the bottom of that—we have a pluralism of cultures that each generates a different context, establishes a different language game. And through all this they each concoct a sense of order, traditions, and customs, an in-house way of linking word and world.

When we look closer we see that any grand cultural narrative itself breaks up and extends, as in the United States, multilaterally, east coast to west coast, north to south. It's interesting that when you are thinking laterally there is only a sort of equal rivalry, like between Los Angeles and New York, right brain and left brain. But when you think vertically you think hierarchically. But since postmodern truth is multiple and local it doesn't travel well. Not legitimately at any rate. So the criteria of judgment necessary to make distinctions of good and bad, civilized and primitive, First World and Third World, advanced and retarded, order and disorder, are lacking.[1]

Postmodernity, then, doesn't proliferate questions in the same way the Modernist Project does. Rather, postmodernity hears questions in modernity's answers, and questions from voices modernity has discarded. Feyerabend tells the story of planet discovery: for as long as the answer to the question "Could there be other orbiting bodies in the solar system?" was "No" then no new bodies were discovered for eons. When one person answered, "Possibly," a new celestial body was discovered. The answer then became "Yes" and within the context of that answer a slew of new bodies were discovered.

So in this fashion postmodernity *is* an answer, a different answer than modernity, an answer that is out to register and attend to the varieties of play of order and disorder. Out of this play different questions and answers emerge that do not fail to clash. But they clash only *if* they are not already sorted, graded, and discarded in the light of context-free universal standards of judgment.

Free market play engenders multiple questions and multiple answers from multiple locales in our society. Nevertheless, it has stepped forward in a time of economic crisis as well as a Habermasian crisis of legitimation. This crisis of legitimation transmits to the culture as a whole through our present incapacity to solve all sorts of societal, family, and personal crises that we feel would have been brought to clear resolution just fifty years ago.

"Earth Last. Business First" is the banner line for the June 16, 1992 *Village Voice*. Business is the economy is the play of the free market is jobs is being rich is the American Dream. The whole chain fills the popular culture. What isn't linked here is either inconsequential or regulatory. Questions may continue to multiply but if they're to be answered at all the answer comes out of free market play.

This chain of utmost significance fills the Big Screen as well as TV; it's heard in rap music, soap operas, on Oprah and Donohue, NPR, it overwhelms the 1992 presidential campaign, it's lurking behind the protest against the Rodney King verdict, Bush takes it to the Earth Summit, it puts the fall of the Soviet Empire on a back burner, it has the American Dream slipping into murky memory as the new millennium dawns over the Pacific Rim.

Economics is hot, red hot, at the very moment the Marxist base/superstructure, for so long too vulgar for Neo-Marxist theorists, goes down the toilet with the Soviet Union. A postmodern cultural pluralism killed the monologic Union, cracked its unity in more places than we can count. The Soviet master narrative lost its hold; if it had hung in there, economic hardships would have meant as much to the Soviets as torture to a martyr. Contemporaneously, the Reagan–Bush regime makes a decisive break with America as Camelot, with government as knights of the Round Table sent out on a mission to create anew the democratic spirit of the land and its people—Arthur's mystical mission that gets linked in unspoken ways with the young JFK. The ineffable, spectral values of liberty, equality, and social justice are brushed aside in the '80s and the raw materiality of wealth and possessions, of wanting to be rich, is identified as the pursuit of happiness.

Constructed and put forward by the wealthy, the Reagan–Bush regime polishes one of the major links historically made between the American Dream and meaning: greed. "Mo' money" for everybody. It trickles down from those who already have it and who will employ it so that everyone will be employed. Money can be earned, saved, and used to educate the next generation. Social mobility is happening; the American Dream is working. Until the many Americans who are not working begin to note that the American Dream is not working for them, that the Dream is always promoted in ways that work for the 'Players.'

A Marxist critique is certainly not now positioned to be heard since it went down in the popular imagination with the Soviet Union. But it is that sort of critique that could communicate that there are Players already positioned to shape the ways we connect the signifier "American Dream" with the world. Both reality and dream become more and more market developments. The players play and the rest of us—our discourse, our democracy, our lived experiences—find their shape in that play.

Our popular culture doesn't advance this one-sided story of mine as gospel-truth. Rather it spreads everything out—the history and politics, the play of the market, the social issues—into local linkings or pockets of meaning. Conservative, liberal, and radical meanings only seem to cover if we stop attending to all the other local struggles-to-say that go on. Popular culture doesn't ignore the play of what discourse has already brought to order, and the contingencies of lived experience that we can only speak analogously about. Even the questions speak of popular culture the way we used to speak of the Soviet Union—as if it were really one-voiced. Is popular culture an instrument of prevailing power? Is it totally controlled by the free play of the market? Does it cooperate in those very real-izings of the world that trouble us?

Film, for instance, enacts what troubles us, what provokes us, what is struggling to be brought to a level of conceivability and expressibility but is yet bound by ways of saying, of signifying, which block us off, as if these narratives already in sway suffice. But they don't. I most certainly stick to my salvo against modernity, corporate rights over individual rights, *Machina sapiens* over *Homo sapiens*, an uncontested free market, any anti-ecologism, Dan Quayle as a voice of communicative rationality, Perot's "just do it" philosophy as anything less than a dangerous undermining of democratic values, and so on. But film can set up unsayable regimes against, or indifferent to, or other than what we might interpret as its own meaning.

Most important, popular film engages popular matters. I mean by this matters that hold the populace bound because they cannot free themselves of them.

Is this not a major departure from popular film as only escapist, as taking the populace away from what remains ungraspable in their lives? Popular film certainly allows its audience to escape the boundaries and bonds of their own lives. At least for a time. But it is not so easy to either escape or bring to meaning a postmodern world as it is to escape or bring to meaning a classic realist or modernist world.

Both pomo lives and pomo world are too fractured to be treated to one escape world, one escape route. Women are alert to the patriarchal narrative, nonwhite to the white narrative, non-Western to the Western narrative, environmentalists to the progress narrative, and so on. Inner landscapes so richly embroidered in a Virginia Woolf world are telecommunicated into mediascapes. Everyone's inner life is drawn into external imagery. Realization is through photo-ops.

We share the outside more intricately, drawn into conversation with late night TV talk shows, early morning America, mid-morning with Sally Jessy Raphael, lunch with Regis and Kathie Lee, late afternoon with Oprah, Maury, or Donohue, tonight with Jay Leno, late night with Letterman. The afternoon TV soap operas take us through a crisscrossing of lives, the unspeakable replaced with the overspeaking, crises and controversies flung out over shallow, hasty, but endlessly proliferating story lines so that in the end—and there is no end—no one, including the burning issue, gets out alive. We watch until we drop.

Is this escape or a helpless entanglement in our culture's myriad ways of representing itself?

Let me say that while modernity was in its heyday the specialists were busy handling society's disorder. They were cataloguing it, defining it, experimenting with it, and repeatedly resolving it, just like W. C. Fields solved his drinking problem thousands of times. There simply was no need to transmit an unsayable issue onto the screen, there to torment and fascinate us. Nonetheless, we think of film as becoming a serious art form at the moment when what escapes Enlightenment modernity reaches the screen. These are the subjects we can't get out of our minds, out of our systems, problems that are getting solved only at the cost of creating more problems.

So they slip onto the screen not only as an aftermath of 1929 Depression in films such as those produced by the cooperative Frontier Films, but right at the moment when economically we're second to none—the '50s. The Dean is a rebel without a cause while Brando is rebelling against whatever "ya got." Gregory Peck poses as a Jew to expose society's agreement about Jews. Sinatra's heroin addiction in *Man with the Golden Arm* as well as Don Murray's in *Hatful of Rain* escape to the screen. We see racial issues in *Pinky* and *Imitation of Life*, *The Defiant Ones*, labor issues in *On the Waterfront*, varieties of corruption in *Sweet Smell of Success*, *Elmer Gantry*, *The Big Knife*.

But the Enlightenment Project —in Habermas' words, "the rational organization of everyday social life"—became in twentieth-century modernism divorced and distanced from that "everyday social life." Habermas once again: "The differentiation of science, morality, and art has come to mean the autonomy of the segments treated by the specialist and at the same time letting them split off from the hermeneutics of everyday communication."[2] Aesthetic modernism of the twentieth century also made its very project the distancing of art from tradition and convention, an ongoing advance away from the prevailing narratives of the real toward art's own representing capacities, a sort of self-engagement that signified as serious art the further it got from anything serious in the headlines.

Today's popular film is caught in a postmodern world that does not feel its problems are being solved by an endless number of specialized authorities. Nor does this postmodern world honor the notion that there is a high art that is somehow resolving our dilemmas on its higher, aesthetic plane. This higher, aesthetic order of things has no edge on any other order of things in the postmodern view, nor are the resolutions of Enlightened specialists enlightened beyond or outside their own little and local ordering of things.

While all of the pretensions of modernity can be swallowed as long as we are within its paradigm, they seem no more than pretensions once we're within a postmodern paradigm.

It's not the present populace, then, who are escaping to the cinema, hoping to escape their own lives, but a whole slew of contesting narratives that are escaping ivory tower, courtroom, boardroom, laboratory, executive suites and jockeying for position on the Big Screen. It's the sheer play of order and disorder and not a solemn modernist filmic problem solving—the difference between the 1962 and the 1991 *Cape Fear*—that is now marketable. The postmodern popular audience is targeted all over the place, quite used to the hoopla of violently competing stories. At the same time, this audience is intolerant and suspicious of and impatient with packagings of the truth put forward as objective and absolute, not somehow positioned culturally.

While TV takes on the talk, discourses until everyone is exhausted, film stretches beyond the discourse toward what we have yet no discourse for. And it has to. Its audience already has heard it all, been hailed by TV, addicted, mesmerized. Rapping with everybody about everything is a twenty-four-hour nonstop run. But escapes from that discourse are unsupportable, insulting. Popular film takes on the unchannelled flow but it also flows where discourse is not ready to go.

The postmodern popular film also moves us laterally out of what we've heard, moves us not away from our own lived experiences but shows us how in an unlegitimated world they intersect other life-worlds. Instead of escaping the commotion and din of an increasingly unresolvable world into nostalgic metanarratives of unity and coherence, the popular film today exploits the din and follows the intersections toward what holds us, as a culture, spellbound, fascinated. All of this becomes part of that freak show that classic realists and modernists alike identify as the "postmodern." Indeed, they accuse postmodernism of bringing this freak show to town.

Film is popular, then, because it does not try to rise above or bring to an a priori order the conflicts that trouble and the fears that haunt our culture. The market is *in* this turbulence and therefore in what is potent, fascinating, but unsettling, disturbed, and chaotic. The popular film that escapes and/or conforms and the serious film that focuses and explores obey modernity's boundaries. There is now a new popular film that escapes those boundaries and that nothing escapes from.

When popular film enters the legitimation-free, unbounded, free market world, it is, as a medium of representation, entering the unregulated postmodern world of representations. Popular film may invest as heavily into stereotypes and classic realist harmonies as does a culture seeking free market play while keeping the free play of signifiers within regulated meanings. However, contemporary popular culture cannot ignore our postmodern culture's uneasiness, its questioning and parodying of previously untroubled assumptions, beliefs, real-izings. Background, dissident voices that clashed with the dominant chord can only be muted at the risk of losing connection with the world everybody else is in.

And the popular film cannot afford to lose its populace; it cannot afford to be forging ahead of or behind those buying the tickets. Their present audience/market is a multinarrative audience whose local knowledge is, to use Lyotard's description, incredulous regarding a "universalized knowledge" and whose local knowledge cannot free itself of unsettling interconnections of and interpenetrations by other and different local knowledge narratives.

Jobs and salaries remain foundational for this potential ticket-buying populace at the same time that our free market culture is pursuing its own economic stability not in producers/laborers but in consumers/players. The clash here is brought to the screen, very seldom directly because the issue is so fractious, because there is such a total absence of successful modernist problem solving here. On the other hand, since what I call the "free market narrative" insinuates itself in every local niche of real-izing in every corner of our 'declining' American culture, there is no way popular film can remain popular without wrestling with, in however disjointed and sigmoid a fashion—with short lateral excursions that serve to tell us this popular film is within the pulse of present-day culture—the intersection of the American Dream and the play of the market.

What are the crossings to be made here? Start outside the market, with the homeless. Definition: nonconsumers, certainly nonplayers. Political entitlement: rendered nonexistent by a free market that is, as Bauman writes, "democratically unaccountable."[3] The free market is deeply embedded in the lives of not only the homeless but a whole class of blue-collar workers who face extinction within the play of that market. And they know it. It's as if when Bush voted against the biodiversity treaty, he voted *not* to preserve the working man in this country. And that signifier, "the working *man*" is not only *not* politically correct but its problems as a signifier underscore the problems in reality.

Within different narrative frames the homeless are the by-products of former liberal (read "The Great Society") excesses. They need to be brought to a level of responsibility and accountability. There are no free lunches in the free market. The blue-collar worker is an anachronism and must be retrained to competitive levels of production, competitive with workers worldwide who have not been bred on democratic notions of individual rights and freedoms, who do not set their individuality against society's/business's pressures to conform and maximize profits. The global blue-collar worker has already been diminished in expectations by long histories of political inequities. And the global high-tech worker is already experiencing economic well-being outside our own American experiencing of a democracy, of contentious individualism. The American working man must either move upward or downward, either be trained to fit into technoculture or accept the victimization of unskilled labor (including nonliveable wages) that is the norm in Third World countries. Note that it is the mindless play of the market and its progress to high-tech culture that reduces manual labor—from plowing a field and lumbering to stevedoring and housekeeping—to unglorious pursuits. Is this not a further distancing from not only our ties within nature but with the embodiment, the physicality, of our own existence?

Worker unions founded by legendary 'working-class heroes' are also linked differently on the global scene where they signify only as deterrents and obstacles to corporate teamwork. Danny DeVito's *Hoffa*, opening on Christmas Day 1992, not even two months after Clinton's victory, does not spend itself on extricating Hoffa from dark, whispered connections with the Mafia, but rather brings to the foreground in Dolby stereo and scenes directed in the fashion of Eisenstein, scenes of clash between workers and owners' private police, a connection between the American union movement and the extension of democratic egalitarianism. For all the corruption that '80s conservatives have laid at the feet of American unions, there yet remains a lessening of the socioeconomic gap between rich and poor accomplished by unions. And that effort strengthened our democratic ideals of social justice and political equity while the Reagan–Bush years increased that gap to a perhaps irredeemable point. *Hoffa* then stands as a clear signal of popular film's response to a shifting of ideologies, itself playing out the undecidability of what is now a postmodern clash, a postmodern shifting.

In an uncontested free market play atmosphere the hero is a player (like Milken), not a sweating worker male-bonded to other sweating workers, going out for a few cold ones after the shift. There is a promised freedom from macho, a promised asexuality about high-tech employment. Here women are truly equal to men. What is glossed over is that the value of both men and women is lessened as the market play affixes them to the regime of *Machina sapiens*. Instead of severing macho from blue-collar work, from sweat on the brow, from manual labor, the whole concept of non-high-tech work is pushed as retrogressive, soon to be extinct. Like nature.

Money is not earned, but managed. It isn't attached to hours or piece work, but invested, transferred, floated, leveraged, brokered, exchanged, arbitraged—in short, *played* with.[4] It's not the brawny steelworker but the clever player who gets the girl, who gets the action. The player is sexy; playing the market is sexy. Not only traditions of individual identity are challenged, but the play of the market also severs small businesses from their own roots, the seminal vision of their founders, the sense of original connectedness with both consumer and society. Local origins then are unsettled by global reconfigurations, by renarrating a local history within a narrative that plays better globally. Traditions of individual entrepreneurship confront a sort of free market indifference to all but increased profits for shareholders.

Liberal and conservative ideologies attempt to bring all the strayings and deviations here back into their own narratives. They do not, however, contain these cultural divagations but are split by them. While "liberal" is a signifier no one even seems interested in reconnecting to the world, "conservative" is fast becoming an empty signifier, one whose connection lies in not bringing to a level of signification 95 percent of what is going on in the culture, from the homeless and the recession, to the decline of democratic ideals in the United States.

When today's popular film takes on the free market the viewer has to be agile to keep up with the crisscrossings, to sort out how we are being played, how we are both consuming and responding to linkages haunting yet not fully conceivable. And one must work hard to avoid accepting as one's own sayable what the popular film holds out as what it is saying. The popular film trafficking in our postmodern culture must always necessarily detour into the abyss of our own culture's haunted, perplexed digressions. Digressions, like centers, are everywhere.

Today's popular film only seems to be coming to rest within classic realist or modernist narratives, where a discourse of connectedness seems to flourish, where all the right questions seem to be asked. Causes and effects, determinants, influences, contributing factors, statistical indicators, empirical validations, and so on ultimately come out of life-worlds and language games that shape how things will come out. More and more our popular culture is bringing us into a contesting free play of such unassimilable worlds. Is this a sort of cultural tribalism, a major step backward to a primordial divisiveness that we ultimately brought to order? Or is this a lateral movement into an immense and prolific difficulty we brought to order at an expense we are—except for those players who have profitted mightily—no longer willing to pay?

GECKOID DEMOCRACY AND THE GARFIELDIAN AMERICAN DREAM
OCTOBER 1991

Greed is Good. Greed is Right. Greed Works.
—Gordon Gecko

A dollar is not value, but representative of value, and, at last, of moral values.
—Ralph Waldo Emerson

I don't make anything? I'm making you money. You don't care if you manufacture cable wire, grow tangerines or sell fried chicken. You're a stockholder because you want to make money.
—Lawrence Garfield

It's kill or be killed.
—Lewis Winthorpe III

If you think Milken was ambitious beyond sense and reason, what follows probably won't change your opinion. But self-serving or not, many of his observations ring true. Read with an open mind and you will almost certainly learn a great deal. We know we did. Mike Milken and his accomplishments are no more to be ignored because he broke some laws than Richard Nixon is to be ignored because of Watergate.
—James W. Michaells and Phyllis Berman

117

Wall Street's world excludes me at the same time the film is drawing me in. I become young Bud Fox hoping to rise from the pit of cold calls to become a real player. "If you're not inside," Gordon Gecko, the Player La Superba, tells Bud, "you're outside." You're a "player or nothing." Maybe my joint fascination and disgust represents the same kind of sweet/sour relationship our whole culture has with money and the "players" of "penetrating insights" and "almost un-believable powers of concentration."[1]

Oliver Stone's young Bud is no Billy Budd. This Bud is not tongue-tied. He calls up strangers—cold calls—and tries to talk them into letting him play with their money on the market. But I can't help making the Billy Budd association. I can't help seeing the difference between the two. This Bud, after all, is for us, for our culture. He's an '80s version of Wilhelm Meister, but he's not look-ing for a Goethean apprenticeship into self and then traveling out of that self toward selflessness. The '80s overwrites that sort of appren-ticeship. Bud wants to be a fox. The sheep are at home, "the home," in the immortal words of Gordon Gecko, "of the exposed brick wall and the house plant." Sounds like my house, which I rent. James Spader, Bud's counterpart in the law, has "got a house in Oyster Bay" and Bud, now on the inside, buys a condo on the East Side for "just under" one million.

We've traveled with Charlie Sheen before. We went young and cal-low into Vietnam with him in *Platoon*. He's got a young, open, honest, vulnerable face, eyes that probe the scene as if he were wondering what was coming next. In spite of the fact that America has wound up with a player as a father-mentor, we continue to produce the young and the restless, and since we as a culture are in search of what they are in search of, we follow their filmic journey. Sheen's real-life father, Martin Sheen, appears in this movie as his father. But Bud chooses the wrong father figure. He chooses Gecko, the false father, the false mentor. Rediscovering the true father will be young Bud's pilgrimage. America's pilgrimage.

Stone's moral message: America in the '80s is making Gecko its mentor. Gecko the player, the man of greed, the Terminator, the Liquidator, the Liberator of Companies. What's the true father like?

He's a union rep who "never measured a man's success by the size of his wallet." He also advises Bud to "create instead of living off the buying and selling of others." And he has a heart attack halfway through the movie. He's resurrected but therein lies the rub. Is he resurrected? Maybe he collapses because his wallet discourse and his creation discourse collapse.

What is the rule of judgment that our culture applies to determine the success of a man? Is it a universal rule of judgment? Do we judge a woman's success by it? And is it clearly other than the Geckoid rule of judgment? Martin Sheen's creation discourse intersects Gecko's discourse. Isn't the creation of new market and endless development, innovativeness, creative financing, creative new technology, and all the rest of it the banner flag of the free market and of a conservative ideology as well? We are ceaselessly at our loom. Milken put in fifteen-hour work days. Gecko is a creative force in the flesh. At a moment when the actual production of things has given way to service, when economic creativity lies precisely in the control and manipulation of what we ourselves do not produce, do not create, it is devilishly Geckoid to put forth this coopted, diversely linked creation discourse as a master discourse.

Let's face it. Next to the nonstop, spontaneous, free play of Gecko, his mad spinning at the hub of things, his own power to buy and control the creativity of others, we don't tie the true father to anything but chain smoking, blue-collar attire, a devotion to his men, a nebulous critique that floats in all directions, a clash with his son, and a heart attack. The film's break from classic realism lies in the blurred parts here. Geckoid democracy is clear: only the naive believe we live in a democracy. The richest one percent of the population owns the trillions. Two-thirds of that is inherited, passed down from one generation to the next. What trickles down and out? The question of the '80s. The remaining one-third is up for grabs on the market.

Players are at play for that. To reach into the American Dream is to be a player. And when young Bud gives up that role, turns in his mentor Gecko to the law, and himself faces justice for his past transgressions, have we reidentified our true democratic roots? Have we established our true cultural mentor? Have we somehow checked and regulated the free play of the market? Have we lost our fascination and unspoken admiration for Gecko, Milken, Trump, Perot? When Bud Fox goes up the steps into the Court of Justice at the film's end, have democratic values brought greed into line and has the American Dream been reinscribed as something distinct from young Bud's dream to be a privileged player?

The director, Oliver Stone, rushes to moral closure as if the film had taken us into the play of the market and led us out chastened and reborn. The problem is that we can't really get into the market, we can't become players ourselves, by following Bud's journey. He has reason to turn against Gecko: Gecko used him to arrange to strip the company the true father had given his life to. And when the true father collapses, young Bud, like a hero from the American West, sets out to set things right. Once on this high horse of justice and morality, Bud confronts his girlfriend, incites her to voice her empty values—"To have money and have lost it, it's worse than not having had it at all."

Bud has looked into the abyss and has found his character and that's what keeps him out of the abyss. If you look too long and too deeply into the abyss, Nietzsche, who did both, tells us, the abyss looks into you. Bud gets out with a lesson learned. But we don't. We understand Bud's apprenticeship and how he regains his moral character and both Gecko and Milken are in jail but we're not quite sure what has replaced Geckoid democracy, that '80s form of democracy that whispers to us: "We've gone into a New Age where the players are fulfilling the American Dream and the sheep are getting slaughtered." These are the same sheep that Clarice Starling tries to save in *The Silence of the Lambs*. They're on the factory line, union members, working class. They're on the outside, homeless, poor, not a clue as how to be creative in this New Age, how to get beyond money as a rule of judgment to something else, some fast-diminishing democratic, egalitarian, fraternal rule of judgment.

Blurred, disappearing links in this New Age. Gecko's narrative in the mouth of Dan Quayle as he reaches out for the 1996 presidential campaign. Perot standing in for Gecko in the 1992 presidential campaign, promising to go into the trenches, fight like hell, "just do it," and win. It's understood here that the sheep will get slaughtered.

There is no easy moral closure or sleight-of-hand return to demo-cratic justice in 1992's *Other People's Money*. In fact this comedy bites deeply into the growing American tragedy—the loss of both economic supremacy and egalitarian justice for all. There is an open clash between old-fashioned small town/business America, which is full of all those heartwarming democratic ideals the Sicil-ian immigrant Frank Capra brought so clearly to the screen, and the free play of the market so exuberantly personified in this film by a superkinetic Danny DeVito. As Lawrence Garfield, president and chairman of the board of Garfield Investments, DeVito glee-fully makes money by buying up the stock of an already estab-lished company and liquidating the company's assets at a substan-tial profit on the current market.

It's hard to dislike him. He has so much greater an appetite for life—including sex, the violin, the opera—than Jordie Jorgenson, played by Gregory Peck in the same way he played Sam Boden in the 1962 *Cape Fear*. I mean he's once again at the heart of Ameri-cana, resonating with all the Heartland virtues. When you see DeVito/Garfield from Jordie/Peck perspective he's a mischievous imp, a malignant force emanating from Wall Street, the rapacious Liquida-tor that post-industrial America has newly spawned. And Jordie/Peck is there to defend us, to defend America from its own foul issue. But DeVito/Garfield's energy overwhelms this nostalgic de-fense, this Mass for the Dead that Jordie/Peck wants to call America and doing business in America. The stockholders vote for Garfield's slate, the liquidation slate, and they do so because after hearing Jordie's defense of the way America has done and should continue to do business, they hear and accept Garfield's equation of a per-sonal desire to make money, the providing of a service to the entire economy, and the creation of new jobs.

It's the same speech Ronald Reagan gave in 1980 and then again in 1984. In 1992 Danny DeVito decided to take the part from Washington to the Big Screen. And although Reagan always seemed to be having fun as president, Danny DeVito seems to be having even more fun. After all, the sort of market player Reagan wanted us all to be would be having a lot of fun.

Garfield doesn't have to be brought to justice on the charge that he's suborning the American Dream for profit, pushing it away from its finer moments toward its latent weaknesses, the shadowy areas of too much desire for everything and too little concern for the 'profits of the soul.' But our very inability to wrest the weakness of the American Dream from its strengths, indeed to keep that latent weakness from now replacing the strengths of that dreaming, makes it hard to decide who the hero is here—Jordie or Garfield.

Just as postmodernism compels us to reinvestigate modernism and see what it is that we meant by it all along, so too do various strong and conflicting interpretations of the American Dream compel us to ask "What ever did we mean by it?" In the end we see that the Supreme Court is always only in the process of telling us what it means, that every new president and legislature is busy being at odds rewriting that Dream, and that every citizen is off living within some individually constructed framing of that Dream.

At a time in history when we are aware of and sensitive to the play of contesting narratives, none of which is self-legitimated or whose truth is self-present, popular film shows certain hesitancies. It literally cannot afford to be un-self-conscious, unaware or naive regarding the identity of what is represented and what may be real. Nor can it *profitably* endorse the power of any one representation to come forward as a controlling discourse in a film.

Even Oliver Stone's various missions to problematize and expose and finally bring to a new understanding, say, America in Vietnam, the Jesuits in South America, America in its flower child days, the assassination of JFK, or the play of Wall Street, get crisscrossed with narratives Stone cannot control. This crisscrossing is not engineered by the modernist drive to reach the truth since that drive does not lead to an acknowledgment of other narratives/other truths. Instead, in postmodern popular film, it is the classic realist impulse, the need to seduce the viewer into accepting the film's representations as real, which forces the film to move laterally and therefore away from its modernist directive and into multiple truths/realities, none of which rises to a single truth. For example, in *Other People's Money*, DeVito/Garfield's winning discourse actually intersects Jordie/Peck's. The new, post-industrial overwriting of the American Dream crosses on to the old "a business is worth more than the value of its stock"/"here we care about people" American Dream.

The scene is this: Jordie/Peck has just made a very moving speech in support of people, conscience, tradition, and continued productivity, and against liquidation and quick profits. It is the desire for continued productivity that DeVito/Garfield will transpose into his speech. When Garfield gets up to speak, he's booed. The stockholders are ready to vote for all the old values over profit. Garfield has a long way to go to get them to vote for his slate—liquidation and a quick profit, and against tradition and the well-being of workers and the town. What he tells them is this: You're stockholders because you want to make money. This company won't be making a profit for long because cable is obsolete and fiber optics is the future. If you liquidate now you can take your money and invest in a company that will be productive in this New Age and not merely once productive in an Older Age.

The rest of the trickle-down scenario falls into place: productive company, greater economic growth, more new jobs, workers can consume more (including education that may someday make stockholders out of their descendants), and profits for present-day stockholders. The first link here (desire for money) and the last (the profits you realize encourage further investment, which profits or "trickles down" to all) are pure conservative discourse. The new technology link—which makes this company obsolete—is the kind of link that Enlightenment modernism always promises. It says that there's an indisputable logic to the liquidation. There's ironclad causality at work here—research and development, new technology, increased productivity, progress, profits—and not just the trickle-down discourse, which can be challenged by Jordie's tradition and humanity discourse. But "progress is in fiber optics." It cannot be refuted. And that means that the play of the free market becomes a *logic* while democratic traditions and humanitarian goals—from liberty to equality to justice—become *contingencies*.

Whatever the logic of the free market doesn't have to take account of is simply left on its own to happen, and that includes what you'll find in the Constitution and the Bill of Rights. Outside the concern of the free market these texts either survive in the trickle or they don't. And whether or not our democratic values are supported more by a company that is liquidated, (in accord with the "logic of the market") or a company that is *not* liquidated (in defiance of that logic) is a question already preempted by that market logic itself. Productivity outside the logic of ever-renewing technology and its path of progress in an inconceivable.

Let's do a crosscut of Jordie's and Garfield's narratives of productivity. Jordie's is clear-cut: productivity serves the interests of the community and workers. It is constrained by values extrinsic to productivity's own course. It rises out of the energies and contentions, dreams and satisfactions, of human life-worlds. It can stop before the invention of the wheel (as with our own Native Americans) or the use of machines (as with the Amish) and yet fulfill the needs of the producers, the needs of the human life-world. Something—values—holds the reins of productivity, and therefore of the free market.

Garfield can get his hands on other people's money without being concerned with whether the company he's trying to take over is going to continue to be productive or not. Short-term profits are here and now; future productivity doesn't affect present profits. He doesn't have to be concerned with how the economy will be served if the profits made from this liquidation are invested in a productive company. However, when Garfield is trying to sell other people the idea of liquidating for profit, his selling discourse is productivity. At the same time, Garfield confounds this discourse, this concern with productivity, by telling us clearly, "I'm not a long-term player." Corporate takeover is his business. Someone else must bring a company to a profitable productive level. If unchecked, unregulated productivity is the *primum mobile* of the American Dream, then the free market player, the entrancing hero of post-industrial America, relies on someone else to fulfill that dream.

The player makes his or her money by having someone in Washington who spins the dream of Garfieldian logic and who thereby transforms simple greed and selfishness into something grand and heroic. Skimming the cream off the top of the American economy, taking other people's money and running, becomes an act supportive of democracy when what America is all about is reduced to unimpeded productivity and democracy itself emerges from an uncontested free play of the market or not at all.

Ironically, the players are into making money off of money, into mergers, buyouts, liquidations, trading, and brokering, a myriad of activities that are represented as investment and financial services. Indeed, post-industrial America's New Age only means something when we link it with these signifiers, themselves certainly less substantial than industrial America's ease in pointing to steel making, ship building, lumberering, car making, and so on as what it does. There were long-term players—like Jordie—at work here.

But Garfield doesn't want to be a long-term player because there's less profit and more risk over a longer haul. Contradictorily, the American Dream of an egalitarian democracy arising from unleashed free market productivity rests on the notion that an unrestrained player will choose to be a long-term player, will act for reasons other than making a profit, will work for 'trickle down' rather than 'buy out,' or taking the money and running. That American Dream also of course rests on the notion that whatever the unrestrained player does will lead, in the words of Roger Smith, CEO of General Motors, to making each of us more fully human. The questions as to what productivity does for us and doesn't do for us and what we as a culture dream of becoming that may be antithetical to unrestrained productivity are in the present overwritten by prevailing ways of linking productivity with success, success with wealth, wealth with the hero/player.

Garfield emerges in 1992 as player-hero, after Gordon Gecko apparently was brought to justice in the 1985 *Wall Street*, after '80s players like Dennis Levine and Michael Milken of Drexel Burnham, takeover trader Ivan Boesky, insider-trader Martin Siegel were prosecuted for violations of the Securities Exchange Commission Act, after big brokerages like Merrill Lynch not only brought the deregulated S&Ls to ruin but, after the Fall, they made "a lively business buying and selling the government-owned carcasses."[2] When Larry Reibstein of *Newsweek* interviews Dennis Levine, who has spent seventeen months in prison for illegal insider trades, he writes: "[T]he sight of Levine, granting interviews in his $1 million Park Avenue apartment and wearing expensive suits, raised the question of whether the punishments for Levine, junk-bond king Michael Milken, speculator Iven Boesky and others were severe enough."[3] You might say that the punishments were the sort Jordie/Peck would dole out. This is the censure of the old American Dream that has been proven obsolete by Garfield's new message. And the message is clear: nothing about the Garfieldian American Dream can be really checked or regulated.

It is of course the discourse of untrammeled productivity that makes a hero of players like Garfield, players who shut down any connection of productivity with the human life-world in order to get their hands on other people's money. The privileged player here crosses a number of entrenched American narratives. He's the bold adventurer, the rugged individual. According to Ross Perot, there are lions and tigers and rabbits in this world. Milken may be in jail cleaning toilet bowls right now but he's a lion and when he gets out there's millions buried in secret partnerships waiting for him. "If I could make $10 million and live in a country-club-like prison for a couple of years, I'd do it, too," one stockbroker said in regard to Dennis Levine's post-prison success.[4] Perot is the rugged individualist who speaks his mind regardless of what the Washington spinmeisters will make of it.

   Both Gecko and Garfield share this presumptiveness. Gecko started out poor and went to the City University of New York, not Harvard. Garfield rises from the "shithole" of the Bronx. And now, like Perot, they lead us into the corridors of power and prestige, of fatcat executives and overpaid lawyers, and they speak up for us. Gecko mocks the patrician background of rival player *Sir* Lawrence Wildman, born into profits not played for. In his corporate takeover speech, Gecko comes down hard on self-rewarding bureaucracy management. "We've got thirty-three Vice presidents making over $300,000 a year. That's where your profits are. I say to them 'Do it right or get eliminated.' " Actually, like Garfield, Gecko doesn't care if "they do it right" since his liquidation profits have nothing to do with continued efficiency, productivity, workers and managers forming a team, and so on. Garfield berates and threatens his entire staff of seventeen lawyers and goes out and does himself what they can't do. Garfield is a player who appeals to the nonplayer, to the increasingly disenfranchised worker watching the film. He can sit down and eat with his butler. He doesn't pretend to be a sophisticate (he loves Dawn Donuts) or pretend to be multiculturally sensitive or politically correct (he puts the chopsticks down and asks for a fork).

And with Garfield free play is sex play. Doing business is orgasmic. Liquidating companies is gonadal and takeover negotiations with a sexy young woman is sex play. Making money is an aphrodisiac. When young Bud Fox is accepted by Gecko as his protégé the rite of initiation is conducted by a beautiful woman we never see again who gives Bud a blow job in the back seat of Gecko's limo. One of the major American narratives that the player intersects is thus the male chauvinist one. It's always a masculine American Dream, whether we're dreaming of a working class hero or a market player. When we do get a woman player as hard playing as Gecko and Garfield—Sigourney Weaver in *Working Girl*—she's clearly a bitch and the audience applauds when she gets her comeuppance by the male CEO. Not everyone can be a player here. Nor does the free play of the market seek to extend play to everyone but rather the guiding spirit is male combativeness, men at war. In the words of Dan Ackroyd to Eddie Murphy in *Trading Places* as they enter the floor of the New York Stock Exchange about to do some trading, "It's kill or be killed." Every day is Super Bowl Sunday for market players.

In order to see how the discourse of productivity that supports the player as hero crosses in and out of some of the darkest landscapes in the American Dream, I want to cross to a third film, Michael Moore's documentary *Roger and Me*.

Moore pursues Roger Smith, CEO of General Motors, in this documentary because he wants Smith to accept the myriad consequences of having closed GM plants in Flint, Michigan. Workers were eliminated as eleven plants closed. The city of Flint was put on a very short road toward evicting itself from the American Dream. *Money* magazine warned its readers that Flint was the worst city in America in which to live. So Moore and his cameraman's pursuit of Smith is quixotic: like the don he wants to bring the world back to . . . to . . . Let's quote Roger Smith in the best light on this American Dream. Moore jockeys back and forth between two scenes: an eviction of an African-American woman and her children and Smith's keynote speech at the annual General Motors' Christmas program. Interspersed with the woman's "muddafucker," we hear Smith say, "The more we respect the individual dignity and worth of each human being, the more fully human each of us will become."

That clearly expresses why Moore wants to bring Smith face to face with the consequences of his actions. In order for this powerful CEO to be made "more fully human" so that he will in the future respect the individual dignity and worth of each human being, he must be brought to see and acknowledge that he has not respected the individual dignity and worth of his workers. It's a moral crusade for Michael Moore. It's his way of shoring up a collapsing American Dream that he connects with respect for individual dignity and worth. As Jordie/Peck told his stockholders, caring about people is not in conflict with business but rather business is one of the ways a culture tries to take care of itself, tries to enhance the lives of its people.

If Dickens' Scrooge had phrased his question like this —"What business does a player have but playing the market?"—Marley's response, "Mankind was my business," would remain the same. Business, Dickens reminds us, is in the whole cultural scheme of things more about people than about profits. But I mention Dickens only because Roger Smith does in a Christmas speech. Smith recites nephew Fred's exuberant riposte to Uncle Scrooge's vilification of Christmas: "It has never put a scrap of gold in my pocket. But I believe it has done me good and will do me good and so I say God bless it." Moore films this speech because he wants to bring Smith to an awareness of his own words. It is clear from Smith's treatment of the whole city of Flint that he doesn't have any idea what Dickens is talking about when he elevates his Christmas discourse above business. Roger Smith, in other words, is a yet unrepentant Scrooge. He's a sort of New Millennium Scrooge: instead of being able to fire only one Bob Cratchit, he now can fire thirty-thousand Bob Cratchits.

Clearly if Smith gets reborn into the spirit of Christmas—and there's great urgency here—the fall of Flint could be averted. And since Moore conveys this sense of crisis and an urgent need for recognition and therefore deep, moral regeneration within the context of an America in the throes of the self-same crises, he's in quest of a counter-free market American Dream, a spirit of humanity and not profit. There's a spirit attached to the Christmas season, Dickens tells us, which brings out the best in people. It pulls them away from worldly distractions just as old Fezziwig pulls his young clerks away from their work on Christmas Eve so they can party. He puts aside productivity and obliges it to heed the importance and dignity of what Dickens might call "the human heart."

It's sentimental. There's no getting around it. Moore is challenging Roger Smith's right to put profit making ahead of everything else because Moore doesn't share the free market American Dream. Or at least he holds it accountable to more quixotic, more Dickensian considerations, none of which can be converted to Boolean Logic so that Garfield's bedside computer Carmen can 'understand.' Smith's public relations man gets to the heart of the matter. If I understand you correctly, he tells Moore, you follow a philosophy that says a corporation owes the employee cradle to grave security. And if that's what you think, I don't think it can be accomplished. This same spokesperson has already told Moore that a "corporation is in business to make a profit and does what it has to do to make a profit, to make money. It isn't in business to honor its hometown." Garfield has also written off hometown and employees in his speech to the shareholders: these employees are already getting more than workers in other countries because they've used the union to put a gun to the corporation's head. And the hometown has made the corporation pay through taxes for every bit of land, water, roads, services they've used.

There is no lien or claim on the corporation held by the citizens of Flint, no moral imperative that could detour a corporation from its single intent—to make a profit—and lead its CEO, Roger Smith, on a tour of "the dignity and worth of individual human lives." At the same time Moore's documentary—a slice of American decline—clearly shows that the signifier "productivity," like the signifier "free market," makes a variety of links to the world and to meaning depending upon what American Dream frame you adopt. And all these significations crisscross each other although there is no doubt that for the past dozen years our ability to express what may be challenging the power of global marketing linking, of free market significations, has been quite limited. Perhaps it began with Dukakis's defensive apologies for the signifier "liberal" or with Democratic presidential candidates talking more about corporate rights than individual rights, or with the recession of the American economy, an indication to some that our market wasn't free enough, that we were paying too much attention to people and what they were entitled to and not enough to profits and how they are made.

"Liberal" has come to mean liberal spending, or negative capital investments, or entitlements that the unproductive are not entitled to. The unproductive in this chain of signification are those that want government to play Santa Claus. Paul Tsongas, a Democratic candidate for the 1992 presidency until the "message-media-money" nexus forced him to drop out, repeated over and over again that he was "no Santa Claus." We're back to Christmas but this time it's the 1992 Democratic chastened liberals anxious to connect their message with productivity and not with what has emerged in my own narrative here as the "Spirit of Christmas" narrative, the "productivity and profits doesn't make us more fully human" narrative, the narrative that Roger Smith himself presented in Michael Moore's documentary.

Tsongas and increasingly Bill Clinton run their Democratic campaigns with the promise that they will be tightfisted and not spendthrifts. Will they be Scrooge before or after he repented of his greedy ways? Does the American Dream of unshackled productivity protect profits, however made, and push toward invisibility, toward noncitizenship, toward nonidentity, those outside play? And if productivity only seems identical to play within a certain framing of reality but is in a different framing something different than play, then the player should be pushed toward extinction because his play saps the fecundity and continuing functioning of an economy grounded in productivity. Within this different frame the blue-collar worker is not a player but both a producer and consumer. If, however, the culture as a whole becomes driven by play, then production doesn't produce profits as great as does play. Production, what Tsongas sees as manufacturing which is the engine that drives the economy, is constantly being destabilized and aborted as the player manipulates it for the sake of short-term profits.

It's alright for what was formerly American production to go elsewhere—to Latin America, Asia, Central Europe, Middle East, Africa—because play has no interest in the ways an economy disturbs or reinforces what is intended to be a democratic infrastructure that permeates everyday life. Severed from its cultural roots and tradition—epitomized by Jordie/Peck in *Other People's Money*—and especially severed from the democratic notions of justice, equality, and fraternity, productivity becomes currency itself in that it goes where the exchange rate is most beneficial. And the American blue-collar worker becomes mobile or adopts at home whatever the exchange rate established elsewhere in the world.

Within this player framing there is no need nor is there a way for the American worker, now producing nothing, to keep on consuming. The only sort of consumption that means anything here is player consumption, that is, consuming other people's money through free market play. What can we envision far down the line? Consumption becomes as selective and elitist a thing as productivity and the players—few but rich—who can feed in that rarefied zone. In this player-consumption there is no reason why consumption by fewer and fewer, or productivity that feeds not the culture but the player, should be linked to the preservation and continued expression of a democratic way of life, to all that, ironically, Roger Smith, in his Christmas message, reminds us of.

At this moment our culture lives uneasily within a belief that all these links are in the nature of things, that Gekoid democracy and the Garfieldian American Dream have all to do with the dignity and worth of each human being as well as with the well-being of our planet. We are, like Bud Fox, haunted by the economic order we have concocted, haunted by a conscience rooted in images of ourselves that disrupt the discourse of greed.

THE UNFORGIVEN:
HISTORIES AND "INDIANS"
OCTOBER 1992

How to tell and show the story is more than ever contested.
—Dell Hymes

*If we have survived the 'death of God' and the 'death of man,'
we will surely survive the 'death of history'—and of truth,
reason, morality, society, reality, and all the other verities we
used to take for granted and that have now been
'problematized' and 'deconstructed.' We will even survive the
death of postmodernism.*
—Gertrude Himmelfarb

*[T]he open discussion of scholarly research has made it rather
difficult to conceal or to manufacture facts without arousing the
skepticism or the scorn of colleagues. There are, after all,
canons of evidence and standards of argument.*
—Mary Lefkowitz

*Logic is the attempt to comprehend the actual world by means
of a scheme of being posited by ourselves; more correctly, to
make it formulatable and calculable for us.*
—Friedrich Nietzsche

I expected to see a remake of the 1960 John Huston Western classic *The Unforgiven*, but Clint Eastwood's 1992 *The Unforgiven* was an entirely different movie. Audrey Hepburn is unforgiven in the Huston film because she's an Indian living among whites and endangering those whites because her people want her back. Two cowpokes are unforgiven in Eastwood's film because one of them cut up a whore's face and the madam, Strawberry Alice, isn't satisfied with the punishment the sheriff, Little Bill, has meted out. Two entirely different movies.

Why did Eastwood help himself to the Huston title and distance his own movie so completely from it? I think it has to do with the nature of unforgiving, what and why. Audrey Hepburn can't be forgiven for being an Indian and that failure haunts the film. In 1960 we're at the beginning of representing to ourselves that in regard to Native Americans we're the ones who can't possibly be forgiven. We're at the beginning of actually shaping a discourse, a saying that says we cannot be acquitted here for our actions nor can we efface from our memories our state of being unforgiven.

Ten years later Arthur Penn's *Little Big Man* will straddle—in the person of Jack Crabb, white pioneer and adopted Indian—the worlds of those who are unforgiven and those who cannot forgive. In Kevin Costner's 1990 *Dances with Wolves* the issue is no longer straddled. The only release from the unbearable weight of being unforgiven is to give up one's whiteness and become an Indian. In 1991—coming fast and furious now—*Black Robe* gives us an Indian view of white men: stupid, weak, unable to survive. While the Jesuit lives in the dream of a Christian paradise, he cannot live in it as something connected to the here and now. The Indians, on the other hand, link their dreams and the waking world. The Black Robe has never seen the paradise he speaks of but he knows its laws: no women, no tobacco, a welcoming of death, and nothing afterward but sitting on a cloud contemplating the face of God. This dream that fails to enrich the white man's life but rather diminishes it, is totally unacceptable to the Indians who recognize the hardships of life but also its gifts; who leave this world reluctantly but do so with a more vivid understanding of the spirit world they go to than the white man. It is vivid because dream and imagination, the world as ceaseless symbol of what lies unseen, of the working connection between visible and invisible, has permeated their lives. Not the laws of the Church or the inculcated dictates of conscience shape reality for them but the crisscrossings of world and dream. "Nothing is more real than a dream." The white man's reality is too thin, too lifeless a world for the Indian.

In 1992 a remake of *The Last of the Mohicans* blights the bright beginning of a white New World with the darkness of the last days of the Indians. In our beginning is already a disruption from the ecological order of things, an impossible stepping away from the flux of order and disorder that we, as well as all nature, are already and always within—a place the Indian did not spend energy in moving out of or against, but rather lived in concert with and within. Things were better before we even began to become Americans in our brave new world—a very unforgiving politics indeed.

A grand, lavish, heavily publicized 1992 version of *The Last of the Mohicans* does not come to the screen innocently, apolitically. Our culture's trek to the stars from *2001: A Space Odyssey* to the *Star Wars* trilogy and *The Right Stuff* had us looking toward the technological future, not our rapidly unraveling past. But a series of sci-fi films—*Blade Runner*, The *Alien* trilogy, and the *Terminator* films—dramatically displays the darkness of our cyberspace future, a darkness permeating William Gibson's "book of the year! winner of the Hugo, Nebula, and Philip K. Dick Awards," *Neuromancer*. A Baby Boom generation now in its Jean Brody prime was reared on Saturday afternoon Westerns at the local cinema. The Thoreauvian natural simplicity of life there at the frontier beginnings of our country, out west, living in concert with and within nature, and so on—all Saturday afternoon simulacra—becomes a place to run to as one runs from this: "Cyberspace. A consensual hallucination experienced daily by billions of legitimate operators, in every nation, by children being taught mathematical concepts. . . . A graphic representation of data abstracted from the banks of every computer in the human system. Unthinkable complexity. Lines of light ranged in the nonspace of the mind, clusters and constellations of data. Like city lights, receding."[1]

In the lush greenery and agile heroism of Michale Mann's *Last of the Mohicans* we are treated to subliminal desires of the Baby

Boom generation and, at the same time, the clear imagery of what they know never was but could have been. So doubly haunted by past and future, it is nevertheless those beginnings in nature, in multiple frontiers extending ever westward, which leave us unforgiving of ourselves. While there is something fated and inexorable regarding our cyberspace future, the past remains a ghostly garden of forking paths, all turns taken, wrong turns. We yearn to begin again, to rewrite our history. Yet again.

The West is being revisited in these films at the very beginning of the final decade of the century, as it is in Eastwood's film *The Unforgiven*. But there is a startling difference: Eastwood is not rewriting the historical account, scrutinizing more closely the nature of our guilt, our Western conscience, confounding our origins and our manifest destinies. He is, instead, marking the evanescence of our historical consciousness, the half-baked and half-blurred and half-heard accounts that form our present perceptions of the past, including the West. The flow of past events, words, and contingencies can never forgive us our representation of them. Western films, from *High Noon* to *True Grit*, remain unforgiven. History is unforgivable because it cannot rid itself of the burden of its own deceits, its own lies, its own misrepresentations.

If I were to link both *Unforgiven*s it would be thusly: we cannot in the present attain a proper state of guilt, a true sense of being unforgiven in regard to what we have done to Native Americans because our representations are inevitably a barricade standing between what we are now and what we have been. History only enables us to live with ourselves.

Eastwood therefore doesn't offer another rewriting but rather gives us a look at the way we form our lies, the way we write ourselves and envision ourselves within a state of either extending forgiveness or able to be forgiven. But the whole terrible muddle of telling and showing the American West—from heroes like William Munny and English Bob to heroic acts they performed to whores with hearts of gold—is invariably ensconced in the conscience, or lack thereof, of the teller and picked at by the conscience of the listener/reader/viewer.

Mr. W. W. Beauchamp, dime novel chronicler of the West, follows English Bob the way Boswell followed Johnson. And W. W. recounts Bob's life with a smidgen of poetic license, all of which is contested by Little Bill who reads the account of McCorkle's death, laughs, and gives W. W. the "true story." Because he was there at the time. English Bob, who did the deed, doesn't contest Little Bill's account because he's been too badly beaten by Little Bill to speak. He's been unarmed by Little Bill and several of his deputies and then kicked viciously up and down Main Street until he's a bloody mess. We watch and wonder what account W. W. will give of this beating or what Little Bill will say about it later. Because he was there.

Perhaps we can draw back from the center of town and get a more objective chronicle of the West from Eastwood the director, from the film as a whole, from Eastwood's own telling. Does that telling lead us down the road of truth to the truth? Is there a metanarrative positioning that points us not only to what the West was really like but how we can indisputably narrate what it was really like? Is there a way of showing or telling the past that after many detours we've finally discovered? After all, Eastwood debunks everything he can focus a lens on. What remains after this debunking—isn't that the truth, an accurate, reliable, historical retrieval? What's unforgivable, then, are the inaccurate, unreliable accounts, all those past stories we've heard about the West that we swallowed. Why didn't we cut through the bunk and see the Truth? Like Clint Eastwood has done in *The Unforgiven*?

Or has he? I mean, how could he? Has he in this film appealed to the real historical facts or has he simply replaced an older ideological lens with a newer one? Has he cut through the stereotypes and found the real West? Has he exposed a prior frame of reference by standing on a solidly grounded, stable one? I think he has done a little of this, namely, the debunking, but rather than settle into a stable frame of sorting through the facts he has left us with a sense that there is no such inherently stable frame, that we narrate facts and in that narration fail to tell what that narrative frame doesn't see, can't conceive of, as part of the story. The transparency of historical events and texts gives way to mere reflections of the cultural frames we are in. The transparency of the Rodney King tape turns out to be nothing more than a reflection of the jury's cultural frame.

In this matter both the stereotypical real West, marvelously 'typed' in Huston's *The Unforgiven*, as well as the contesting of such stereotypes, notable for example in the 1991 National Museum of American Art "The West as America" exhibit, ground themselves in the notion that they can distinguish reality from illusion. In Huston's film, there is no marked space between the film's representation and the real West. The story may be artfully presented—this is what makes a great director like Huston great—but the essence of life as it was lived is not belied. In the case of the exhibit, there is an acknowledged recognition that while ideology is determining, we can still from a present nonideological perspective look back and see that imposition of ideology upon the real. In other words, we can see how an illusionary real West was assumed in the past to be the real West.

But unlike Eastwood's film, that exhibit of paintings of the West, mostly American Indians, winds up talking about each painting as if *now* the real story can be told, as if we had now jumped out of our cultural frames and taken up headquarters in that much talked of Archimedean point, that ideology-free perspective upon which we can look back and see the real West. So the commentary about the paintings seems like it comes from where Kevin Costner is at in *Dances with Wolves*: it wants to tell the story the Indians would tell, not the relatively few Indians alive today who have already been culturally severed, but the Indians back then. Back then when they were real Indians and the West, of course, was equally real.

Before saying something more about the real American West I want to stray wider along the history path and discuss two 1992 Columbus films: *Christopher Columbus: The Discovery* and *1492*. Point of immediate connection: here we have a telling of the first encounter of Indian and white man. But the whole matter of the present's positioning in 1992 and our revisiting of 1492 creates other interesting intersections. How much of the 1992 cultural agenda can be read in these tales of Columbus's voyage? Here we have a deeply embedded cultural narrative: the discovery of our own country. The most important date one learns in elementary school. "In fourteen hundred and ninety-two, Columbus sailed the ocean blue." How, we now say, could he discover a land and people that had already been there for eons. From a Western point of view, he discovered. From the point of view of the Indians who were already there, he invaded. Columbus invaded and claimed a land and people for Spain that was already inhabited. Since we are in 1992 quite sensitive to our history as the imposition of Western cultural values upon the Third World, we cannot unabashedly celebrate the folklore origin of our country. You might say that here our need to be politically correct shapes our historical correctness. We deem it necessary to give the people who were already there their due and thus refrain from seeing them as savage heathens needing to be Christianized, or as soul-less and therefore subject to enslavement.

Decentering Columbus and centering the Native Americans he discovered is a ticklish matter, especially since we as Americans would be revisiting the discovery of America five hundred years after not to deconstruct it as a point of origin but to celebrate it. How to celebrate a beginning that can only be represented as sordid if we decenter the Europeans and center the Indians? How to celebrate a beginning that is not a beginning, or only a beginning of the end for the people who were already there? It is not surprising then that for the most part during 1992 we have been undecided about celebration. Already under economic attack by the Pacific Rim, the West does not particularly welcome this occasion to rewrite-in-small its Great Age of Exploration and Discovery, a prominent section in every elementary school history book.

Mario Puzo, who wrote the screenplay for *Christopher Columbus: The Discovery*, does not take on Columbus the way Oliver Stone took on JFK or Costner took on the American West. While they progress along a vertical path with a definite end in sight and a clear map to follow, *Christopher Columbus* depicts this origin of the New World as broadly layered, as a path intersecting numerous other paths, as much a middle of many things, and a natural culmination of others, as a beginning. There would be no voyage to the New World if Isabella had not succeeded in destroying the Moorish hegemony in Spain and looting the Moorish coffers. In the name of

Christianity. And in that name and with the profits of war she supports Cristobal Colon's voyage. Not before both Isabella and Ferdinand have agreed to the immodest demands of Colon, including a tenth of all the wealth of the Indies and the title of Admiral of the Ocean Sea.

The Church does not see Colon as its apostle but rather as a possible heretic, a free-thinker who challenges the teachings of the Church Fathers. Colon stands before the Inquisitorial bulk of no less than Marlon Brando as Torquemada wrapped in forty yards of black cloth, a seminal presence in the Court of Ferdinand and Isabella. St. Augustine had written there were no human souls a certain distance from Spain; Colon disagreed with this, pointing out the discovery of humans in Africa. Colon's beginning is thus already muddied. It already lies in an act of domination—the victory of Christianity over Islam. His course is also a deviation from established truths of the Church. But those truths have Spain in thrall. At the moment Colon's ships finally depart from port, there is a shipload of Jews who have refused to accept the Church's offer to become Christians or to give up their possessions (to Church and Crown) and leave Spain. Brando blesses them both, regretting the fact that the Jews have missed the opportunity to become Christians, and hoping that Colon gets lost at sea.

Europe, thusly, is the birthplace of discovery, the origin of exploration but it is itself fractious, caught between dominating and liberating impulses, between the order of absolute narratives and the interrogation of those narratives.

Colon is also entangled in this garden of forking paths and he never emerges, as does Jim Garrison and Lt. Dunbar, as a hero, romanticized, stereotyped, idealized, Hollywoodized. No mean feat considering he is our euonymous character, the agent of discovery. The decentering here is achieved not by villainizing him as Costner villainizes white men, but rather by depicting him as an ambitious man who has convinced himself that he has a correct map of the world, a man also with a secret, a very practical secret that indeed makes his voyage a success where others had failed. He has knowledge of what he calls "rivers of wind" that will drive him westward and then enable him to return. In short, he wants wealth and power and has the perseverance and know-how to succeed. If given the chance. While this is enough to get him across the waters, it is not enough to see him through when he reaches land and encounters his Indians.

There our historical narrative gives up its multifocused lens and zooms in on "the truth." Whereas the Europe and Columbus that shaped the voyage seem each to fork off in many directions and thus deny us both a definite point of origin—a sequence of events and/or a propelling, hidden force—or a well-documented historical understanding, the Indians and white men who first confront each other in the New World are dominated by a strong metanarrative. The Indians are marvelous, joyful, loving, trusting people and the white men are rapacious and violent. Theses Indians are the forebears of Kevin Costner's Indians. The daughter of the chief, sent as an envoy of peace to Columbus, is almond-eyed and bare breasted, large well-shaped breasts, and wonderful, innocent clear eyes, a lovely face full of natural innocence. Eve before the fiasco. She is met by a rapist and patricide, a tortured, divided soul—a harbinger of what angst awaits *Homo sapiens* in America's technological future, in its reign of *Machina sapiens*. He needs a shrink or Prozac but neither is as yet available on the shores of what will become Club Med.

1492 is an exception in its refusal to undemonize the Indian while demonizing the invader. Ridley Scott's *1492* is less troubled a film than *Christopher Columbus*, although Girard Depardieu's Columbus is certainly troubled within a great romantic tradition of troubled heroes, of tortured souls, of rare individuals who have dreams that enable them to see further and deeper than the rest of us, who cannot give up their dreams regardless of the forces set against them. A very classic realist rendering this attempt to assert Columbus as a controlling presence. Someone is hoping that *1492* will be seen as it would have been when we went to the movies in the '50s, as if Depardieu's energy—and he is almost a force of nature—would seduce us away from our present uneasiness with not only this discovery but with a great romantic tradition of troubled heroes.

Strangely, in spite of Depardieu's overbearing presence, his wresting our attention from the dark corners of the event being narrated, the narrative is lackluster, dead-in-the-water. There is no fire here, no clash of what we in the audience are already troubled by. There is no playing into the dark corners of our culture's need to be unforgiving to itself. The angst of Depardieu's Columbus intersects deadened Hollywoodized angst. The voyage has been made too many times, always in less self-reflective times.

A hackneyed conflict of hero and villain conceals the real conflicts with this voyage and this voyager. Armand Assante conspires against Columbus but this villain in the end admits that his name will only be recorded in history because it was linked to Columbus's. Villainy, too, must bow to the presence of canonized history. Because this moral rivalry is foregrounded we do not in *1492* get a playing out of the turmoil of the European stage as we do in *Christopher Columbus*. But inertia is disrupted at one point in the film: the representation of Indians whom Columbus meets.

In contrast to the Indians of *Christopher Columbus*, who are edenic, these *1492* Indians are described by one Spanish nobleman as "monkeys." They are scrawny, dark, with twisted features and look very much like World War II racist caricatures of the Japanese. Every time Depardieu/Columbus speaks with the Indians, he is told that they are lying. Ridley Scott's camera plays on their scowling features, as if we, too, should believe they are liars, that this Otherness is to be feared.

The most electrically charged scene is when Depardieu wanders as if in a dream through a fight between the Europeans and the Indians. Like frightening monsters from the Id, the Indians appear and then disappear before Depardieu's eyes. It is as if not only he but the viewer were engaged in an unrepresentational confrontation with the people we conquered, demonized, and then destroyed. It is as if we were still trying to grapple—but in an unspecified, unrealized way—with the people we dominated. At the same time there is visual buzz that links that originary New World Western domination of nonwhites, that first move on the Manifest Destiny chessboard, with a present '90s economic domination of the West by the East. Destiny has transferred itself to the Pacific Rim, back to Asia, the conjectured home of our Native Americans. If there is no easy way to continue in 1991 to demonize the Indian, then the appropriate

Hollywood move to make is to translate old demons into new ones. This is a brief scene, a brief departure from a romanticized narrative that tries to package itself the way heroes and commemorative, cultural-legacy narratives have always been packaged.

Judging by the "West as America" exhibit, Costner's acclaimed *Dances with Wolves*, and the New World narrative of *Christopher Columbus: The Discovery* we are now ready to revise the history of our relations with Native Americans. We're finally telling the truth. We're finally separating stereotypes from hard realities, fictions from facts, and so on. Before I go along that road I want to take up Arthur Scheslinger Jr.'s notion that we can take sides on historical matters—and therefore sort through the good and bad of the past, guilt and innocence—by applying certain humanitarian, democratic guidelines that foster "liberal democratic political regimes"[2] that we believe are "expressions of the natural order of things."[3] What we want to sort through in the past is the workings of a progressive emancipatory spirit, a growing acknowledgment of individual worth and freedom, a movement away from oppression, chauvinism, superstition. Can we, in other words, agree to a fixed humane narrative of historical review, a perceptual lens that looks for the fulfillment of these certain ideals? Our historical accounts would then be relative to this communicative rationality—the past would be filtered to us through it—but that would be okay because it would be encouraging us or chastising us in a way that does us the most good. History becomes our culture's report card and the criteria of evaluation are at the highest, most estimable level.

In his *Atlantic* article, "Was America a Mistake: Reflections on the Long History of Efforts to Debunk Columbus and His Discovery," Arthur Schlesinger Jr. defines the criteria by which we can judge the past and according to which we can know what perspective on the past to take. The issue of whether we have any reliable way to retrieve the past becomes irrelevant; the important thing is that we have the means to sort through conflicting representations of the past and to attach ourselves to the one that moves us further along this inscribed path of what we should be, or what any culture should be moving toward. We move along by distinguishing what impedes and what hinders a culture from achieving "the great liberating ideas."[4]

What are they in Schlesinger's view? "Individual dignity, political democracy, equality before the law, religious tolerance, cultural pluralism, artistic freedom . . . ideas to which most of the world today aspires."[5] Before we begin to inscribe matters in a pro-Aztecs manner, Schlesinger argues, we should realize that both Europe and Mexico in 1492 suppressed individual freedom and human rights and that Latin America's failure "to achieve humane, stable, and progressive democracies" cannot be blamed on Columbus.[6] But while we cannot know whether the Aztecs would have "learned to read and write and would have abandoned their commitment to torture, obsidian knives, and blood-stained pyramids," Europe did evolve "great liberating ideas" out of anguish, self-criticism, and bad conscience.

The issue here, as Schlesinger presents it, is not whether European culture ever did wean itself away from mass extermination ("ethnic cleansing"), high-tech weaponery, and blood-stained jungles and deserts. The issue rather is whether we can settle on these "great liberating ideas" as a means of sifting through history and establishing historical accounts that clearly show the ebb and flow of these. We encase the past within the metanarrative of these ideals and recount it within the implicit universal rule of judgment such a framing affords. The actual grasp of the past in itself is too clearly a visionary enterprise. But the capacity to grasp it within a certain order of things, within a universal thrust of all cultures, gives us a rod by which we bend history. We bend it but only for the purpose of placing it within the compass of "a new and generous vision of our common life on this interdependent planet."[7] This is not a little and local bending of history that perhaps is not so generous to those in other locales. No, it is presented to us as natural and universal.

What is presently in 1992 going on in a balkanized Yugoslavia between Serbs and Croats, Muslim and Christian, clearly indicates that Europe's ethnic rivalries produce Aztec-size bloodbaths. Democracy is foundering in a contemporary America of rich and poor while the Soviet attempt to ground *its* "great liberating ideas" in economic equality has collapsed. The play of the market is indifferent to any liberation except its own liberation from "great liberating ideals" that intrude the common life of humankind into market play. Western cultural hegemony has achieved no determinate, fixed, absolute hold on individual freedom and dignity, human rights, political democracy, equality before the law, religious tolerance, cultural pluralism, and artistic freedom.

We are propelled, however, by our own cultural linkages of these, linking them with vague but grand chunks of reality whenever we narrate what we're all about. That we are now sensitive to the local positioning of our own cultural linkages is, of course, demonstrative of our present self-reflexiveness—our urge to jump back from the results of our own real-izing. But this acknowledgment of cultural relativity is a new shifting and while it is carried through in Eastwood's film it is not present in Schlesinger's ostensibly more astute meditations in *The Atlantic*, which claim to have a firm hold on the natural order of things.

The point is that we don't get to the other side of our culture's local biases by, for instance, going at history under the guidance of a series of inflated and floating, puffy, and abused signifiers like "individual freedom" and "equality before the law." We can't do so because at the present moment the power of the free market reconnects grandiose notions of individual freedom to matters of product choice. We become free of any regulations that will hamper needs creation and the ethos of "I shop, therefore I am." That ethos makes all past demands for individual freedom forgettable, unrecognizable, of little interest. We fail, for instance, to recognize the lack of freedom of the underclass nonconsumer. That feeling is repressed by the play of the market.

History becomes a long fight to get us to this point—market seduction and repression. And because we have a fallen sense of individual freedom, there is no way that we can preserve that equality which makes individual freedom possible and also tempers it with a recognition of the existence of others no less important than ourselves. Instead of supporting cultural pluralism, this economic privileging reduces it to a new moral hierarchy: consumption matters most, those who can consume the most matter the most, those who cannot consume have no existence, although they remain tantalized by the whole culture's urgings to fulfill themselves through consumption.

Enough. Sufficient to undermine our confidence in "great liberating ideas" as the way to deal with the past. The day of blithely imposing a grand narrative scrutiny of the past, of weighing and discarding, is now itself past. To do history now is to observe how one cultural inscription is exposed by another, how a questioning of stereotypes exposes its own shaky premises, and how our narratives of the past must foreground the narrative protocols we have assumed.

Let's head west once again.

Huston's *The Unforgiven* and Costner's *Dances with Wolves* are two contesting Western narratives while Eastwood's *The Unforgiven* is about how history itself is narrated. How does Huston's film abide by the stereotypes that Costner exposes? Doesn't in fact Huston show us that how we see and respond to things emerges from where and how we're brought up? No one can assume an objective position from which to observe and recount the truth. Ben, the older brother, can't hate his sister Rachel when she's revealed to be an Indian because the way he sees and responds to her is already shaped by his love for her. Cash, another brother, rejects Rachel when he finds out about her because his real-izing is already contorted by his hatred for all Indians. Rachel herself cannot jump out of her upbringing within the white narrative and suddenly see the world as an Indian. She can neither see herself nor her own brother, a Kiowa chief who comes to claim her, as they are, as real Indians. The mother, the only one who has always known Rachel to be an Indian, cannot see Rachel as anything other than as that sweet baby girl who, in reality, died at birth. The truth emerges in every case from a frame of representation, different frames producing different truths. Indeed, the film has begun with the Voice of One Crying in the Wilderness, a fiery prophet who announces himself to be the God of Vengeance so that "Truth Be Told and Wrong Righted." It is this promise to reveal the truth, to fix guilt and establish the right, to lay bare what must not be forgiven but damned, that Huston's film does not fulfill. All that is laid bare as the film ends as it begins—

with the flight of geese overhead observed by the players below—is the multiplicity of narrative worlds both individuals and cultures are already in and the drama of their collisions, as many histories as there are collisions.

Costner, on the other hand, clings to many classic realist formula elements: immediate and steadfast identification with Costner, clear-cut opposition of good and evil, presence of a historical record (Dunbar's journal) that says this is not illusion but reality, and a determinate moral closure. In his zeal to set the record straight and to allow the Indians a chance to tell their side of things, to relate a countermemory, Costner falls prey to some prevalent Western stereotyping he wishes to debunk. Indians become noble; nature naturally fills them with good humor. They have a deep, abiding sense of brotherhood and equality, a grounding tradition of ancient wisdom, a harmonious relationship with nature, and so on. White men are guilt-ridden, sadistic, debauched, and just plain unnatural.

While Huston is aware of the difficulties in the telling, in showing the past, Costner just wants to tell his side of things and tell it so that it doesn't seem like a positioned telling but the real truth at last. It is not the tentativeness of making such pronouncements regarding the truth here in the '90s that Costner reflects but an absolutely unfissured certitude, an infectious bravado that doesn't take a moment out to doubt itself. In this he intersects that same desire for a determinate past and present, a return to firm categories of right and wrong, truth and falsehood, which propelled Ronald Reagan into office. And just as Reagan turned out to be launching balloons full of hot air, Costner's dance with the real West is danced to a tune of his own.

But views of the past must always be forgiven because we cannot hope to assert that unpositioned truth of the past, that stable record of historical reference, which would have no need of forgiveness because it is the truth. By means of this truth it would be possible to point out which stories of the past, which histories, are so pernicious, so destructive of our humanity, so deceitful and beguiling, that they must remain unforgiven. Blessed are we when the truth of the past is revealed, when no conflicting narratives emerge.

When has that been? Skinheads today venerate Hitler while others assert Hitler was not a fascist but a liberal. Others assert that the Jewish holocaust did not happen and challenge anyone to prove it did. Truman has been evoked by both Clinton and Bush as a historical mentor—clashing evocations, same historical entity. The very foundations of Western culture are being rocked by histories of Asian and African origins.[8] Serbs recount a different history than Croats, Croats than Bosnians. The American South still has a different history of the War between the States (Civil War?) than the North. And the assassination of JFK has led to a state of parallel historicizing that continues into the present. Everything from Vietnam to the Reagan–Bush era is recounted in multiple ways from these universes of parallel history. These conflicts are orchestrated—sounded or silenced—by the present, another disturbing feature of a postmodern history.

The past draws us to it not because of its variable vividness but because we wish to bring something in the present to life and often find it easiest to do so in terms of a record of life we have already lived. In making the present vivid, often for political and/or economic reasons, we use the past like a palette of colors. We take what we need, win the day, or sell the product despite the fact that someone will always be protesting our exploitation of the past, challenging its historical accuracy from the presumed pedestal of totalizing truth telling and determinate retrieval of the past.

We are always in the process of transgressing someone else's construction of what really happened. Accounts other than our own are always unforgiven. Their history is always unforgiven. It is to Clint Eastwood's credit that he shows us that all stories about the past are equally unreliable and therefore equally unforgiven. It is the universality of this plight that must render all our histories forgivable. Even those of the real American West.

ROBBIN' N' THE HOOD N' THE NABE
NOVEMBER 1992

*I've been blessed with the opportunity to express the views of
Black people who don't otherwise have access to power and
the media. I have to take advantage of this while I'm still
bankable.*

—Spike Lee

*Well, maybe as a class, white males aren't allowed to look
good in the nineties. Western culture is instead painted with a
broad brush as giving us the imperialists who killed the infidels
in the Crusades and oppressed Native Americans in America.
Never mind an objective, balanced view of history. Never mind
those little Western contributions like democracy. No, it is the
Muhammad-inspired Muslims and the pantheistic Native
Americans who are the real good guys.*

—Charles Colson

After the mass-culture victory of *Dancing with Wolves*, Kevin Costner
took on the mantle of Robin Hood. In the same year the Brits had
released their most recent version of the Hood legend while PBS
was running a weekly series on the same. Why this popular culture
revisiting of the young patrician who, deprived of his property, took
to Sherwood Forest, formed a band of brigands, and robbed from
the rich to give to the poor? As legend would have it.[1]

Robin Hood—a most powerful tale, absent of all historical corroboration. Like King Arthur and the Round Table, a legend that provided the horizon for JFK's own 1960 Camelot, a presidential administration that ran idealistic (spiritual?) values into politics. We strain to find the real Arthur, the real Robin, the real JFK.

Costner's Robin is a leader in the cultural diversity movement. His life enacts a celebration of difference, of Otherness. There is an Eastern grounding to the West and to prove it Costner's Robin brings back an Arab with him to England. A black Arab (Morgan Freeman, who introduces Robin to the telescope, gunpowder, and, I guess, the scientific method). Now, Morgan Freeman appears here just after his *Driving Miss Daisy* role, a role that won him a Best Supporting Actor Oscar. While Costner's follow-up reetched his liberal sympathies for all kinds of difference, Freeman's follow-up contested his loyal black retainer role in *Driving Miss Daisy*. Now, as Azeem, a Muslim Moor in *Robin Hood: Prince of Thieves* he was no longer a servant but an equal, one among equals in Robin's band. And the culture he represented was now portrayed as the seminal cultural force behind the wheel of Western culture. It was an ennobled part. Where once he had driven a wealthy old white southern woman around in her Packard, he now stood before us as a representative of a culture that put us on the road to science and reason, to the technology that eventually built that Packard.

White America obviously found it ennobling to convert Hollywood's longtime 'Stepnfetchit' view of white southerner and black southerner to a bond of true, heartwarming friendship between Jessica Tandy and Morgan Freeman, old white lady and her black chauffeur. It straightened things out. Everything went warm and equal. Black and white could live together not as servant and master but as loving, mutually respecting equals.

If we revisited our past, we could clearly see that. If we revisited the Old American West, the Great Frontier, Westward Expansion, and Go West Young Man! we could clearly see that the Indian was already a Native American wrapped deeply and profoundly in an identity replete with all those personal and family values, that ecological respect, that staunch individualism and fraternity that non-Native Americans have lost.

If we revisited the legend of Robin Hood we could clearly see that what made him special was his political correctness, his multicultural sensitivity, his uneasiness with patriarchy. He gave to the underclass an identity that the prevailing order denied it. If we went back far enough we would see that all along Morgan Freeman had been our equal. In fact, he had been more than our equal. He had been culturally superior to us. When you take that bit of history and reintroduce it into post-slavery America, you really get the equal historical balance that white America so much wants to connect itself to. You take a past superior black culture, add it to black slavery in America, and you get a black not put too high nor bent too low. You take a past African/Asian dependent Western culture and you add it to a Western hegemony and you get a white just at the right, equaling out height. This is the point where black meets white.

At least it is if you follow film: cinematic representations of history, of Robin Hood legends and American West folklore, of black and white equality, or stories about the same. The bonding between Jessica Tandy and Morgan Freeman and then Kevin Costner and Morgan Freeman—cinematic bonding of black and white—holds off the real play of order and disorder going on. But it can't hold it off without touching upon it, touching upon it the way a hurt, troubled mind touches distractedly, over and over again, its own fears.

I start here with the Robin films because the sudden and repeated appearance of this legend in our contemporary popular culture seems to bear its own concealed secret. Costner will replay Robin Hood to accord with that money-making multicultural mentality displayed in *Dances*. And maybe Morgan Freeman took the part because he wanted to stand, as a black man, a bit taller than in *Driving Miss Daisy*. Both narratives cross the theme of equality. Was it equality of opportunity that Robin Hood sought to disperse among the poor? Was it equality under the law that enabled Morgan Freeman to spend his whole life driving Miss Daisy around? Is our secret fear as a culture a fear of equality because to us it always deep down means economic equality, which means loss of free market and loss of free market is always linked with loss of individual liberty? Must we then always foster a sham equality, an equality restricted to the level of the signifier—"under the law," "of opportunity"—to words and not world?

The legend of Robin Hood is a marginalized tale, a tale of the need to generate equality by being outside the law that stands. There is a pressing need to reach equality by robbery and violence, by withdrawing from home and hearth, by forming an outlaw ghetto in the dark wood. A new, alternative neighborhood, a 'hood for those seeking equality and bound to break the laws of the land to get it. "Robbin' n' the 'hood."

At the very same time that we are apparently reaching back to the past and reexploring the Robin Hood legend, we are being taken —finally—by young black directors into the 'hood, the inner place, the dark recesses of the wood, of our own held out of sight psyches, into the unsightly part of our glorious technoculture. The legend of Robin Hood, that persistent bit of undocumented memory, draws us because of that signifier of recessed/repressed darkness, the physiognomy of the dark face that haunts white America—the 'hood. There was then a 'hood of outlaws who robbed from the rich and gave to the poor. A 'hood of unrestricted entitlements, of expeditious, nonbureaucratized welfare, of strenuous recuperation of economic and therefore social equality, a movement therefore toward the true creation of political equality, a revolt in the name of the underclass that would move the whole culture toward equality-beyond-the-signifier.

Farfetched? Are the boyz n' John Singleton's 'hood set on equality? Are they deep in the recesses of places whites don't want to go? Witness Tom Wolfe's *Bonfire of the Vanities*. First scene: rich whites lost in the black 'hood and fearing for their lives. Like the Sheriff of Nottingham's men venturing into Robin's 'hood—scared for their lives. And Yusef Hawkins wandering into Bensonhurst? Like one of Robin's men wandering into Nottingham, being recognized and then pursued. But what will these boyz that matter to us now, today, rob? Forget Robin and his men; they're just nonthreatening masks, concealments, surrogates for the boyz here in the present that worry us.

We focus on Robin the way Freud said a boy who fears and loathes his father focuses in dream upon not the real father but some harmless but linked representation of the father. What will these boyz rob? How do they threaten? Robin Hood is looking at a nightmare from the best side: a little violence against Prince John's entrepreneurship, a series of ambushes of the idle *Fortune* 500 and we return to an egalitarianism, a brotherhood and sisterhood that has already been given up in the last dozen years in America by a "coalition of white ethnics, middle and high suburbanites, God-fearing reborns, neoconservative intellectuals and stalwart country-club Republicans that Reagan led into the White House."[2]

What's the worst side of the nightmare? It's a toss up between our fear that the Robin Hood safety valve doesn't work and we have open revolt, or it does work and we slip out of our free market American Dream and back into an egalitarian one. The movement toward revolt is already underway: "first comes fear, then depression, then anger and finally, if the traditional political safety valves fail, outright rebellion."[3] Our present fascination with Robin Hood on the screen indicates that we've already accepted, amid this 1992 presidential campaign, that traditional safety valves, valves located conveniently *inside* the plant, will not work. We go *outside*, outside the prevailing order, just as the South Central LA revolt for justice had to happen outside, in the streets, because justice had already failed in the courts.

The appeal of the outside candidate Ross Perot lies in this—that he is outside the entrenched two-party system. America turns to a billionaire entrepreneur to release the pressure of pent up frustration caused by the indifference and neglect of the entrepreneurial '80s to egalitarianism and fraternity. The move is as inane as dragging out the Robin Hood legend as a cinematic safety valve, as a symbolic configuration of both our dilemma and its solution. It is inane to see a solution to our culture's failure to spread itself laterally in an Entrepreneurial Prince who has spent his whole life moving vertically—right to the top where he knows how to speak to others. It is equally inane to put forth as a vindicator a Prince of Thieves who is white, male, nobly born, a signifier picked clean of any connections to fear, depression, anger, rebellion by countless

TV, film, and cartoon send-ups, a massive hyperreal to which America seeks to play out its hauntings.

What could this inanity mean? It means that the real brother n' the hood is too hot to handle, that we can approach this threatening violence—sort of—on the screen if we cut all the hot linkages and retie them to what we're able to take. Dream politics. And we turn to the Entrepreneurial Prince as our designated outsider because he promises to bring those of us who are ready to climb and weren't ready in the '80s up the ladder to where he is. Perot knows how to make money. He knows how to make billionaires out of people. He knows the formula. He knows, in short, how to inscribe the divisiveness of this country—its economic, social, political inequalities—so clearly and naturally that America can settle without further restlessness into a cultural verticality that the rest of the world accepts as the norm. He is, now on the eve of the 1992 presidential election, a newer, more efficient model of Prince John's entrepreneurship than what George Bush represents. But the envisioned utopia is the same: the underclass somehow acknowledges its underclassness and settles into a life of service. The entrepreneurial class joins hands across the globe, denationalizing their purses and their psyches, and engaging in a play that the underclass, now spectators, applaud and encourage, knowing in every fiber of their beings that without this play they'd be baffled as to how to get on in the New World Order.

Once clear, firm lines of identity and difference are drawn, once creeping lateralism is beaten back, once the technocultural elitism makes it impossible for pretenders to claim an equal footing, then America has reclaimed that Hollywood American Dream Reagan communicated so well. Difference and Otherness is economically silenced; a whole technoculture/entrepreneurial discourse that instrumentalizes and proceduralizes egalitarianism becomes tied to the signifier "education." There's no more lateral spread because all the sideroads, the detours, the forking paths, are buried. Brotherhood, sisterhood, and equality get linked in a whole new chain of signification, sort of the way people at AT&T or IBM or Toyota or Time Inc get reconstitutionalized when they come to work. And the New Constitution? It's what Garry Trudeau calls the "Owner's Manual."

America is running away from equality because it means bringing into the cultural fold an increasingly disturbing diversity, a
multicultural diversity that can't verticalize within a prevailing hierarchy but wants to stretch laterally in all directions. The Heartland
would have it's heart un-niched, Quayle's core of family values would
attenuate, meander down mean streets, and disappear into the privacy
of homes that Andy Hardy wouldn't recognize as home. The global
market becomes an excuse for ignoring this lateralizing democracy,
the postmodern multinarrations that create a community without unity.
We have to win in the global market despite any loss in egalitarianism; if we have to destroy our labor unions in order to compete in this
global market, then we will. If we have to substitute company procedures for the Bill of Rights, then we will. If we have to divide into an
entrepreneurial/managerial elite, Third World labor supply, and an
underclass not costed in at all, as a global economic necessity, then
we will. If we have to ignore environmental issues or make them a
lower priority in order to succeed in the global market, then we will.
If we have to give up spreading outward to those on the margins
because the play of the market urges us to look only upward, to pant
after those at the top—whose lives we can catch glimpses of on TV's
"Lives of the Rich and Famous"—then we will.

It is not then the boyz n' the hood that have instigated their
own threatening persona. Our culture has already written them off
and therefore our culture fully expects a violent reaction. It's a
dangerous game but both Reagan and to a lesser extent Bush have
shown that they are prepared to play. And prepared to defend against
the revolt they themselves are orchestrating by establishing as a
prevailing order the stochastic play of the free market. Quite simply,
this play turns a nonconsumer/nonplayer into a nonperson, a creature scheduled for extinction. Therefore, the homeless, unemployed,
untrained, computer illiterate, assembly line worker, imprisoned, men-
tally ill, abused, sociopaths, and so on are not to be reached for but
waited out. What the free market promises is eventual annihilation
of all its casualties and victims. It's called "creative destruction."
It's the New World Order.

It's not going to go down well but in this trickle-down vision
America will have to give up its egalitarian dream, just as the market

players already know that this dream has nothing to do with their market play. Paradoxically this market necessity is playing itself out at a postmodern moment: a moment when a discourse of difference is forcing the monologue of verticality, the discourse of a mythic single cultural identity, into a diverse polyvocity, a carnival of Otherness. The clash is up there on the screen; market forces can't hold it off. This clash makes profits.

You get this sort of polyphony in *Grand Canyon*, a film in search of an analogue of meaning, meandering laterally into lives and events that don't seem to connect. The journey to the Grand Canyon provides closure, a Grand Canyon sort of closure, a huge hole, an awesome emptiness, a monumental gap, an unexpected fissure, a fractal ending. If it were E. M. Forster's Malabar Caves we'd be expecting to make something out of the experience, a mystical resolution, a transcendent harmony. But the Grand Canyon is more of a break in the path of meaning as the eye wanders down in long sweeping laterals. All the paths the film has taken us on come here in the end and disappear within the multifoldings of this grand break in order and continuity. The characters stand there at the canyon's edge and join together in experiencing the sublimity of the moment: their answer lies there, the connectedness lies there in the labyrinth of the canyon. No one line can be freed of its interconnectedness with any other; every path is a crisscrossing path, our own passion for smooth surfaces from coast to coast is mocked in the earth's own implosion here into the difficult, twisting traceries that comprise not only a present scene but a record of the past. We are in rapport with nature's forked paths but at the same time we assert the separate singularity of our lives, as if we were discrete observers, capable of erecting a hierarchical order, up and out of the canyon, no swerves, no holes in our monument.

This Grand Canyon provides an answer to the film's most profound question, the question Danny Glover asks Kevin Kline when Kline, feeling indebted to Glover for rescuing him from the boyz n' the hood, offers to help Glover's sister get out of the 'hood and into a better neighborhood. The move represents the move upward, the move from the 'hood, which already beats in the blood of Glover's young nephew, into a mainstream cultural assimilation. It's that part of the American Dream that has to do with social mobility, with rising out of Otherness toward Americanization. It is that part of the Dream that has to be fulfilled despite specific legislation, like southern segregatory legislation against native-born African Americans, the Immigration Act of 1924 against, among others of Southern European latitudes, my own Sicilian forebears, the forcible removal of Native Americans from their homes and into government-run boarding schools, the internment of Japanese Americans, and the recent denial of access to our shores to countless Haitians. The examples are many: we legislate against this dream of Americanization simply because this signifier doesn't open up to us like the Grand Canyon. Instead we link it tightly to some *mythos* of identity grounded in purity, determinateness, and lack of lateral deviations.

Thus Kevin Kline wants to help bring Glover's sister and nephew into the American Dream but the egalitarian version of that dream has always been a threat to the Heartland. And in 1991, when Kline faces Glover in that parking lot, there is a further complication: democratic egalitarianism has been eroded by a free market indifference to anything but its own play. And that play can get along nicely with a certain rate of unemployment, a certain dispensing of the underclass. The only problem with the expendables is to make sure they don't sap through entitlements the profits of play, or, through crime and violence, the lives of the players. It is not hard to see then why taxation for egalitarian reasons is verboten in the present and infrastructure taxation, which will make us better global players, is acceptable. Accepting capital punishment as a deterrent, attacking the rights of the accused, constraining the individual in legal battles with corporations, taking the rehabilitation out of internment, building more prisons, eroding the powers of the Equal Employment Opportunity Commission, and throughout, unremittingly and pervasively, replacing individual rights with corporate rights are all measures taken by a culture that knows it has shut down this part of the American Dream and is setting itself in a defensive posture.

Lawrence Kasden's *Grand Canyon* doesn't take any of this on. Glover's response to Kline's offer to help doesn't go into any of this. He doesn't say, "What's the use?" He doesn't say that unless Kline is willing to stake the boyz n' the hood to a college education and then use his connections to find them jobs afterward, there's no sense doing anything. He doesn't say that perhaps what lies behind billionaire Michael Jackson's urge to have a white face is the haunting belief that nothing gives a black face equality in America. If the money is made available, who will give countless other African Americans the desire to be what they have thus far set themselves not to be? Who will give them the desire to join the white Heartland and the means to do so—implant the rules of that game in their heads while sucking out the rules of the 'hood? Will Kline step in as a private-sector benefactor motivated not by the market but by his heart? Will he do what the federal government has failed to do? Is it too late for the teenage nephew anyway? If there was a viable Headstart program, shouldn't he have been in it years before so that now he could move out of the 'hood and into the Heartland? And if he had been, what was he getting a headstart on? Isn't it more accurately an early *waylaying*, a detouring from the start the 'hood can give him? Wouldn't he then be making a headstart from his own identity, an early move out of difference and into that identity which will do what? Make him white, marketable, perhaps a market player, put him into play. Conservatives speak of allowing corporations to educate our youth, the most efficient headstart, an early jump into the free market weltanschauung before there's a chance for anything different to seep in, before your own 'hood brings you into its life-world, a life-world always conceived as the abyss from the perspective of the market world, in the view of *Machina sapiens*.

Danny Glover could have said all this but he didn't. What he said was less politically hot, more universally neutral, more abstract, perhaps—in modernism's terms—the dark, though ultimately graspable heart of the film. Until we get to the Grand Canyon and verticals give way to laterals. But Glover's answer is grist for my mills. My paraphrase of what he says: "Don't you think that it's not our duty to stick our noses into other people's lives, to get poking around into private lives that we can't hope to know and therefore can't help." Sort of the Hawthorne privacy of the human heart message. In my terms, what he's saying is difference can't be probed by our tools of identification; we can't state the problem in other people's lives that we identify *from within our own identifying frame.* Therefore we can't do anything about what we can't really see. And if we did something, it would first entail a reworking of difference into our identity, which might be the underlying problem itself.

Kline answers that later on he'll berate himself for not having offered any help, for having taken the course of doing nothing because respecting the inviolable Otherness of the boyz n' the hood is to wind up doing nothing for them. And that's what Bush does. Nothing will come of nothing. Something then. But what? Judging by the posters of "Four More Years of Reagan/Bush" shot full of holes in the opening scene of *Boyz n' the Hood* this sort of federal 'do nothing-ism' doesn't sit well with the boyz either.

The boyz suffer from a very postmodern sort of wanting: they want to inscribe themselves into the culture at the same time that they want to 'scribe' against it, rap being the scribing of choice. They want to shoot straight out of Brooklyn like Dennis in Matty Rich's *Straight out of Brooklyn* or out of Cabrini Heights, Chicago, like Truth Harrison in *Heaven Is a Playground.* But you don't shoot straight out of the 'hood by seeking your visa in the 'hood. Dennis has no connection with anything but the 'hood and that won't do anything but keep him there. And Truth Harrison, brilliant on the basketball court, is already too much in revolt against both the truth of the 'hood and the truth of white America. Both young African-American men have tragic endings. Both cases point to the isolation of black identity within a white power-frame. You need to wrap yourself in that identity that has been denied you, that is out of reach, before you can fly straight out of that difference a polarizing identity establishes.

Countering this desire to leave the 'hood is Spike Lee's version of *Our Town, Do the Right Thing.* The 'hood here is cast in a sort of *Our Town* veil. It's certainly not Mister Rogers' neighborhood but a cross between that and the 'hood. Lets' call it the "Nabe." Bugging Out, the resident militant, objects to a white yuppy presence, a dreaded regentrifier. The black street corner chorus objects to the intrusion of the Korean grocer. The white man in his convertible enters the scene at his peril. But the Italian-American pizzeria, Sal's Famous Pizza, stands alone as a white outpost at the heart of Spike's Nabe. It's there so Spike can work at the black/white thing, the terms of identity and difference. Is this exile here in the Nabe? Abandonment? Or is this the homefront? Is this the beginning of a new multicultural identity that does not, as bell hooks observes, speak out for a black essence or deny black experience? "There is a radical difference between a repudiation of the idea that there is a black 'essence' and recognition of the way black identity has been specifically constituted in the experience of exile and struggle."[4]

Spike Lee thus breaks up the unitary essence of blackness, of the Nabe as a place where we hear only a monologue. His Nabe is polyphonic, carnivalesque, multiple voices sounding the multiple identities, shifting, crossing, moving laterally, of the Nabe. Difference here may join together in singing Public Enemy's "Fight the Power" but they are joining together to fight the power that masses them in one big stereotyped pile, which is blind to differences because the color linkage doesn't open up, it doesn't extend laterals in all directions. Both Spike's Nabe and Singleton's 'hood never extend into awesome Grand Canyon difference under the white gaze. And while Singleton and Matty Rich show us life n' the 'hood as a realization of black difference within a white gaze, of the assimilation of a white chain of signification by blacks, of an adoption in other words of what Derrida calls "white mythology" by the boyz n' the 'hood, Spike Lee is always already deterritorializing that mythology. He is both filming within it and filming outside and against it. He doesn't want to deterritorialize the hood but simply transform it into the Nabe, a neighborhood where blackness spreads out into multiple crisscrossings not restricted to the vertical polarities of white and black.

It is not only an Italian-American crossing that has been made in Spike's Nabe but an Asian one and a Hispanic one. Mookie, Spike's observing presence, his Nick Adams on the scene, crosses the path of women, the elderly, the handicapped, the militant and the peace-loving, the wise and the blind. There is a steady jostling of cultural differences in this Nabe, a stylized, utopian Nabe that has multiple ways of handling its differences, of both having an identity and breaking that identity up into a polyphony of voices.

Spike's Nabe, however, is utopian, not only because it envisions a getting along of differences that Matty Rich's more gritty *Straight out of Brooklyn* collapses into twin paths of numbing bitterness and desperate longings, but because it holds the destructive power of a white real-izing of the black identity as something that is everywhere not in sway but challenged. Spike's Nabe holds the vibrant harmony of difference of the Nabe as not already twisted by the white hegemony, as not already the force of real-izing that has made the 'hood not a Nabe but the 'hood of Singleton's and Rich's films, as well as Mario Van Peeples's film, *New Jack City.* In *New Jack City* Nino Brown, played by Wesley Snipes, sets up his crack house as a fortress. You can't have any identity except the one that is white identifiable. Spike's utopian Nabe becomes in *New Jack City* a defended fort.

In Spike Lee's view the white identifying *mythos* does not prevent a black attempt to gaze at its own heterogeneity. Spike can set utopia, this peaceable kingdom, this Nabe of workable difference, against that white power that only empowers a white identifying, the superiority of a white essence, of a single white cultural identity. Spike's *Do the Right Thing* Nabe isn't already some ring in Dante's Inferno, the ring he clearly shows in *Jungle Fever* when Wesley Snipes as Flipper enters a Harlem crack house in search of his crack-addict brother, Gator. Here, in this scene, Spike's Nabe quickly descends into the worst part of the 'hood, the anus of the free market logic. Facing this urgency, how could there be time or opportunity to work out Spike's vision of blackness rising in a self-recognized difference not already victimized by a a white frame of representation?

There's no Nabe in *Jungle Fever* or in *Mo' Better Blues* precisely because *Do the Right Thing* led Lee out of visionary politics and into local politics. Not only did Spike's Nabe have the 'hood beating at its door but since his postmodernist polyphony dispersed white linking everywhere and yet not wholly anywhere—in Sal's pizzeria and yet not there —he had to draw closer to what was already clearly coming down in the culture. He had to drop back from the universal themes of an *Our Town*. It is significant that *Mo' Better Blues* begins with a camera shot that draws us into a window, into an interior scene, and that *Malcolm X* begins with a close-up of Spike's shoe being shined. The visionary turns naturalist.

In *Do The Right Thing*, Sal's pizzeria turns out to be only sort of the enemy, only sort of the threat to the peaceable kingdom. There are really multiple openings here for Spike's polyphony. When Spike looks closely he sees only difference trying to preserve its difference yet at the same time work with, deal with, interact with, an identity outside itself yet somehow already interpenetrating. Sal himself enacts this sort of exchange between identity and difference, living both within his own ethnic experiences and living day to day with other experiences. This self-contained compact is exploded in his two sons, one a racist, the other not. The racist links only one way: black is always and only what the white *mythos* has signified. The nonracist has slipped past the grand linkage and is open to the multiple ways of difference around him.

The attack on Sal's pizzeria mirrors a real-world event—Howard Beach—and does not emerge from the visionary politics Spike has been following in *Do the Right Thing*. He has been problematizing grand, stereotypic linkages, and tracing both white and black identities into a smorgasbord of differences that implies that both whites and blacks face the same dilemma: How do you have an identity and yet deal with others who don't have that identity, who have different identities? Spike shows us that monolithic blackness breaks down into a Grand Canyon of differences and that monolithic whiteness does the same. There's no one psyche privileged in this film. Mookie isn't our existential hero, a black avenger, or even our narrator. He doesn't tie things together for us or provide us with a running commentary. He is, in short, not pursuing the Modernist Project. Our visa to interpret, to come in and find the meaning, is canceled. What he does is perform this getting along of identity and difference, this daily, minute by minute accommodation of what one is with what is constituted differently. He doesn't transmit to us his grasp of or agreement with Radio Raheem, Bugging

Out, his Puerto Rican girlfriend, his sister, the Mayor, Sister, Pino, Sal, and all the many characters of this Nabe. But he enacts a way of being Mookie and yet allowing for others to be themselves.

It's what I have called a visionary politics. And this goes on until Spike brings the headlines—Howard Beach—into the film. That real-life tragedy must be responded to in film. Out there in the real world there is and has been no getting along of black difference and white identity. While the visionary "right thing" is clearly a dissolving of grand narratives of identity—black or white—and a living through of intricate, Grand Canyon patterns of difference, the Realpolitik "right thing" is give the black answer to the white Howard Beach. But that real-life incident was already whirling in the same kind of undecidability as Spike was to present in his film. Although it was clear that three black youths spotted in front of a Howard Beach pizzeria had been attacked and beaten and one chased onto a highway where he was struck and killed by an auto, neither surviving youth was willing to testify in court as to what had happened to them. Without such cooperation from the victims it became difficult to both define "the right thing" and do it. And yet clearly justice had to be served. But if justice is only justice in granting to each his or her due, doing right by each individual, then the refusal to cooperate is itself a questioning of justice. The implication is that the "right thing" can't be done under a white system of justice.

Enter Spike Lee who brings the question before blacks—not as a question but as a command. The assertiveness comes from a man who, alongside his desire to link laterally across the culture, feels obliged to express the views of black people, to put up there on the Big Screen a black differing, a differing that has in the past mostly had outlets in violence and riots as well as peaceful demonstrations. In both Malcolm X and Martin Luther King. The categorical path here forks off into a divided path: Malcolm X and Martin Luther King. Spike has to lateralize to pursue "the right thing."

In response to a question as to whether he was advocating Malcolm's path or King's path as "doing the right thing," Spike said he was advocating a synthesis.[5] That synthesis, however, cannot be found in the ending of the film—in the murder of Radio Raheem by the police and the retaliatory attack on Sal's pizzeria. That is pure

Malcolm X before his journey to Mecca. When the interviewer pressed Spike on this point Spike told him he had it wrong, that he meant both paths were being taken. In Spike's visionary politics he can have both a difference acting to defend itself and a difference not acting in order to free itself of this yoke of difference. A defense of difference necessarily entails a defense of multiple differings, no single identity to difference. A difference seemingly not acting, a chilled difference, is one struggling to slip the binds of that single identity. Sal's pizzeria then cannot be transformed within Bugging Out's notion of the black identity not only because its difference must be allowed but because Bugging Out's linkage cannot be privileged as a single identity of blackness. And both Sal's and Bugging Out's assertions of their own identities parallel Malcolm X's own: "We don't want to be transformed into anybody's sense of who we should be."

While Spike's visionary politics has shown us how *our* identity gets along with *their* difference, that the whole Nabe is nothing more than differences rapping with each other, he must respond to real-world challenges to this. What Spike extends to Sal's difference is already not extended to the world outside the film, not certainly to Howard Beach. And it is in this outside world that Malcolm X forges his defensive politics against the determination of black identity by white signification and therefore the annihilation of black difference. At the same time it is Rev. King's intent to put aside such self-assertiveness that opens the door to Spike's visionary politics. Only by doing this does blackness open up to its own variegated voices, a full chorale that checks the imposition and force of any one Master Voice and allows the full panoply of differences, both black and white, to be realized. And it is the Malcolm X who becomes Shabazz after his trip to Mecca who symbolizes this yet unrealized visionary politics. Spike Lee's own work, including *Malcolm X,* becomes then a fulfillment of what Malcolm X might have enacted if he had not been assassinated. 'By any means necessary' moves from oppositional dualism to postmodern heterogeneity.

The "right thing" according to Spike's visionary politics is to give equal justice to our different identities. To fit the means to the difference. In the Nabe, he says, we do it all the time. And what of pursuing actively this sense of equality, this equality that does not speak of opportunity but rather of life-world, of, in a postmodern sense, narrative? We cross that path once again: How does one man or woman cross into another's life in order to help him or her? Is the mission of equality to make life-worlds equal? And our sense of what is less than equal or more than equal—within what identifying frame does that emerge? I fall back on what Spike's Nabe enacts: narratives that interpenetrate *other* narratives shape a lived-experience that is not aloof from others but already imbricated in the lives, in the narratives, of others.

We see this sort of identification in *Boyz n' the 'Hood* among Tre, Doughboy, and Ricky. Doughboy's mother asks Tre to let some of his fine qualities rub off on Doughboy who has just been released from prison. Tre needs no such encouragement because although he has developed into quite a different person than Doughboy his identity does not establish itself in unconcern for Doughboy. Rather his identity is nothing but a daily round of recognizing and responding to, of giving equal justice to, others. Even a film publicized as zany madness like the Hudlin Brothers' *House Party* takes us into an interpenetration of identity and difference and the ties of fundamental concern that such an interpenetration creates. Kid and Play are very different from each other, differences they set to words in a contestatory rap, a rap of differences that they nevertheless perform together, a dialogue that performs the connectedness of their lives.

Equality limited to equality under the law, to a provisional equality of opportunity, cannot therefore sustain a democratic sense of equality because ultimately the free play of the capitalist market polarizes—as it has done—the culture. Such economic polarization privileges an identity of power and wealth, an identifying frame that paves a main road through the culture's discourse, practices, and institutions. What is ejected as difference by this framing can only be recognized and admitted through transformation, recuperation, redemption. Nothing unidentified is offered equality. And since this polarizing identity comes into being by denying others what it accrues for itself, there is either a fear and loathing of what is different, or a nurtured indifference to difference. Justice is served as long as the laws of the land do not inscribe this invidious polarization, as long as there is no written law denying an equal opportunity to all. In actuality, however, democracy has become plutocracy, liberty is extended to those who have the means to shape identities for themselves, equality is only extended to the identifiable, and fraternity comes out of the play of the Global Market or it doesn't come out at all. Justice happens when an identity that inscribes itself in the culture says it happens.

And if no real justice is extended to the unsignified—as it is not—then Spike needs to rise up like Malcolm X and show the black people who cannot speak for themselves that they won't be burned down. They won't be forced to take their heroes off the wall and put up the "right ones." They'll fight for the recognition of their own difference. Like Sal, the Italian American, does. In this fashion do we circle back from Spike's visionary politics, from Nabe to 'hood.

GUNS AND PROVOLONE:
'WILDING' AND WISEGUYS
DOING THE WRONG THING
DECEMBER 1991

The attacks [on a Central Park jogger] had been committed on
April 19, 1989, by a gang of some 30 youths who went 'wild-
ing'— a term which came to mean rampaging through the park
perpetrating random assaults. The brutality and unprovoked
nature of the attacks, together with the fact that the victims
were white and middle class—the jogger was a vice president
of a leading securities firm—whilst the assailants were black
or Hispanic, meant that the case received a massive degree of
publicity and became symbolic of US racial tension and urban
violence.

—Keesings, August 1990

Yusef Hawkins had entered the predominantly Italian area of
Bensonhurst in order to buy a secondhand car, but had been
pursued, attacked and killed by a mob of 40 white youths who
were intent upon preventing blacks from attending the birthday
party of a local white girl.

—Keesings, May 1990

If Mr. Gotti—Italian, devoted to his family, and in familiar
criminal businesses—is the old face of crime, Mr. James is the
modern one. He is 19, black, has fathered two children by two
separate women (girls really) and is said to be associated with
a cocaine ring whose headquarters are a few blocks from the

*Capitol. Maybe it would take a moral philosopher to distinguish
between the two men's characters, but it takes someone with a
lot less brains to work out who frightens the average American
more.*

*America's underclass does not merely shame or exasper-
ate the rest of the country; it frightens it. Some of its members
display a random amorality to which fear is a rational
response; and where fear is present, loathing is rarely far
behind.*

—Economist, December 7, 1991

"Little Man" James, the "Mr. James" in the above quotation, shows
us the face of the abyss—the human mind sprung loose from any
personal or societal sense of order, a mind whose composure is
maintained through random acts. "On the night of the recent murder,
he was driving along an inner-city expressway with some friends,
who allegedly have testified that he said he felt like `busting some-
one.' So, it is said, he took a pot-shot at a passing car, and snuffed
out a 36-year old life, just like that. When arrested, he was walked
through a Washington police station with the press in tow. He was
asked what he was doing the night of the killing. With a diabolical
grin, Mr. James replied `I was out maintaining my composure.' "[1]

"Little Man" James was just wilding, advancing, you might say,
the cause of contingency, the disruption of what lives we should be
living at age thirty-six or nineteen or whatever. "Little Man" James
jumped outside the moral imperative. The Central Parkers who went
wilding also made that sudden, unexpected jump into the disorder
zone. And the "press is in tow" because the public wants to know.

We want to know what? I suppose we want to know the causes
for the wilding. Maybe if we're liberals we want to know the root
causes so we can solve the problem. Maybe if we're conservative
we want to be able to identify potential wilding types so we can
install the most effective self-protective system when we're home
alone. Meanwhile in the absence of root causes and proper IDs we
have put in our law books a felony crime—"depraved indifference
to human life." Sort of what I recall of the Vietnamese "conflict."

These are not merely the words of a court-appointed psychiatrist or a TV evangelist. To demonstrate a "depraved indifference to

human life" is a punishable crime in this country. It's on the books. This fear has been legally signified. When human minds become lost in contingency they cannot be linked by means of the signifiers we already possess. If there's no on-scene arrest or eyewitness account, no VCR tape, they leave no trail, forge no chain, we are able to follow.

Is this perhaps the New World Order? The old order of signification under attack by other untrackable significations that we seek somehow to corral within the depraved indifference regime? If we can classify them, order them, then we can possibly deal with them. But if this contingency of the human mind domain is amorphous, spreads laterally, undetected, like AIDS, like the new, lethal viruses from the rain forest coming north, looking for a new home, if it infiltrates regardless of the normalcy, the consistency, the orderliness of our lives, regardless of our antibiotic defenses, then how do we remain 'we, the public' and not 'them, the randomly amoral'?

Has our culture already slipped into a "depraved indifference to human life" and do we see the face of that slippage in the act of wilding? Is Central Park wilding as natural to our postmodern world as organized crime is natural to modernity? Does the disorder of postmodernism configure wilding just as easily as the order of modernism configures the Mafia?

Let's follow the Mafia style of wilding first.

The Mafia stands as the reverse image of the corporate state, John Gotti, the "Teflon Don," as the reverse image of President Bush, the "Patrician President." The sacred order of Mafia Otherness is precisely that: a secret ordering of what is seen as unidentifiable, or only identifiable as being other than what is and what should be. Excluded from both market free play and the play of the dominant culture, Italians transport from Italy to America their tradition of response to such exclusion. The stage has been set: Gotti is in "no light, but rather darkness visible." And this darkness remains visible and distinct within our cultural order of light, our way of attaching ourselves to the truth, as long as Gotti does not cross over into our domain of light.

According to *Forbes*, Gotti won't confuse matters because his sort of businesses "cannot easily be capitalized with commercial bank debt; they cannot be taken public as a multiple cash flow." The don's "dirty profits," his "dark dealings," can't cross over into "clean profits." [2] Or can they? Las Vegas now stands within the American *mythos* as the place where dark money supplies the voltage to keep Vegas's bright lights shining. Meyer Lansky and Moe Dalitz were canonized in *The Forbes* Four Hundred in 1982 precisely because they were able to take their ill-gotten gains public. They formed conventional business organizations.

Michael Corleone in *Godfather III* takes his 'family' out of businesses that cannot *show* a profit—illegal activities—and puts together an investment portfolio for the family. They go from being thugs and racketeers to free market players. The darkness diminishes into the light of the free market. Clear boundaries of darkness and light fade.

Don Corleone's activities are a form of organized wilding from the perspective of a culture that knows only too well what it has to exclude. Mafia violence may not be fully comprehensible, seems always to be ensnared in arcane and primitive rituals of Sicilian bloodletting, but it jolts the mainstream culture and at the same time it provides a leverage of violence that proves a results-oriented way to 'do business.' The lens through which the darkness of the Mafia is visible to the culture is the lens of violence. Violence becomes the nexus of cultural identification, it becomes a means of empowerment within a culture that metes out power stingily to the dark skinned, dark haired, dark eyed.

When Michael Corleone progresses toward making the family a bunch of market players, he is, in essence, putting aside the values of the alienated family and adopting Quayle's family values. He risks losing family values in the shuffle of a value-less free market play that puts both democratic and Mafia valuing in the it-doesn't-matter pile, is equally indifferent to Founding Fathers and Godfathers.

Michael Corleone will return to violence, to 'family ways,' at those moments when the indifferent amorality of free market playing, the play of the kill or be killed human exchange, expects that its play is subject to no outside regulations. Michael has, however, inherited what you might call a "tradition of response and regulation." When he does employ it we feel that justice is being served.

It's as confusing a response as when De Niro's Max Cady in *Cape Fear* rises up and attacks his attackers. Francis Ford Coppola is not only engaged in making conceivable to the American audience the strange folkways of the Mafia, a process of translation of one signifying system into another. He is also using the difference of the Mafia to explore what the culture chooses to keep out of sight—the culture's preference for corporate values above individual/democratic and family values, and the Mafia's preference for family values not bound by the cash nexus but by blood, that is, values of the heart. It is not surprising that the culture will downplay its own dehumanizing preferences while demeaning and mystifying Mafia values.

The Mafia discourse blows the whistle on connections among politics, finance, and crime that pervade the culture as a whole. "Politics and crime, they're the same thing," one don tells us, and another tells us, "Finance is a gun. Politics is knowing when to pull the trigger."

While there are businesses that the American free market cannot legally pursue, that free market is at the same time pushing mightily for the freedom to practice, to do business unrestrained by law or principle. In other words, there is an acknowledged and even praised order of ruthlessness, of kill or be killed, which is shared by free market players. Their crimes can do further violence to the whole American underclass and in this way erode further democratic, egalitarian principles. However, this is signified as not crime but "playing hard ball." The casualties of this game need not be costed in. The path to this acceptable order of unscrupulousness, the path to becoming a player, is either inherited wealth or patent-leather credentials.

The former head of the Justice Department's Organized Crime Strike Force, Edward McDonald, admitted that if John Gotti "had an education, he could be chairman of General Motors." [3] I extend the education here beyond academic degrees and into the Heartland American image. Gotti would have to be educated within the recognized image of the corporate executive, the market player, the financier, all of whom are concerned with making a *bella figura* as defined in ways that the Mafia don, equally concerned with making a *bella figura*, cannot relate to, cannot identify.

The Mafia's use of violence in the service of business and finance then is uncoded whereas there is a coded form in the culture as a whole that seems to be bound by less nonmarket values than the Mafia. This uncoded practice of violence serves to define violence for the culture as a whole. It stands in for the violence of the free market play itself. That playful violence must be signified differently since the Mafia has already established the link between the word "violence" and its worldly signification. I am reminded here of Baudrillard's take on Disneyland's existence: it is there to assure us that it is unreal and that its environs, Los Angeles, is real. Each day millions of Americans flock to the Disneyland gates to reconfirm their foothold in reality. In this same fashion do we need the Mafia in the headlines, in our best-sellers, on our soap operas, in our films.

The whole relationship here is demonstrative of an important aspect of wilding: the Mafia's violence seems not to be provoked by the culture as a whole. In terms of our own moral concern it seems only amorally indifferent. Our concern for human life distinguishes itself not by our free market practices but in our condemnation of the Mafia's depraved indifference to human life. While our culture's present concern for human life is mocked by the increasing hopelessness of the underclass, by the felonious greed of American entrepreneurs of the '80s, by a trickle-down sense of democracy and egalitarianism, the open revolt in our inner cities, the sheer weight of our cultural rhetoric regarding our concern for human life renders contradictions merely problems to be solved.

The violence we do to the underclass is already caught up in a way of doing business, a discourse of power, an impersonal cultural logic that allows us to practice, to enact, to real-ize a "depraved indifference to human life" while signifying it as concern for human life within this formalized cultural discourse. Our free market culture then provides an analogue of meaning that blocks from view the play of what in our culture, multiple dissident voices, would bring to disorder that analogue. Wilding then crosses the narrative of Otherness, always occurring in ways the culture has set itself up not to understand, or understand only as what is not itself. In this way is Mafia wilding, like all underclass wilding, a Deleuzean deterritorialization of the culture, of the prevailing order, and especially of the coded linkages among market, politics, violence and power. The organized nature of the Mafia denotes its own reterritorialization, what women and ethnic minorities, for instance, are struggling to attain.

One of the reasons the press is in tow during the Gotti trial has to do with Michael Corleone, Brando's and De Niro's Godfather, Al Pacino's Scarface, Joe Pesci's Tommy DeVito. John Gotti's presence in real life crosses laterally into or 'intertexts' film. Film makes the darkness of the Mafia visible, but it does so only after Gotti, for instance, has been penetrated by the film. Gotti is in hyperreality, which is only another way of saying that the culture is imaginatively invested in this *mythos* of good and evil, of inside and outside. The film must always Hollywoodize the outsider because its audience can be more easily fascinated with what breaks the rule of order than what obeys it. At the same time the cultural *mythos* of what is order and reason, goodness and justice, is writ large on the hyperreality screen.

The inexplicableness and strangeness from the mainstream culture's point of view of the actions of the Mafia subculture are deflected into the film's own narrative paths. What are only contingent events within the culture's own reckoning of the real attain connectedness. The plot may seem to achieve this connectedness through sleight-of-hand, but in point of fact it is only because Gotti and Don Corleone have crisscrossed already, the real person has already responded to his representation in film, that the underworld is made visible to the overworld, its darkness made visible.

The hyperreality of the film becomes the place where we work at our fears, where we try to consume and respond to what we have repressed and yet has already responded to us and threatens to consume us.

Our discourse of human concern is bolstered at the same time it is punctured. And the counterpoint here leaves us speechless; the discourse of human concern that we've come in with begins to sound like a voice-over that isn't quite in sync with what we're taking in, what we're consuming. There is a way of doing business with, say, *Godfather III*, that puts in question the way we've been doing business.

In response to Don Luchesi's warning that Michael Corleone must fall in line with the prescribed way in which this international corporation does business, Michael replies, "You want to do business with me, I'll do business with you." While his response expresses a willingness to deal, it clearly shows that Michael is ready to counter Don Luchesi's way with his own. It is this 'other' way of doing business, the nonprescribed, outlaw way, which the film pushes us toward consuming and ultimately responding to. And what we finally digest after all three *Godfather* films is that just as politics, economics, and violence are linked, so too is business and family, the impersonal and the personal, heart and hard bucks, food and fortune.

Profit ventures laterally into people and people into profit. If, as Michael Corleone tells the bastard son of Sonny Corleone, slain in the first *Godfather*, that his father had too much temper, so much it clouded his reason, it is that comingling of emotions and reason, of making the way we do business answer to the way we feel, that directly counters our culturally privileged way of doing business, from Wall Street to the White House.

The only way Gerry Grinberg of Lyndhurst, New Jersey, could send a letter to *Forbes* stating the following—"Many of those who attack Mike [Milken] fail to realize they are denying opportunities to the best capital this country has, the American entrepreneur"—is if he or she had already barricaded profit from people, the human life-world from entrepreneurship.[4] Supposedly, what counters this humanizing of entrenpreneurship, this personalized way of doing business, is the explicitness of violence and murder that is the Godfather's way of doing business. Wilding is ultimately their business. They represent it. It is what we can from our dominant cultural perspective focus upon.

In the same manner but from the opposite perspective, both Vito Corleone and Michael Corleone will focus on the lack of honor, respect for tradition, for family, for the place of the underclass in the family. From their dominant perspectives as dons within their subculture, they stand for doing business within a human life-world, within a context in which human needs and emotions regulate all forms of doing. Whether the tribal valuing of market entrepreneurship or that of Mafia family is closest to—or furthest from—Enlightenment notions of universal truths and absolute values, or whether those, too, have now been exposed as tribal, are all considerations made within some framing of order and disorder. This is a vying of difference and identity, one always staged/signified by identity.

Coppola chooses to end *Godfather III* with a sequence of shots that assert the human life-world as the *primum mobile* of doing business. Michael's daughter, Mary, has been slain on the steps of the Palermo opera house and Michael remains, mouth open, frozen in a silent Munch-like scream. In the next scene he is an old man in a garden who topples slowly from his chair. The man who has been able to invest $600 million has done, Coppola tells us with this abrupt passing of time, no more business since his daughter's murder. The heart has shut down entrepreneurship.

What this underworld of the violent underclass brings us to consume must in some way be averted. We rush to humor. It is our bridge to an Otherness that has not been neutralized—'Disney-ed'—through the hyperreality of the screen but has instead disturbed us. On our immediate horizon is the knavery of Iraqgate, the erosion of democratic justice and equity through Republican conservative tax legislation that left "just under a quarter of all wealth . . . held by 1 percent of the population,"[5] the abandonment of the Kurds in Iraq, the rejection of Haitian boat people, the Wall Street racketeering of the '80s, the south central LA revolt, the politics of the Clarence Thomas appointment . . . It is difficult in this setting to take a holier than thou attitude.

Popular film will not avoid the tensions. Neither Scorsese nor Coppola, for instance, has been interested in giving us an unhaunting view of the Italian-American subculture. They have not analyzed the Mafia into some historical resting place. Rather we see this subculture work its way provocatively and disturbingly into the main culture. That haunting is box office. But so, too, is the defense of itself made by the prevailing order: it reduces the threat to comedy and farce. We are to laugh at what frightens us. The bogey-man in the closet is just a clown.

Marlon Brando, *The* Godfather in the minds of the American public, appears in *The Freshman* as a parody of his original Godfather role. When Matthew Broderick first sees him he is about to make the identification but is cautioned not to do so. This comedic don doesn't like to be compared with the cinematic don. He's the real thing and of course he's a scream, a riot. He confuses Vermont with Kansas and then in defense humorously discards all claims to difference in America: "Kansas? Vermont? What's the difference? We're all Americans." Later on we discover that this comedic don is only pretending to be like the cinematic don. He turns out to be not only funny but a nice guy who in the closing shot strolls through a cornfield with Broderick, telling him about how he has some connections in Hollywood that could help Broderick get a start. In the movie business.

Paul Benedict plays the part of Profesor Fleeber, a professor of film who is deeply attached to films about the Mafia and who has written a profound essay entitled "Guns and Provolone" which he advises Broderick to read. As *Godfather II* is being shown in his class, Fleeber mouths the lines along with Michael Corleone: "It was you, Fredo. You broke my heart." Mafia emotion and sentiment, the power of *la famiglia*, the heart that tempers profit, are just plain funny. Of course, if this screening within a screening takes you back to *Godfather II* the plain funny gets muddled.

In *Spike of Bensonhurst*, a film made before Bensonhurst became a poor choice in which to locate a comedy, Ernest Borgnine, who began his career as Marty, the homely, Italian butcher in *Marty* (a '50s film that typically focused not on the difference of Italian-American life but on the universality of the unloved seeking love), turns the Mafia underboss into a sort of slow-witted clown, a buffoon from the *commedia del arte*. *La famiglia* becomes thoroughly domesticated in *Moonstruck*, a sort of Big Screen family sitcom in which Nicholas Cage's violent volatility, reminiscent of Sonny Corleone's, begets only farce. In *True Love* any threat made by *la famiglia*, by life-world attachments, to our own mainstream market indifference is rendered ludicrous.

From a market player's perspective, say Gordon Gecko's or Michael Milkin's, these people don't represent a challenging difference to the values of American entrepreneurship. They're just losers. They don't know what's really going on nor do they have a snowball's chance in hell of getting into play.

The thrust in *True Love* is again not toward isolating difference but toward universalizing: Michael and Donna are young lovers who go through all the ups and downs that all young lovers do just before their wedding. That the Italian-American jeweler wants to sell them a "real hair-loom" and the Italian-American caterer tells them that blue mashed potatoes will go well with the gowns the bridesmaids will be wearing is just comedic background. The distance between the wedding as a personal, family matter and the wedding as a business you get someone else to do for you, between the wedding among *la famiglia* as in Rodney Dangerfield's *Easy Money*, and the wedding conducted by wedding specialists and consultants, as in *True Love*, is unlinked in *True Love*. And it is untouched because that distance between the Otherness that *la famiglia* creates in this subculture is to be minimized. The more pressing need is to see that "We're all Americans" and that differences are really only idiosyncrasies, in the case of Italian Americans, always funny.

Even Coppola's *The Godfather,* the "great American Italian-American film," sees something funny in the Italian-American difference. But the comedy here is linked with tragedy, smiles change to frowns, joy to anger. The plate is indeed very full, everything overflows, nothing is restrained or diminished. Distinction lies in wholeness, however complex and contradictory, and not in unity. Community without unity. When young Michael Corleone gets a lesson in making "gravy" (tomato sauce) while the house is under siege, Sonny Corleone, a Hotspur of revenge, slices through the comedy and urges the perilousness of the moment on us. This is real, he is saying. Bad things can happen here. We can all get killed. When you understand what's at stake you don't laugh. Your fears are justified.

Martin Scorsese's *Goodfellas* is self-consciously at play with our nervous rush to humor when faced with a deadly difference. The film begins with three men (Joe Pesci, Robert De Niro, and Ray Liotta) driving down a road in the dark of night. A strange sound gets them to stop and open the trunk in which a bloody body—the classic Mafia body dumped in the trunk of a car—is still moving. They shoot and stab the body repeatedly and then the voice-over of Ray Liotta's Henry Hill—"As far back as I can remember I wanted to be a wiseguy."

We go from inexplicable wilding, mayhem with a French kitchen knife, and then segue into a Copperfield entre. If we follow Copperfield's own narration we will, I think, discover that the issue of whether he is the hero of his own life is undecidable. Similarly, if we follow Henry's narration, we will discover or not discover the story, the reasons, the causes, for the bloody opening scene. He will have told us a story that links wilding with the order of our own lives. Everything connects within this ordering of things. Scorsese intends to do no less than give us what he spoke of in regard to *Mean Streets* as "an anthropological study." "It's not about Henry, really; it's about the life-style. It's about all of them together. Henry's the one who gives us the in; he opens the door for us, but basically, it's about all these people. So it's more a comment on the life-style than it is on Henry."[6] But this is a postmodern anthropological study: no objective distance. We get swept in. We get swept in, not suspended. We take our ordering frame with us. How could we not?

The lifestyle rushes at us in the first twenty minutes of the film as the young Henry, like Pip, germinates before our eyes, apprenticed to the neighborhood wiseguys. There's a distance between Henry's enthusiastic recollections of tampering with the U.S. mail, arson, swag cigarettes, alcohol, furs, being arrested, and so on and our own judgments, but the film doesn't allow us that distance. Upbeat lyrics punctuate Henry's own fascination with the lifestyle. He has to introduce us to the awesome varieties of life here, really a Dickensian cornucopia of characters whose very names reveal their life-worlds. "It's like a Dickensian world," we then say to ourselves, a world full of farce and good humor. We are willing at this point to see the difference here as a laughable difference and therefore inconsequential. The wilding isn't understood but it's not serious so what's to be understood?

We get pulled up short almost at once. Joe Pesci's Tommy De Vito is regaling his fellow wiseguys with a very animated account of a police interrogation. Henry can't stop laughing. "You're a funny guy," he tells Tommy. "Whatya mean funny?" Tommy shoots back, suddenly very serious. "You know funny," Henry rejoins, still laughing. "No, I don't know funny. You tell me. How funny? Funny like I'm a clown? I'm here to amuse you? Funny like the way I talk?" "You know. The way you tell the story. You're a funny guy." "What the fuck is so funny about me. Tell me what's so funny?" The exchange is unnerving. As Henry stops laughing and begins to sense the danger, so do we. We made a mistake.

There's nothing funny going on here. We are drawn back to the opening scene, to Tommy with the French kitchen knife in his hand stabbing over and over again the bloody body in the trunk. Henry was just laughing. We were just laughing. And now our lives are threatened for no reason. Unprovoked. Random. This difference is dangerous. We're not going to be able to laugh it off so easily. We relax in our seats when Tommy tells us, "I had you going. I really had you going."

Joe Pesci wins the Best Supporting Actor award that year for that very scene. He really had us going. The stakes are always high when we are brought to fear. We live to reward it and Joe Pesci in turn redeems himself by coming back to us as a funny guy who learns the rules in *My Cousin Vinny*. Finally, difference has to be here to amuse us. Or it has to fit into the Hollywood protocols of fear. It is when images fail to order and therefore dispel fear that loathing sets in. That no longer sells tickets.

It only attracts votes.

All this said, there is a difference between the Mafia's wilding and that of "Little Man" James. Modernity went after the Mafia as a problem to be solved, a provocation to the order of things that needed containment. That difference organized itself both within its own unsignifiable difference *and* as a reverse image of the culture's identity. And it did so both offensively and defensively. Postmodernity has sort of whipped the problem-solvers out of the temple and made an endless crisscrossing of provocation its order of things. Easy oppositions have interpenetrated and firm hierarchies have fallen to sidelong paths. What we fear most is what we've become: a culture that has lost the means of tying things together, a culture that has lost its Beatrice who guided intellect toward the light. The random, stochastic, the contingent await us in the dark bushes as we try to jog on the jogging path in Central Park.

But there is no Central Park. Just a Lateral Park. You can get to places that you don't know how you've gotten to. Your mind arrives at the sensible after having wandered all over. You can see things you don't understand. Things can happen to you that make no sense. And the sense people live by, their own framed sense of real-izing, comes undone, unframed, as things happen sidewise, spreading out into each other, crisscrossing, erring, digressing. The undertow, the subliminal, the repressed South of our own psyches, are no longer under, sub, or south. The heights get spread out, the grand narratives get leveled. The jangle of the psychic boiler room explodes into the parlor. It gets on TV, makes the newspaper headlines, and reaches the Big Screen. Fear of this fall propelled Reagan and the politics of metanarrative recovery, of revived logocentricism, into the White House, into 1980. It's the fall of America into random contingency and it comes to the screen variously.

Mafia wiseguys have been wilding on screen long enough for cross-pollination to have occurred. As it has. If not a problem solved, a Gotti found guilty, at least a problem coopted. A haunting that doesn't rob us of our sleep. But the vestiges of an originary wilding can be seen in the wiseguy versus player clash in *Godfather III* and also in the wiseguy film's own objection to being considered funny. So the press is still in tow because Gotti is a media event, a photo-op, a spectacle. We know *what* we're viewing even if we don't quite know *how* to view it. This draws us, like a murderer back to the scene of the crime. Nevertheless, the wilding here has almost lost its wildness, its capacity to wrench things out of order and leave us fearing that order's—our own as well as society's—survival. This Mafia wilding has been played out on the screen. And anyway, there is a new wilding out there that comes almost image-less.

The press is in tow when a Central Park jogger is beaten and a motorist is shot to death, both without reason, because there is unbelievable fear here. I mean, this reality hasn't quite been brought to the screen. There's been no hyperrealizing here. We can't make a screen identification. Jeffrey Dahmer's weird psychopathology gets some play through *Silence of the Lambs'* Buffalo Bill and Hannibal Lector but the new wilding is different. It's newness is like the newness of the working poor in America, people who work forty hours or more a week and still can't afford to pay for food and rent. This new wilding comes out of everydayness, not out of pathological deviance. Yet it meshes a depraved indifference for human life into this routine everydayness.

Needless to say we're far from thinking it's funny. The wilding here is questioning our own narrative-making capacities. We can't tell ourselves an explaining, soothing, or funny story about all this. In fact, the Central Park wilding and "Little Man" James' wilding are only perceived as contingent because our culture wants to tell a modernist story, a problem-solving story about these events and that story can't be told. Or, when it's told we hear phrases like "random amorality" and "depraved indifference." The underclass is wilding because modernity's metanarratives—from political to moral—have already been thrown into a wilding of embattled narratives. Our culture is rapidly being deterritorialized. Our ordering constructions are, to our dismay, being constructed against. This new, stochastic wilding is only possible within modernity's increasingly frayed order of things, an order that has for the past dozen years or more tried to retailor itself.

The new wilding may have ontological rather than political roots and therefore our fear turns on our very being-in-the-world. The problem is deep-rooted and has to do with a fundamental change in our consciousness of ourselves or, more exactly, a retrogression in sensitivity to the full palette of our own human natures. Perhaps this is due to the bombardment of computer logic, of being drawn increasingly into computer-generated virtual reality, of being drawn into the hyperreality of Big Screen, TV surrogate stimulation and response, the play of an indifferent free market. The list of possible culprits is almost endless.

What happens if our minds get lost in hyperreality shuffle, the blitz of simulacra, and we lose our sensitivity to human life? I mean, we literally shape a harder consciousness, the kind that more easily blows off (or away) the "sacredness of human life," a phrase that ecologism ultimately leads us to interrogate if a defense of the equal sacredness of other and diverse forms of life on this planet is to be achieved.

We may be propelled toward this depraved indifference by the indifference of a market economy to any but the cash nexus, the loss of so-called humanistic metanarratives in the face of a postmodern anarchy, and the absorption of people within simulated or virtual realities that order *Homo sapiens* toward the ordering of *Machina sapiens*.

We do not go gently into that darkness. Ironically, we hold it as our greatest fear, as if we had looked into the abyss, saw what we would become, and drew back in horror but not before that abyss had crossed over into us. While the Third World, the ecological South of the planet, fights in the open against hunger, poverty, oppression, the North, the economically sound, the culturally proud, wrestles with its own self-disordering, of minds, settled in the crud at the bottom, like clams at the bottom of polluted oceans, contaminated, poisoned. The waters are poisoned and there are myriad causes for this pollution. We are sensitive now to the fact that minds go awry in unfathomable ways, that Sherlock Holmes' deductive method would fall into a crack, that our logic is something nature does not follow. We cannot continue our line of investigation. That line now spins a web.

The wilding of the underclass is the force behind recent African-American films. That wilding has been narrated rarely and always from the outside, which means from the inside of a stereotypic narrative frame. Whites brought to the screen what they could identify and they could only represent what their own lives had already presented to them. One African-American filmmaker, Spike Lee, makes repeated lateral crossings between film and culture, narrating at the crossroads of fears felt by whites and blacks, bringing to the level of representation—of giving shape to what heretofore had no identity in our culture —what seems so alien to our representing powers, so aloof from our capacity to enclose it safely within a story. He brings into the fold of a continuous narration the lived experiences of African Americans, lived experiences so far in the two-hundred-year history of America that have been plotted like stochastic events, contingencies waiting for a metanarrative of linking.

The message is clear: as long as films weren't being done and performed by those who are the marginalized underclass we could only identify Italian Americans, African Americans, Asian Americans, Hispanic Americans, women, and others from inside a sort of homogenized, Hollywoodized, cultural identity that played to the folks in Indianna. Willard Motley's *Knock on Any Door* is a novel about African-American street culture but translated into Italian-American street culture because nothing else would work in our culture at that time. And that novel comes to the screen in that disguise. The boyz were in the 'hood but they couldn't get to the screen. James Olmos's *American Me* is perhaps just the beginning of Latino films done by Latinos. But the clearest sign of the Native Americans' diminished presence has been the absence of their own self-representation in film.

Robert Redford's documentary, *Incident at Oglallah*, shows clearly the sort of problems his nondocumentary film of the same subject, *Thunderheart*, will face. The documentary focuses and refocuses on the shooting incident, probing, investigating, questioning, representing testimonies from everyone involved. But the closer we get, the more the horizon from which this incident emerges grows inexplicable, something we can no longer apprehend. We have no way of intersecting the Native American life-world. We are outside it. We observe the aftermath, the explosive results of a long, slow silencing of the Indian voice.

Thunderheart can then only offer a liminal presence—Val Kilmer, FBI agent, three-quarters white, one-quarter repressed Sioux. Liminal entities, according to Victor Turner, "are neither here nor there; they are betwixt and between the positions assigned and arranged by law, custom, convention, and ceremonial."[7] But the film narrates from 'our side' of the threshold; we don't—because we can't—step into that *communitas* (a social state of being that is yet not a social order) which *was* the Native Americans'.

Val Kilmer can be no less outside this *communitas* than we, as viewers, are. We all finally make Hollywoodish nods toward that mystique but it's just Hollywood stereotypic nonsense. All our representations invariably show what whites *did* to that *communitas*; and, as *Thunderheart* shows, we are still trying *to do* things to Reservation survivors.

I have already discussed African-American film in the previous chapter, but here I want to say something about black wilding. A foreshadowing of the LA revolt appears in *Do the Right Thing* as does a foreshadowing of the Bensonhurst murder in *Jungle Fever*. The murder was of Yusef Hawkins by Bensonhurst white youths on the prowl for any blacks heading for Gina Feliciano's birthday parth. The Rev. Al Sharpton led a protest march through Bensonhurst on May 19, 1990, and the Bensonhurst community showed up to display their racial hatred of blacks. For the camera. *La famiglia* obviously meant something very little and very local, tribal more in what and whom it excluded than in what it valued and respected.

Rather than being narrative-less the forty white youths who attacked and killed Hawkins clearly found themselves in a world in which there were suddenly too many narratives, rather like present-day Germans who took to bombing out the alien Turks in their community. In each case someone's own narrative was threatened. You might say that whereas a modernist order of things generated a hierarchy within which the boys from Bensonhurst could find their place—or at least place everyone else—our culture's postmodern shift put everyone's neighborhood, so to speak, inside everyone else's. If one's center was everywhere, why not travel around?

If forty years before a Gina Feliciano had preferred black lovers to white ones, she would have had to move out of the 'family.' Neighborhood territories are like Deleuzean territories in that they lay claim to modes of being and realizing. In the postmodernizing of the 'hood, Yusuf walks into Gina's neighborhood, the Italian-

American narrative. It's that free lateral strolling on the part of Yusef, unprevented by cultural barriers in place, which brings the forty heroes to fighting pitch.

It's the already present postmodern climate that has enabled narratives to cross each other's path. It brings a long-time racism into the daylight. And it leads to murder. No middle of the night fire bombings of a black family on their first night in a 'hood that doesn't want them. No quick, muffled, back seat pummelings by the Mafia of blacks who "didn't know their place." In short, the clandestine retaliation of a cultural order of things that needed every so often a bit of fine tuning is now an open confrontation. *La famiglia* is being reterritorialized. The 'hood is interpenetrating it. The irony is that family bonding and 'hood bonding have already interpenetrated within a culture that has increasingly given itself to only one kind of bonding—free market bonding.

Baseball bats in the hands of a mob running through the streets after a sixteen-year-old Yusuf Hawkins. And then a long, tiring outpouring of racial taunts and insults as Rev. Sharpton and some five-hundred African Americans march in protest of the murder. In response to taunts Rev. Sharpton throws kisses. The contesting gets filmed and appears on *Frontline* where Bensonhurst can see its own image, where their racism goes public. Where to go to now? Certainly not back to a racism secreted carefully in the cultural order of things. On to another murder? I think not. Once the cameras march laterally into your 'hood, it's never yours again and the narrative of identity that was shaped in its very own niche is invaded, penetrated, riven. Your own image on the TV screen contests your own identity. You shrink back.

Four Italian-American teenagers from Bensonhurst, Brooklyn, were accused in regard to the murder of Yusuf Hawkins, the African-American teenager shot to death on a summer night in 1989. That tragedy crossed my own life, twenty-one years gone from Bensonhurst, my old neighborhood, the place I grew up. I was in the Heartland of America in 1989, in mid-Michigan, a part of the country I have come to overgeneralize as a locus of balance, of centeredness. Here is a weltanschauung that doesn't move laterally very well for fear of losing the center, for fear of losing its balance, for fear, I think, of falling off East and West Coast edges. New York City is an abyss in the mid-Michigan mind; Bensonhurst, a circle of hell. I get as many questions about what Bensonhurst is like as I do, as an American of Sicilian descent, about John Gotti and the workings of the Mafia. I know now how events that connect with what our culture has become can be signified as wilding. It's just a matter of linking word and world from within your own 'hood.

Identity in mid-Michigan takes surreptitious, calm glances at my difference. But they only look at me through the lens of the Big Screen and that screen has both commodified me and linked me with what is sociologically problem-solvable. For Italian Americans, the wilding is being quelled by its own cinematic image. I am not feared nor loathed, perhaps because I'm funny like all my *goombata* on the screen are funny. And my younger Bensonhurst *goombata*—Joseph Fama and Keith Mondello and the others—are they funny, feared, pitied, hated, irrelevant? As long as they can be connected with racism there's a reason for their actions. And that's soothing in the Midwest. Their minds hadn't gone off on flywheels, their sense of right and wrong fly out the window. They just let their racism consume them. They live on the coast of things, on the extreme, Eastern edge. They've lost a sense of the middle. They just let hate lead them to a public display.

In the Midwest at the center if people are different you ignore them. You certainly don't go public. Difference is to be made invisible not openly encountered. When difference walks through your neighborhood you go on about your business without looking up. If it hangs around, you relocate. But if the center is everywhere, where do you relocate?

Four were charged with "depraved indifference to human life" but their depravity is in a different category than "Little Man" James who fired at a passing car for no reason. The sense out here at the center doesn't want to come undone. We want as much protection from what ails "Little Man" James as we do from AIDS. And we go to the movies to find the linkages we've missed. It isn't accidental that African-American film and rap music are at a fever pitch of representation in the present. They have an audience looking to be brought out of the play of order and disorder and into some supplement of meaning, of understanding.

Since our culture is incapable of linking wilding to revolt, of solving the problem of difference, of regulating its free market indifference in accordance with the needs of human life-worlds, our culture is bound to go the movies, there to consume what it cannot express, there to see made conceivable what it doesn't want to conceive.

Can we construct an African-American image that will not frighten us and that we can rear future generations of African Americans on? Can we make African Americans funny again, not the same way two white men made Amos and Andy funny but a '90s way of funny? Can we bring order, in short, to African-American wilding? Has order already transformed/deformed difference into what it can identify? Or can order only cast it out as an Otherness that identity must shape itself against or leave alone?

And the tribalism of not only wiseguys but of any ethnic group, any 'hood—is its order, like all postmodern order, little and local but because of this must it then necessarily be blind and hostile to what lies outside itself? Can we not move laterally into each other, preserve the 'hood and each other's difference? Not be one but instead be a difficult whole?

What is clear is that these questions and dilemmas are already representing themselves on the screen apart from the needs and requirements of any one order of identity.

AFTER *BOB ROBERTS*: WAS THIS A POSTMODERN PRESIDENTIAL CAMPAIGN?
DECEMBER 1992

> *Politics and entertainment have always been the same business.*
>
> —Linda Bloodworth-Thomason

> *The right will always invoke an enemy within. They will insist on a distinction between real Americans and those who say they are but aren't. This latter is your basic nativist amalgam of people of the wrong color, recent immigration or incorrect religious persuasion.*
>
> —E. L. Doctorow

When we were deep within the Reagan attitude, the Rightness of the Reagan Right, very few of us could journey far enough out to touch the framing of that frame. Criticisms of everything from the voodo nature of Reaganomics to the competency of Reagan himself seemed carping, partisan, just so much sour grapes. No indictment of grounding axioms such as "Greed is Good," that the down-and-out are parasitic slobs, that democracy was grounded in "merit," that egalitarianism was secured by equality of opportunity, that the Bill of Rights is *really* about corporate rights, that market contingency and volatility *is* Ameri-

No barb was ever really sharp, telling. The Democratic Party seemed to blur; liberalism in the mouth of Michael Dukakis pled nolo contendere to the charges Bush brought against it. Modernist satire, whose last vestige seemed to be an already coopted-by-the-market *Saturday Night Live*, and a PBS owing more and more of its existence to corporate sponsors—needed—and wasn't getting—a secure Archimedean locus from which to deliver sharp, telling blows to the Reagan grand narrative.

We have a perspective now on it, now after the Clinton victory, as if we woke up and could look back and see where we've been and what was happening to us. How could the naked barbarism, the crudity and inanity of the New Right have so effectively turned the table on any opposition, indeed, successfully represent that opposition as retrogressive, degenerate, anarchistic, deeply threatening to American values? I think we are realizing now that the powerlessness of that opposition lay in its own increasing deconstruction of Enlightenment optimism and its problem-solving methods. In other words, the place from where a formidable critique should have been launched was itself already under attack. And not by the rightists, whose rightness inheres in the rightness of its own foundation.

Reagan came on the scene the way water flooded the *Titanic*, the way nature abhors a vacuum. The Great Perotian Sucking Sound was the collapse of the Modernist's Project. The final shuffling of twentieth-century modernism's own attack on modernity was toward a *horror vacui*, an abyss from which no justifiable attack could be made. The firm bedrock of one reality and at least a chance to reach it, to touch it, was cracking up into multiple fragments.

This was all in process, not completed, and thus the vibe we get now of what was going on then is one of uncertainty, of a deep ontological uncertainty, a *crise de conscience*. And at that moment of increasing dishevelment, a proud unquestioning, un-self-reflexive Absolutizing Certitude stepped forward, a third-rate Actor-Construct (it's easy to adopt what traditionalists take to be the poststructuralist position regarding subjectivity and look upon Reagan as fully constituted by outside forces) here about to assume its one Big Role. Infinitely appealing at a time of inner angst, this presumptiveness spread into every camp. Even its obvious victims and casualties—minorities, the working class, the poor, the young, and the old—took up the banner, only momentarily looking over to see if someone could voice any clear reasons why they shouldn't do so. Clear reasons were precisely what any oppositional voice had in short supply.

The rhetoric of the Right seduced and where it couldn't seduce, it advocated repression. Caught without a logic of integration, an enlightened critique, and unwilling to see truth as merely a rhetorical matter, any opposition to the Right remained stuttering, incomprehensible, defensive, showing all the signs that weakness shows before strength. Modernity balkanized before the Soviet Union ever did. The Reagan Right slipped past modernity's epistemology/ontology and niched itself in a rhetoric of the Right, and that rhetoric sought to construct various classic realist scenarios with which to make its case. But that classic realism is not the kind I have been redefining here—one that plays out the turmoil and undecidables of the culture—but an old-fashioned, B-movie, Hollywood kind, the kind Ronald Reagan made a career out of.

There was a powerful correspondence among Reagan's effectiveness, the power of his communicative rhetoric, and his Hollywood film career. Against a backdrop of postmodernist chaos, Reagan played out a tight, clearly etched classic realism: good guys against bad guys, background mellow muzak, and the solemn recitation of heroic speeches, call to arms, glorious sunsets, proud traditions, noble legacies, yellow brick roads.

The Democratic Party was caught in the chasm between the old certitudes of "E Pluribus Unum," of truth and reason as the stuff that stuck people together, that brought difference around, and troubling nightmares of a future in which difference could no longer be brought into line. While the Democrats held on to, with shaky hands, the pretense that differences were incrementally and slowly being cleared up, the Republicans were spinning stories of firm foundations and centering presences. Only the lost were pathless and the pathless were those facing the aporia of undecidability; there were examples all around us of people who had found the right path. You could see them on TV, on "The Lives of the Rich and Famous."

In Tim Robbins' film, *Bob Roberts,* we are no longer bit players in that metanarrative of the Right, waiting in the wings as it were to come on and get our share of the fame and riches, bask in the light. Robbins hasn't picked up the old corrective rod of liberalism and he hasn't honed another, new corrective rod out of the old. And this absence of an enlightened *Ideologiekritik* doesn't lessen at all the force of the film's undermining of the metanarrative of the Right.[1]

There is no implicate order or external point of reference that Robbins enlists to dismantle the Right's rhetoric. The sureness and dexterity of Robbins' narrative on small matters as well as grand don't fit the MO of an unsure and undexterous counternarrative that was spun in the '80s. Nor could it come out of that Old and New Left fervor that after the collapse of the Soviet Union is unsure of both itself and its audience. Nor could it be merely representative of our culture's rediscovered centeredness, or our culture's new rootedness in some totalizing, holistic vision. At the moment of the film's release American culture is more than ever divided by ever-increasing differences. Marginalized voices are wearing out with unassimilable dissent that unifying foundationalism that had heretofore managed to keep them silenced or managed to remodulate them into a preexisting notion of harmony.

I therefore disagree with Terrence Rafferty's praise of *Bob Roberts* as a deft satire on the conservative Right enacted by the liberal Left.[2] That would mean that liberalism had reconstructed itself and so far distanced itself from the conservative attack that it had itself become a foundation from which to launch a critique. *Bob Roberts* is a joyful immersion in a way of real-izing that no longer frightens or frustrates. The reascendant Right is at every turn so patently absurd and wrong-headed, so solemnly intent on its own Rightness, so infatuated by its own manipulations, that all this is transparent to a focused lens, which is what the Brit documentary filmmaker is doing in the film while we're watching the film. And often what we are watching is that documentary film.

We have come a long way here from the insecurity of liberalism in the '80s to a confident faith in the power of a focused lens to parody that Right-wing soap opera of American culture that for so long was not something we viewed but something we were in and had no idea of ever finding our way out of. We have traveled that distance not because a New Liberalism has discovered new paths to a universal rule of judgment but because we have settled down—finally—into the morass of our own multiple, diverging constructions, the Bob Roberts narrative being one of them.

We aren't anyplace firmer, more stable, better, but we are someplace *different* and that makes all the difference, makes the film not a modernist critique but a postmodern parody. And it is that spirit that finally finds its way into a real-life Presidential campaign—the Clinton–Bush narrative clash. But let's first stay with Bob Roberts' senatorial race.

Bob Roberts tours the country in a bus that is a trading floor on wheels and speechifies through song, a New Right version of Bob Dylan. The Times Are Changing *Back*. This Land Was Meant for Me. *Period*. And since the world turns its back on God, Bob must fight to protect Him (surely God is a Him). Bob's songs protect God from the Godless. The times, which are shifting toward the unregulated diversity of postmodernism, have to change back to a vision of secure and firm foundations, to moral certitude, to a universal rule of judgment and the ability to preserve hierarchies.

Modernity ultimately generated only an ambiguity that twenthieth-century modernism tried to be at home within. The mission of establishing a Determinate Rightness, in other words, collapsed under its own ponderousness. It collapsed into postmodernity, a state of being-in-the-world that tolerates only collapsed metanarratives. There is no changing back on this level, no going home, where home was home base, the place/presence where stable linkages of word and world could be made. It is postmodernity itself which puts into play the yearning here, the strength of this narrative of return and retrieval, of reclamation of the world as a stable point of reference for the rational, for those who have not strayed into a postmodern garden of forking paths. This is not the opposition; this is an unrelenting strong narrative of unity, coherence, and identity, one that is slowly changing as it finds itself not distanced from postmodernity but interpenetrating it.

If postmodernity seems at first to be nothing more than a symptom of modernism or a new face to modernism it is because postmodernity's purpose and meaning are, by definition, construed

within the overall frame of modernity. It is also because the difficult or unbroken whole of postmodern narratives, their imbrication
and intersection, is not oppositional or hierarchical but exists on a
similar plane, a lateral, crisscrossing plane.[3] Postmodernism lives
in an Otherness that does not subsume modernity, does not replace
it in the way modernity replaced scholasticism as well as the spirit
of the Renaissance. It is that evident failure to replace modernity
according to the replacement rules of modernity itself, which leads
to the belief that postmodernity is merely a brief detour off the
main highway of modernity. If it were any good, it would prove it
was better.

It becomes inevitable then—within the rules of this game—
that just as we have in the twentieth century taken the detours
of Dada and the absurd, nihilism and positivism, existentialism
and Freudianism, of structuralism and poststructuralism, of
deconstruction, and semiotics and those have dead-ended (in
modernity's solve-or-perish calculation), postmodernity will likewise
fade away. It is interesting that postmodernity's resurrection of all
supposed casualties of the modernist method has already led to multiple codings of self and world. Such a rhizomic intercrossing has
encouraged the diversity of our culture in deeply affective and perceptual, if not cognitive, ways. There is no going home, and if there
is, the house has been designed by Robert Venturi.

How does the nostalgia for a firm Teutonic *Aufhebung* by which
to bring differences into an order of identity wind up flying the
banner of self-interest? Why is a reality sui generis, a reality that our
Aufhebang supposedly mirrors/captures, nothing more than an invi-
tation to plunder, to line one's own pockets? My point is that the
establishment of a universal, neutral Rightness, an order by which
truth is legitimized through reference to this reality sui generis,
enables exclusionary politics and Deleuzean dominant forms of
signification.

The way is cleared for Bob Roberts and his followers to sing
"This land was meant for *me*." When asked how he became so self-
determined, Bob answers, "Rich. I wanted to be rich." Everything in
the world can be there for a few to grab only if everyone else in the
world has already been handicapped by their difference from, their

diminishment and exclusion by, what modernity offers as a natural and necessary order.

Bob Roberts doesn't run for senator on a platform of ultimate unity, of ultimate social justice, of a reality and truth whose last pieces are put together under his administration so that "we can all be real together," which is the promise of his opponent. Bob Roberts does exactly what Reagan and Bush did and did successfully for twelve years: he tells people that only by holding off differences that threaten a legitimately grounded cultural reality, a truth neutrally and rationally based on a sui generis reality, can any one individual hope to be rich.

To have the world and all its riches one must seek the preservation of a dominant and domineering chain of signification and deny any validity to a Derridean *différánce*.[4] The obstacles to any secure positioning—including one of wealth and power—arise out of this notion of *différance*. The play of differences over word-world linkages, of meaning and truth, cannot be resolved within any one linkage. Difference is never sorted through by any rod of sameness. At the same time, stability and determinacy are endlessly deferred. Modernity's foundationalism provides the underpinnings of inferiorization and therefore the underpinnings of ceaseless self-aggrandizement for those already favorably positioned within what postmodernity would call an arbitrary cultural ordering.[5] The fascinating thing is that Bob Roberts' campaign on film is not made to show these connections. They are the wellsprings of the parody. They have already been made in the 1980, 1984, and 1988 presidential elections. All the film has to do is draw on them. The audience already comes in with a horizon of hauntings. Has the 1992 presidential campaign been different? I think I see in it a clear shifting toward postmodernity.

With Bush-like 90/90 hindsight, we can now look back and see the unity, coherence, and continuity in Bill Clinton's campaign for the presidency. A former negatively linked slickness now has very positive connotations: he kept a steady course through the confusion, worked his way skillfully through fragmentation, and wound up being more decipherable than George Bush. Perhaps this is just strategy, skillful campaign tactics; perhaps a unified vision is lacking and therefore Clinton cannot bring the country from fragmentation to coherence. Without a unifying vision how can there be any continuity of purpose and intent, any sense of entirety, totality, and system? Or is the vision thing here with Clinton the way it was with Bush: everything works best for everyone concerned if the president's unifying vision is to have *no* unifying vision?

That turns out to be not only a vision thing but one the voters have just rejected. After twelve years it became very palpable to them. It's Quayle who sets us on the right track here: if Clinton, Quayle said, runs the country the way he ran his campaign, we'll be alright. Is it therefore enough to be a slick tactician to be president or is the point here—the one I want to extract—that Clinton displayed a gamesmanship in his campaign that reveals a different way of handling the vision thing?

The Soviet Union is not a solitary instance of collapse into balkanization. Reality has balkanized, and in this country, committed to a melting pot unifying vision in the face of an endemic balkanized population, that reality has quite naturally shifted to multiple, fragmented realities. The vision thing is always little and local. One has to find one's way through a garden of multiple, crisscrossing visions.

The slickness of Bill Clinton's campaign is that it, too, shifted into this New World Order in which order always emerges from some cultural positioning, in which difference is merely that which some positioning, some framing of the real, cannot identify, in which coherence and continuity are no more than disruptions and instabilities outside their constructed modes of real-izing.

Clinton played out his moves on the postmodern bottomless chessboard: there was no foundational, universalized, absolute grand vision upon which all the varieties of crisscrossings between himself and the American people could be modulated, brought to meaning, or judged. What ultimately revitalized the Democratic Party was this movement away from one totalizing grand narrative of truth toward the recognition of multiple truths, of a national diversity that could neither be held under a free market/trickle-down truth or any new, unifying ideology the Democrats could come up with.

It took three presidential elections before the Democrats put modernity's Quest for The Truth on a back burner and went postmodern. Truths and the platforms they create are culturally relative and therefore there are as many out there on the campaign trail as there are culturally diverse people. Americans are not hyphenating the signifiers that identify them because they are pieces to be placed in one Big Picture of America but because they are making every effort to distinguish their difference, a difference that they live within and out of which they link themselves to their own identities and the world outside themselves. Truths and realities are therefore always mediated from within narrative frames, stories people live within.

Clinton listened to the stories. Ideologically you might say he trafficked locally and wound up being accused of indecisiveness and pandering. But the skill we now admire in the way he carried through his campaign has to do with his ability to escape being connected to messages struggling for universalizing status while at the same time being able to plunge into the discord of local voices. This success depends upon him being able to interpret the nature of different settings and to respond effectively. His responses become pertinent because they are not shaped by a prior universal rule of judgment but rise out of his own intersection with the ways of real-izing of those he encounters.

Such pertinence and relativity of response becomes clearly a matter of hypocrisy and pandering if Clinton had already attached himself to a grand narrative of truth, if indeed he had shown that he was committed to some absolutist program and had not grounded himself on that most relativist of notions—change. A postmodern politics recognizes that truth is relative, changeable, local and little, that there is no way to say that one relativist notion of truth is rooted in reality and another is not, or that local truths are incremental, noncontradictory, and can be added up objectively to bring us closer to reality.

Finally, all encounters are culturally positioned but that positioning itself has no stability. What is called for are repeated intersections of truth-narratives, of stories of identity and difference. The play of postmodern chess on a bottomless chessboard is not preempted but goes on with an unleashed energy and constant contesting that antagonizes the apolitical and disgusts those who already possess the truth.

If postmodernism were truly 'post' the temper of modernity, from the early Enlightenment faith in reason to the twentieth-century angst-filled variety, and 'post' the temper of blind faith to take us beyond the many representations of reason to reality itself, postmodernism would be caught in the oppositional politics of modernity itself. It would be asserting its new-found truth above all others and presumably doing so because it had assumed some Archimedean point outside the fray from which it could pass judgment on the truth or falsity of lesser narratives. This postmodernism cannot do. It finds itself one narrative among others, but for the first time since the Renaissance not a narrative that synthesizes or integrates others, or subsumes or denies others.

It enters the fray with a joy because it is neither burdened by modernity's urgency to prove its reason to be more reasonable than another's or by modernity's consequent angst over its failure to stabilize and make determinate one construction of self and world. Fragmentation signifies only as multeity, discord as unrepressed contesting, decisions as only "for this place at this time" and therefore always to be revisited, and change becomes the natural toppling and unraveling of limiting narratives.

The campaign was a delight for a postmodernist to watch, each and every bit of it, from the character assaults to the steadfastness of the message, from the TV debates to the battles of the pundits, from the charts and statistics to Perot's "let's just do it." An intricate webbing of classic realist, early modernist, late modernist, and postmodernist threads. No one voice could silence another, no story could elide another, all solutions proferred by one candidate elicited from another candidate a litany of new problems, and the dualism of true or false, good or evil, right or wrong, standing behind the two-party system expanded laterally.

We cannot confer too great a significance to this: the vertical hierarchy, a cultural ordering that is not total or absolute but merely ingrained and imposed, collapses onto a horizontal plane. Truth is not in any one position but lateralized and narrated differently along the plane, as is falsehood. The viability of Perot and his campaign presents a difficulty to our dualist mind-set; it wreaks havoc with our attempt since the Enlightenment to not disperse truth and falsehood, good and evil, into many locations but to distinguish them clearly and defend against their intersection.

That there must be one telling the truth and one lying or concealing it gives way to three, each of whom is narrating a truth from within his own construction of reality. That there must be one who steps out of his own views and assumptions and grapples objectively, from a distance, with reality, gives way to a three-way mutual parodying in which no one ascends to an unreachable higher ground.

When we look at how each candidate gathers supporters and patches together necessary though unstable coalitions we are looking for meaningful connections. The reasons, however, are not in facts but within stories: not only the stories the candidates spin but the stories they themselves are obviously ensnared within. And these stories intersect the stories voters, either as odd individuals or in lobbies, tell themselves. We are not tracing the flow of an argument here, sorting through clear avowals of fact and the intelligent assimilation of them in order to come to the correct answer. Who is George Bush? Who is Ross Perot? Who is Bill Clinton? Who is Charles Foster Kane? There is no 'rosebud' signifier here to crack open and thus reveal the kernel of truth within.

There are three noteworthy modes of perceiving and responding, of feeling and thinking, which crisscross each other in any presidential campaign but in this one most dramatically. Why in presidential campaigns? Because the difficult whole we call the United States, polyphonic and polydimensional, comes into play. And this year most dramatically because the confusion, fragmentation, and indecipherability of this difficult whole is no longer being repressed, a repression directed by a third-rate screen actor with a nostalgic Hollywood Golden Age script.

You might say that our cultural shifting toward a postmodern paradigm had taken a last desperate detour down a Hollywood classic realist path. If we just stopped costing in individual human life-worlds, stopped hindering corporate destiny with individual rights and ecological concerns, stopped valuing those same rights above corporate rights, a few of us would do well and the rest would benefit from that success. If we ignored a rapidly increasing gap between rich and poor we could still aspire to the American Dream of one day being at the top ourselves.

Although this path was just one of the many forking paths in this campaign and was no longer the superhighway to progress and prosperity, to the American Dream, the classic realist attitude, the attitude that says "this is the truth as everyone knows it is," always threatened to take over the campaign as well as the minds of the voters.

The spin here is to simplify everything, from dramatis personae to issues, to conceal all contradictions resulting from clichéd and stereotypic representations, to spread such a smooth patina over everything that the voter glides easily toward the best candidate, to make as many links between a candidate and a voter as possible, and to do that by providing openings for the voter to identify himself or herself with the candidate, to make a candidate's message the truth and not a representation of truth.

None of the candidates abjured this representational mode nor did it fail to seduce voters for all three candidates. Bill Clinton was caught but broke free of a number of classic realist spins: philanderer, draft dodger, radical organizer, pot smoker, soft and indecisive leader, perhaps pathologically damaged by a traumatic childhood. What had to be concealed (and of course an opposing narrative would not allow to be concealed) was that JFK, among other highly esteemed presidents, had been a philanderer, Clinton had not been alone in protesting Vietnam, a war that not even John Wayne could reduce to a classic good guy/bad guy formula, and the very cultural diversity of the country demanded that a leader be not already possessed of a single truth and what course of action to immediately take.

Clinton responded in a postmodern way: he contested each and every charge, immediately and specifically, leaving it up to the voter to decide which representation, in effect, was stronger.

Not so with Perot, who presented a platform totally within the classic realist frame and therefore it seemed not to be a platform at all but a playing out of a Hollywood script. His "I can fix it and let's just do it" fit one of the strongest of American mythic fixations: the no-nonsense practical American who gets the job done and avoids all the talk that the Europeans get bogged down in. Like a home-spun grassroots American hero Perot would go to Washington and sweep out dirty politics. What broom he would employ—his ideo-logical corrective rod—is, in Perot's story, unimportant. There are hundreds of good ideas lying around. The trick is to pick one and "just do it." In the debates Perot stands alongside two men repre-senting conflicting ideologies, two men who want to "just do it" in two different ways, and yet Perot staunchly maintains that a conflict of ideas and beliefs is not at stake, is not important. He doesn't want to contest representations. After all, he is in possession of reality and truth.

The strength of the classic realist formula derives from the connection it makes with mythic/stereotypic narratives in the cul-ture. Certain stories reach what Jean Baudrillard calls the hyperreal, a realm of simulated images and sounds constructed by powerful forces of marketing and media, as well as politics, so that the surest, quickest, broadest connections can be made to an otherwise dispar-ate and diverse body of voters/consumers/viewers. The dirty politics Perot inveighs against are not outside the voter but are made pos-sible because the voter has already invested his or her own story within excluding and dehumanizing simulacra.

One reason why politics may therefore be dirty is because politicians must appeal to voters who are themselves already lost in racist/sexist/elitist attitudes. Politics may also be dirty because there are heated differences. Classic realist clarity gets muddied. The con-testing of views that both Perot and his running mate Admiral Stockdale saw as the problem, as symptomatic of dirty politics, is the playing out of democratic governance. Their appeal to the power of stereotypic simulacra is nothing less than an attempt to replace the free play of democratic contesting with immoveable, unreach-able, nondebatable biases.

The American voter may be sick of politics because he or she is not completely ensnared by classic realism's simulacra but cannot quite stop measuring things according to the limiting rod of simulacra. Doubtless this produces frustration. Or voters may see through the realist spin by applying an Enlightenment rod: reason enables them to see through the smooth facade of realism to the tensions beneath. But since the world has shifted out of that simple rhetoric of knowledge and rationality to a different sort of primacy—the primacy of cultural difference itself—and the universalist assumptions of the Enlightenment are everywhere brought to a local contesting, the staunch Enlightenment voter can do nought but rail against the fall of rational aspirations into the present postmodern abyss. Of dirty politics. One does not quite know how any longer to make things clean, or when one does—as in the case of the Three Pats (Buchanan, Robertson, and Boone)— rival narratives of cleanness emerge as well as those postmodern ones that express a deep incredulity toward any narrative that claims it can make things clean.

The postmodern response to these classic realist webs is to simply point out what has been left out, denied, elided, oppressed, shackled, or constrained. Although Perot relied on a classic realist platform he went after the other candidates with the energy and joy of a postmodernist, repeatedly pointing out what other narratives were concealing or leaving out. And, as already mentioned, his third-force presence fractured modernity's dualist narrative, its reduction of diversity to an 'either or' rather than an 'and also' mentality.

While Perot cast his own platform in the classic realist mold but assailed others as a postmodernist, George Bush's campaign was clearly forced to spin classic realist tales of itself and of its antagonists. The Cold War had provided Reagan with endless openings to gather the diverse under one banner. Bush held on to the Cold War spin: that if a threat to our national security arose, he could lead us as decisively as he had led us in the Gulf war. Even the end of the world survivalists had a hard time buying into this tale. And the family values spin was not only undermined by its own rigidity and exclusionary drive at the Republican Convention but was challenged to great effect on a popular TV show, Murphy Brown standing forth as a surprised but ready adversary.

Without a powerful connecting myth to ensnare the voter within, Bush turned to his opponents. He hoped to ensnare them as well as the voters within spins that would divert attention from his own campaign. And that campaign suffered from the absence of any way of connecting with the American voter.

George Bush was fractured in a typically postmodern way: he had a hard time asserting one representation of himself. He looked frenetic most of the time, his whole body, his whole speech moving in an erratic pattern, the syntax that joined both words and body into a comprehensible unity was set in motion, was in flux. If Perot was a postmodern challenger, Bush became the postmodern body, a clash of dissident voices that began to ventriloquate him as he failed over and over again to thrust forth one image, one representation, one story, one voice to the American people. The "folks out there, Mr. and Mrs. America, the hair dresser, the cab driver, the little people, the middle class" and on and on as George Bush struggled to find a signifier that would link him to that chunk of reality out there he had to appeal to if he was to be elected president, not as Reagan-2 but as George Bush.

This was, in effect, his first presidential campaign as George Bush, and "George Bush" was not only multiple, caught in multiple competing frames, but none of those framings of the real provided him with a personal, working linkage to the American people. If the voters by and large detected something pathetic in his bid, something tragic in his campaign, it had to do with this failure of one man to connect himself to his own brethren.

We sense that Bush's loss brings welcome release and relief to him, a man torn in many directions by the difficult whole of American diversity, a difficulty and diversity his own life had up until now successfully blocked off. The patrician/country club Republican who has had to interact with people who have no country club membership, people who wouldn't be in his life had he not campaigned for the position to lead them, can return to the country club. The man who had to stand behind the banner of free market play and trickle-down economics, unfortunately for his own peace of mind, could not wean himself away from seeing the mindless, voodo aspect to Reagan's mythology. The man pushed toward upholding a politics of do-nothingism had to conceal not only from the American people but from himself the recession, the riots, the erosion of egalitarianism, and so on because he could not identify what he was compelled—by programmatic affiliation—to do nothing about.

There are very interesting lateral issues here: Why did Bush pick Quayle and then stay with him? And why did he desperately seek to be not himself but a dead Democrat, Harry Truman?

Quayle almost immediately was pinned within a classic realist frame: he was one of the sons of affluence who bought his way out of Vietnam. A scion of the elite with no brains. After four years as vice president the spin on him only got worse: at first a thoroughly frightened and intimidated idiot, he became, in the debate with Gore, a confident, feisty idiot. Quayle himself seemed to be writing the script for this spin but so potent was it that it is hard to conceive that Quayle could ever buy into the spin Clinton did—"the comeback kid." At once giving the impression of an intimidated idiot and then coming back as a feisty idiot proved not to be a winning comeback for Quayle.

The modernist also rejected Quayle but they did so on the evidence. From neither representational mode—classic realist or modernist—could we answer the question why Bush would have chosen Quayle twice. This is a modernist puzzle, a conundrum, a problem to be solved. But if we entertain the postmodern notion that choices are narrated, that they, in short, come out of stories people live within, then the question of stupidity is extraneous to Bush's choosing of Quayle. It's not costed in and doesn't signify because Bush makes connections to Quayle that are socially compatible and not socialist. I mean by this that precisely what keeps Bush distanced from the American people—his total lack of imaginative identity with the concrete particulars of their lives—makes Quayle comprehensible and acceptable to him. Quayle is just as removed; they're kindred spirits.

Quayle doesn't have to prove himself efficient and functional within the bureaucratic-instrumentalizing order of things, a march toward a well-oiled, rationally based democracy. Bush and Quayle are not in that flow, not in that loop. They are already somewhere untainted by it; they're both, you might say, up there in the Manor House. For the rest of us, this connective logic is inaccessible. It's a chunk of the real our own chain of signification doesn't link us to.

Why did Bush link himself to Harry Truman? For that matter, why did Clinton? And, why do many think Perot is more like Harry than the other two although Perot himself didn't make the connection? First of all, both Bush and Clinton had to reconstruct Harry Truman to fit their present needs. While modernist historians were scambling to put the real Harry Truman before us so we could clearly judge who in this campaign was really like Harry, the candidates were both postmodern historians. They knew that the modernist retrieval could haul up no determinate Harry Truman but only a variety of contesting narratives. Harry, in short, was up for grabs.

What mattered on this bottomless chessboard was making your moves fast and with aplomb, and then making them before as wide an audience and as many times as possible. Once postmodernism made Harry so available the next thing that was needed was a classic realist spin to weave him into, a spin that would conceal the cracks in each man's campaign, as well as the cracks in any spin of Harry Truman, a spin that would spin against the crack-making spins.

Bush needed Harry's fixed, stable, unified, coherent self-identity. Bush desperately needed a mask, a persona, to cover his own multifractured 'I.' The buck would finally stop here and not meander, like a Bush sentence, into untrackable nooks and crannies, not spin out of conflicting representations of self but out of one dominant, controlling, fully mastered selfhood. And this was something Bush's spin represented Harry Truman as having and something Bush yearned for. Other, challenging representations of Harry Truman—a shoe salesman from Missouri —could only bring Bush back to that state of self-fracture, of having old self-confidences intersected by alien narratives (from the homeless to AIDS to Arkansas to the American people themselves).

Clinton didn't need Bush's nonschizoid Harry but he did need a decisive, "I can drop the bomb if necessary" Harry. Harry would cover up that widening fissure in the polished surface of Clinton's campaign—that Clinton had no mind of his own, that he wouldn't act but would remain listening to an endless variety of counsel and advice, always caught in the spinning, never stepping boldly forward and doing something. Clinton didn't attempt to totally rewrite that classic realist frame. The world had fractured into rival multiplicities. There was virtue in not being driven by what William Blake called "Single Vision." Listening to other voices was a virtue. The linkage with Harry was not to be played in a major chord. It was a note, among others.

Clinton was steadily throwing out linkages from within a postmodern frame. Unsaid, they yet amounted to this: what the New World Order really meant was that without a universal rule of judgment and in the face of ever more vocal cultural differences, we would have to value the absolute less and the relative more. We would have to make cultural differences primary. The majority was already breaking up into cultural differences; the pluralism was already overspilling the unity. American democracy was being called upon to represent/recognize more voices at the same time that our Enlightenment claim to being able to impose a rule of rational order was being exposed as a rule of law that disenfranchised, oppressed, ignored, or silenced differences. A democracy grounded in this Enlightenment order was being exposed as just something narrated from strong cultural biases, as really an emperor without clothes.

The postmodern paradigm infiltrated a campaign struggling to remain within the laws of two countries—classic realism and modernism. In the former, harmony is something we know all about, and, because we know all about it, conflicts stick out like sore thumbs. The enemy is always clearly visible. And because we all have a common sense of harmony we know how to overcome difficulties, correct those who make waves, the people and ideas who are strangely lost in turmoil and have therefore lost sight of what it means to be a real American.

In the case of modernity, we must rely on the specialist of reason and method, the value-free and theory-neutral, to define the true and the real, either authoritatively establishing the whole truth or putting it together by increments, extracting it from a variety of relative locations. Problems here ultimately give way to a systematic assault of unimpassioned reason. Or in the dark, angst-filled form of twentieth-century modernity, we work at the real like a great labyrinthine puzzle with numerous hands, gradually replacing darkness with light, gradually coming closer in our representations to a stable, external reality. Such a reality moves our representations toward determinacy, a reference point that with great difficulty we bend to, and according to which we ultimately define our true shape, our true being.

Is it any surprise that all that bending and shaping in the name of "truth" and "reality" would lead to a Bob Roberts campaign, a campaign for those shaped well and against those bending low? While Bob's campaign relied upon the real campaign for the force of its parody, the real campaign—Clinton versus Bush—had to go on within the frame of that parodying, a state of affairs that froze Bush's play and liberated Clinton's as well as the Democratic Party's. The world of postmodern parody was clearly a world Clinton was at play within and clearly a world inconceivable to Bush. You might say, the campaign was played out on Clinton's turf. Ironically, then, it was Clinton who had the home court—our present world— advantage.

THE FINAL DANCE AROUND THE PLANET: GREEN SPACE VERSUS SELF SPACE
JUNE 1992

The coils of a serpent are even more complex than the burrows of a molehill.

—Gilles Deleuze

It has been estimated that as many as 50,000 jobs associated with logging are at stake in the spotted owl and old forest growth controversy.

—Gerald K. Kreyche

I call him the ozone man because he's way out there on the environment. I mean he's way out there, man.

—President George Bush

Our greatest contributions to the environment will come when we're farthest removed from it—in the laboratory, in the voting booth, and in the marketplace.

—Martin W. Lewis

What would the quality of our lives be without nature?

—John Terborgh

There's a way to live with earth and a way not to live with earth.

—Robert Redford's Thunderheart

*This World is for Sale. Yammer all you want about the global
village, the global this or that. The only real topic on the
UNCED agenda is the* global market.
—Marc Cooper

Time to get that shit out of your system.
—Wim Wenders' Until the End of the World

*He is a tiny machine, I suppose, depending on what you mean
by* machine, *but it is his occasional moments of randomness
and unpredictability that entitle him to be called aware.*
—Lewis Thomas

What really is the tragedy of one more extinct species?
—Gerald F. Kreyche

*And what will it mean to be human in a society where com-
puter brains are fashioned from organic 'biochips' and the
human mind can be downloaded into a cybernetic matrix?*
—Mark Dery

*[T]he spectre haunting nearly all postmodern SF—the uneasy
recognition that our primal urge to replicate our consciousness
and physical beings (into images, words, machine replicants,
computer symbols) is* not *leading us closer to the dream of
immortality, but is creating merely a pathetic parody, a
metaexistence or simulacra of our essense that is supplanting us.*
—Larry McCaffery

When an MTV interviewer asked President Bush in the final week
of the presidential campaign why he called Al Gore "ozone man"
Bush responded that it was not because Gore was concerned with
ozone depletion but because he was *too* concerned. To which the
interviewer asked whether it was possible to be too concerned about

such a truly global threat. Bush made eye-contact for the first time with his young interviewer: What could he have expected from such a "really out there, man" world such as MTV but a "really out there, man" view? I got the sense as I caught that megasecond disappointment in Bush's face that what really tormented him was the disrupting thought of voters out there who always wanted to go too far and who had to be stopped for all our sakes.

Reagan tried mightily for eight years to restore us to a Hollywood back-lot where nature was to be rapaciously consumed. Bush, who could no longer make use of that stupefying *mythos*, must argue for reelection sake that environmentalism had gone too far, that "it's more than high time to restore human values over those of the world of nature."[1] It was time to hook up the economic rationality of the marketplace as the engine that drives human communities. The well-being of human communities is purely and simply a market matter. Human values, presumably, are only a matter of present polemics—being seen as either restorable or in need of drastic change—because we embrace capitalism. If we had not given ourselves over to the creative destruction of the market, had not redefined moral processes and social relations as *products* of the activities of research labs and product engineering centers, then we, as humans, would have no well-being.

Well-being, then, is a product of the market, of doing well market-wise and not something that has ever been erected on a foundation of determinate, universally accepted human values. Nor has a human community been generated out of those nonmarket values, a community that would have the right to intervene and regulate the free play of the market. The market determines well-being because a universal foundation of truth and a universally just civic order are forfeit. Forfeiture is already a market reality.

But let's say a community built on absolute values did exist. I suppose it would know how to keep track of, how not to lose touch with, how to show respect for nature. Anything other than this sort of connection would doubtless lead us back to that divisiveness, that furor of contesting moral truths, of undecidabilities, which market reality protects us from. If the Enlightenment had ever created that utopian community whose well-springs were indisputably just and right, the whole matter of justice and moral foundations, of a social as well as individual construction of the truth, would be, by definition, outside the market-technology-wealth-well-being loop. They would then, ideally, provide a universal rule of judgment that could be applied to the market loop.

Alas, that's all a dream. To be outside the market loop is only to be subject to it. Outside is neither transcendent nor grounding. It's just unneeded, inconsequential, not even "costed" in.

What puts a priori notions of human valuing outside the loop here is the fact that postmodernity has already noted the cultural positioning of all our human valuing, of the dignity and integrity of our Western cultural valuing. It is clear that narratives of liberty, equality, and fraternity, of privacy, individuality, and intellectual freedom, of a community somehow built on diversity, of a unity rising out of pluralism, of one, commonly acknowledged American Dream—all these have become not foundational but incendiary, hotly disputed because of their very undecidability. In the wake of this fall, the master narrative of the market has come forth and America is in a new loop, one that modernity's quest for the truth, incrementally shaped perhaps but still respectful of a single reality commonly shared, can only counter by proliferating its own ambiguities.

The only way to leap over the ambiguities of modernity is to treat market well-being and its fulfillment of self-interest as the culmination of the Modernist Project. In other words, while the determinacy of order project was having its last gasp under Reagan, a contemporaneous supercession of that whole project by a market metanarrative was underway. Well-being had to be rescued from a sinking ship. Pools of modern ambiguities were becoming an ocean of postmodern undecidability. That undecidability was already unnerving foundations, hierarchies, and loops.

In its public unraveling of the myriad modernist narratives regarding the vital sources of humanity postmodernity is also challenging the market as the arbiter of our culture, from what we do to what we are. Modernity's vital sources always turned out to be vital to someone, someplace, at some time and *not* vital to a lot of other people. And the market mentality seems to want to perpetuate that lopsidedness, with or without grand Enlightenment justifications.

My interest here is in how neither modernity nor market is vital to nature. Certainly nature is not vital to them. By the light of modernity, nature was not costed in in the same fashion that modernity's vital sources of humanity are not costed in by the market. By the light of early modernity, Enlightenment modernity, nature was something we *had*, not something we *are*. "The more we learn," Lewis Thomas writes, "the more we seem to distance ourselves from the rest of life, as though we were separate creatures, so different from other occupants of the biosphere as to have arrived from another galaxy. We seek too much to explain, we assert a duty to run the place, to dominate the planet, to govern its life, but at the same time we ourselves seem to be less a part of it than ever before."[2]

But this same Enlightenment anthropocentricism and its notions of human dignity and cultural integrity are now just "side effects" of "unfettered free trade" which "is the only hope for a prosperous, healthy world."[3] Such "side effects" are not to be directly pursued because they might be used to "fetter" that free trade. If, for instance, a linkage is formed between egalitarianism and democracy then a negative critique of the free market's indifference to such egalitarianism emerges. The market cannot allow its own contingency course to be preempted by Enlightenment valuing. The market's grand narrative is meant to replace with its own focused drive to greater productivity/greater consumption/greater wealth the undecidability and fractiousness that now seem to be the cultural heritage of Western Enlightenment, prefigured in the tragic vision of twentieth-century modernism.

When Bush went to the Earth Summit in Rio he had the global market—and America's losing share of that market—in mind and not the global environment. As far as the market master narrative is concerned nature has already been replaced with technologies. It is not an active player. Only people who pay more attention to either human values or to nature than they do to the market narrative are a problem. Some human valuers want nature to be at their disposal because "it is high time to restore human values over those of the world of nature."[4] But these people suffer from what Martin W. Lewis calls a "green delusion"—namely, that "economic growth rests fundamentally on the exploitation of natural resources."[5] In Lewis's estimate, those loggers in the Pacific Northwest who care for their livelihood more than they do spotted owls don't realize that the market needs technologies and not their lumber. The market's creative destruction will make them just as extinct as the spotted owl.

It's just a matter of time. And no interference. Whether technology is itself just the medium and not the message, whether new technologies do not inevitably alter us and our valuing, is a difficult question and I will use Wenders' *Until the End of the World* to see how both question and answer are played out. But it is the market that drives the technologies and the human community follows in their wake.

Whatever sense of human community that has been developed in the Pacific Northwest, and the human values grounding that community, will, if they themselves were grounded in the logging life, either vanish completely or become reshaped by a new market-created situation. 'Human Valuers' see the 'Greens' as their opponents and not the play of the free market. However, 'Human Valuers' are a potential source of opposition to free market play. When the market eventually erases their community as it erases their livelihood they may rebel against rather than applaud the creative destructiveness of the market.

'Human Valuers' therefore do not oppose 'Green Politics' in a really market acceptable manner. They fail to be market correct. There is still need for an anti-'Green' coalition that understands and accepts the credo of the unfettered market. The 'Wise Use' group comes forth. This group gets the support of Bush's administration (a photo of George Bush embracing the author of *The Wise Use Agenda* is on the book's cover) because one of its stated principles—to make anyone protesting corporate activities liable for civil damages—acknowledges market values as superior and prior to any human values. Indeed, human values arise out of market values.

Democratic narratives do not shape the market in their own image but rather the market shapes them. Since our democracy is already being eroded by the economic inequities of the '80s (up to 70 percent of income increase went to 1 percent of all families), only oligarchy could come forth as a shaping logic. But market logic has already supplanted any political logic so the widening canyon between rich and poor in this country can stay in the background, out of the limelight. It doesn't matter that our American cultural diversity is finding its many and different voices and discovering at the same time the inadequacies of a democracy built not as a community of diversity but by a culturally privileged unity. It doesn't matter because we no longer need to sort these matters out. That sorting out is done by the market. Some dissident voices will wind up extinct, victims of a creative destruction that the free market engenders.

Those people who want to fetter the free market in the name of the environment, for nature's sake, may be out to preserve as much of the earth as possible as an untrammeled Eden. There may be a sort of visionary/mystical quality to this because one is able to put aside the global politics of pollution, of technological disenfranchisement, of consequent domination and social injustice, of rapacious overconsumption by the North. Politics, the market, and all inherited Enlightenment anthropocentric real-izings are not costed in here. It is with this group that Bush wanted to link Gore. Nature is the divine Logos, a divinity long bespoiled by man's progress.

Is this the underside of the Enlightenment Project: humankind's own disavowal of itself, a last refuge in nature in order to silence forever humankind's inexorable will to power? The unbelievable determination and energy to hold the line for nature against the assault of man, to fight tooth and nail for the sanctity of each and every species, and, most glaringly, to never heed the pleas and arguments of the human community—is this not part of that modern temper that railed against the very absurdity of man's own efforts and accomplishments and opted for nihilism and absurdism rather than become party to the blindness and cruelty of our self-applauded humanity? Is there not despair and a tragic self-denial in this last grasp at a nature that can be the last holdout from our own will to destroy? Destroy ourselves but let us at least leave the planet to go on to better things. Everything in this 'mystical Green' narrative is represented from within this late modernist frame. All the angst of the twentieth-century tragic vision is here.

I want to go on to a postmodern 'Green' and then on to Wim Wenders' *Until the End of the World*, a film that not only gives us the images of our own fears regarding the market, the environment and technology but shows us how 'we can go on.' But I cannot ignore another way of handling this vague and nebulous fear we have that we are destroying the world outside ourselves because we cannot seem to continue to live or end ourselves without doing so. I say nebulous because no part of it is personal in the way that a 'mystical Green' can make it personal, whether that is pathology or pantheism remains undecidable. The deep troubling quality of this haunting has to do with our apparent helplessness as individuals. It is on the order of the bomb dropping nightmare that was wrapped in the dark, incomprehensible shroud of the Cold War. Now lurking behind every spell of warmer than usual winter weather is the greenhouse effect, an insidious global warming that ultimately melts the polar ice caps and inundates us "while we sleep!" I can see a terrifying cinema lobby poster with those words slashed at the bottom.

There are those who face this haunting with a modernist problem-solving optimism. We can maintain a clean habitat if we isolate, describe, experiment, hypothesize, and make changes based on our nonpartisan, objective analyses. Once the truth is known regarding global warming, toxic wastes, population growth, urbanization, secondary smoke inhalation, desertification, water and air pollution, biodiversity, energy conservation, electromagnetic fields (EMF), food production, chemical additives, non-biodegradables, harmful emissions, and so on we can adopt the right solution and solve the problem. One by one. And adopt whatever technology is needed to do so.

Zgymunt Bauman captures the viciousness of this cycle:

Problems get bigger. So do their consequences. The less relative one autonomy, the more relative the other. The more thoroughly the initial problems have been solved, the less manageable are the problems that result. There was a task to increase agricultural crops—resolved thanks to the nitrates. And there was a task of steadying water supplies—resolved thanks to stemming the flow of water with dams. Then there was a task to purify water supplies poisoned by the seepage of unabsorbed nitrates—resolved thanks to the application of phosphates in specially built sewage-processing plants. Then there was a task to destroy toxic algae that thrive in reservoirs rich in phosphate compounds.[6]

It is no doubt a bedrock difficulty for modernity's method to be able to isolate and fix an autonomous event in nature, to first decouple the observer from the observed and then to decouple any one form of life from the sum total of life, and finally to decouple that isolated form from the sum total of all internal and external circumstances.[7] If indeed our own awareness does not arise from any linearity and consecutiveness in our trains of thought or streams of consciousness but arises out of contingency, an unpredictability that we share with all living things, then the first problem to be resolved is our own awareness.[8] There is a related but not fully realized awareness of this in the modernist's admission that problems in nature, like global warming, are too interlaced with unfixable variables, too replete with contingency, too imbricated in contemporaneous goings-on, too "implicate" to use the word David Bohm has adopted, to allow us to isolate facts and come up with definite answers.[9]

The market take on this is that the market can only proceed in an unfettered way because we have already decoupled ourselves from nature. We have already taken ourselves out of the flux of natural forces and asserted our independence through technology. The only way to maintain this freedom and mastery is through technologies. We cannot stabilize the flux of nature but we can create a market-driven alternative technopoly that leaves the contingencies of nature far behind. We could enhance our well-being even though nature ceased to exist.

I would associate a postmodern green politics with a kind of politically radical environmentalism. What these deep ecologists want to do is *not* ignore the socioeconomic logic of the unfettered free market, *not* ignore the social injustice and ecological injustice this logic causes, and *not* ignore the fact that "there may come a time when we face a choice between preserving human beings or preserving nature."[10] The problem-solving, instrumentalized reasoning and systematizing, the distancing and objectifying of nature were initiated and carried on within the Enlightenment paradigm. An earlier, opposing Renaissance temper mediated nature and consciousness through magic, thus coupling different narratives without imposing either dialectic or hierarchy. But that chaos of correspondences, none of which could be brought to a universal rule of judgment after the Reformation, left nature and man unfettered, unaccountable. A modernist scheme of accountability begins with Descartes and only begins to end now when this white mythology begins to unravel itself. [11]

This enlightened white mythology led us down the path to ever-increasing economic growth based on the continual creation of new needs, both inspired by and fulfilled by endlessly proliferating technologies that have no purpose other than generating needs, enabling consumption, and thus increasing economic growth. Gilles Deleuze points out that what we have in the technologically advanced countries is "no longer a capitalism for production but for the product, which is to say, for being sold or marketed." What this market wants "to sell is services and what it wants to buy is stocks." Thus a former logic of production that created distinct "analogical spaces that converge towards an owner" has now become the logic of the product whereby "the family, the school, the army, the factory are no longer . . . distinct analogical spaces" but "deformable and transformable." Deleuze categorizes the journey society has made thusly: *societies of sovereignty* ("to tax rather than to organize production, to rule on death rather than to administer life") led to *disciplinary societies* ("the individual never ceases passing from one closed environment to another, each having its own laws"), and finally to *societies of control* in which individuals are kept in "states of perpetual metastability"—"in the societies of control one is never finished with anything—the corporation, the educational system, the armed services being metastable states coexisting in one and the same modulation, like a universal system of deformation." [12]

If humanity itself is now deformable and transformable within this market-created society of control, what is nature but obviously something that has, like egalitarianism in American democracy, already been written off, already been superseded, surpassed, scheduled for extinction? This knowledge is at the heart of deep ecology:

that a market logic has decoupled itself both from nature and humanity and that decoupling began with the distancing and objectification of both. This logic, which is nothing more than a loud whir of contingency, drowns out all living voices, sets them within its own flux so that no opposition is possible because both identity and difference become market products, or, they are made to serve the flux of the market.

The deep ecologists display a deep incredulity toward the master narrative of a current, capitalist market logic. Nature cannot be saved without dismantling this logic. And this involves an unraveling of the modernist spin that has divided humankind from nature while celebrating decoupled technologies. These technologies promise us, via the market they service, a materialistic well-being as long as we, nature and humankind, are kept in a perpetual state of metastability. We are in state of ever-readiness to be retrained and reprogrammed, deformed and transformed, controlled and modulated.

Deep ecology cracks this grand narrative deeply, down to its bedrock foundationalism. It points out that we pay for this well-being with the diversity of nature itself, including ourselves. Our market well-being has already proven that it can do no more than retain "as a constant the extreme poverty of three quarters of humanity, too poor for debt, too numerous for confinement."[13] Deep ecology sets up a postmodern contending by setting up a challenge to the current socioeconomic logic. It questions the uninterrupted play of the market and also the paradigm of modernity out of which emerges the presumption that there can be such a thing as one indisputable narrative of truth, in this case, the market narrative.

Well-being became identified within this market narrative and thus reduced our American Dream to self-interest. That path of self-interest and fastest possible economic growth is not a detour off the path of modernity. Rather it is a fulfillment of that decoupling of matter and mind that Descartes began when he 'cogitated' himself out of a Renaissance spirit, a spirit that has been reborn in present day postmodernism.[14]

Those arguing that biodiversity enhances the quality of life and that man has no moral right to permanently destroy nature claim eternal and irrefutable status for these arguments. "These arguments are based on intuitions of fundamental values: but they are tragically lacking in persuasive force in our materialistic world."[15] The problem here is that this whole sense of foundational values derives from modernist "forms of civic culture, grounded in Enlightenment universalist conceptions of reason and knowledge."[16] The market has already raked through fundamental values and has extracted what Deleuze calls "dominant forms of signification" so that what "enhances the quality of life" signifies only within a privileged chain of "ceaseless consumption, planned obsolescence, and inexhaustible resources."[17]

These same fundamental values have already been technologically "morphed" ("morphing is the punningly named, computer-based image processing technique that gave *Terminator 2: Judgment Day* much of its technodazzle") so that the whole dualism of man versus nature and the need to applaud technology or defend nature is facing extinction.[18] The new "morphed" identities of man, nature, and machine involve man's "joint kinship with animals and machines."[19] "In this possible tomorrow," Mark Dery writes, "the physical body is intertextual and endlessly recombinant, offering itself, like the bits that make up computer memory, for read/write activities." [20]

The foundation of fundamental human values is a value call and values change although it is the mesmerizing quality of modernity to leave us feeling we have an unbroken legacy of such values, that our values are legitimated by an unimpeachable naturalness and "necessity."[21] Deep ecology voices its differences from the imperialism of modernity's technopoly and in the absence of any legitimizing *Aufhebung* such differences cannot be denied.[22] Deep ecology's own differences are not grounded in a sui generis reality, however. Green space and self space parody each other in what may prove to be humankind's last dance around the planet.

The film *Until the End of the World* begins with catastrophe and our indifference to it: "The year the Indian nuclear satellite went out of control Claire couldn't care less. She was living her own nightmare." Claire's dance around the planet is her own but we soon realize that it is a mythic journey we are all making in the present, a journey that begins in a market notion of well-being and plays out that well-being as a nightmare, scenes of the immediate future that haunt us now.

Claire is nothing more than what we have become by the year 1999. She is all ours: her indifference, her single-minded pursuit of her own well-being that finally locates itself in a 'beloved' ("a man with whom I would at this moment be making love"), her deformation and transformation as she becomes part of Henry Farber's attempt to visualize through technology "the human soul singing to itself," her ultimate narcissistic withdrawal as she drowns in the "noctural imagery" of her own mind, and finally her recuperation and redemption through "the healing power of words," words written by another that tell a story of a world outside herself, of a world of difference outside her own totally decoupled life-world.

"We can go on," we hear sung at the film's end by "breaking the rules." What rules we ask? What rules but those that have led Claire on a frenetic pursuit of her own pleasure, endless self-gratification, endless consumption, endless ministerings to one's own well-being? She begins in decadence in Venice, waking up hung over, the party still going on, the man she slept with unconscious beside her. There is no satisfaction here and she journeys on until a traffic jam—which her auto computer reports but cannot prevent—takes her beyond the "End of Map Zone," beyond the world that the computer has mapped.

Contingency, chance accident, again intrudes and she meets two thieves with a bag full of money. She can earn 30 percent of that huge sum if she takes it to Paris, which she does. That money—the source of what our American democracy now identifies as our well-being— has its own journey in the film: it is tossed on Claire's bed and we feast our eyes upon it, some of it is stolen by her beloved, Sam Farber, it is counted, wrapped in packets and frozen, it is used to hire a detective to find Sam Farber, it is used by Claire to go from one country to another in pursuit of Sam, it is stolen by a crazed used car salesman, it enables Sam to get the pictures his father needs to carry on his "computer visualization of dreams" project. And then, after we have followed the money to Henry Farber's laboratory in a cave in Australia's outback, it vanishes.

The trail of money has led us to scientist Henry Farber's laboratory where he is in the process of "extending the envelope," of breaking the rules that have up until then enveloped our reality. Here "science is more important than the end of the world." The end of the world is feared when a nuclear blast in space knocks out all electromagnetic power. Indian technology has already led to a nuclear blast in space and begun an "end of the world" scenario, the scenario of the film, the scenario that haunts our technological dreams. Stranded in the outback, Claire, the Farbers, her former lover and narrator of the film, a thief, and a host of aboriginals who work in the lab with the Farbers, cannot put an end to their total absorption in their own aggrandizement, their own empowerment through technology.

Farber has invented an odd-looking pair of goggles that capture what goes on in the human act of seeing. It records the brain's activities that are fed into a computer and then available for retrieval, for visualization. Farber has found a way to plug into the brain's circuitry as it pictures for itself the world out there, how it brings into itself representations of the real. There is a two-stage journey that Henry Farber makes: at first he wants only to use the technology so that his blind wife, played by Jeanne Moreau, can see, and then after she dies, he decides to use the computer to capture the "human soul singing to itself" in dreams.

This may be the epitomy of narcissism, the deepest contemplation of self, the dark journey into self space. Is this not the place where personal self-interest and market needs creation must finally wind up? The future of needs creation market lies in the unexpressed desires within. The future of self-interest lies in the uninterrupted viewing of the self's inner spin. All nature can hear a "huge sucking sound" (to use a Perotian image) as man turns inward and links his once outwardly reaching five senses to the dance within. The introspective gaze cannot remain distanced as it is drawn into the inner spin. Life is now totally reduced to individual self-interest as it is brought to visualization by the computer. Interaction is with these inner visualizations and no longer with the world out there.

Both Claire and her beloved, Sam, are no longer in a dance around the planet but now in a dance within themselves. They are not only blind and deaf to nature but invisible to each other. The computer has brought them to a state of catatonia, held immobile before monitor images of their own inner workings. Is this not the culmination of the technological journey itself, namely, that well-being is a totalizing satiation of all conceivable human needs? Here in this computer-mediated navel-gazing, humankind winds up needing only more of itself, more of what does the wanting, the dance out of which all needs and desires arise. Both Claire and Sam consume themselves, the last service performed for human-kind by a technology geared to bring us to ever-expanding levels of consumption.

The aborigines, who assist Henry Farber with the project to make Jeanne Moreau see, leave him when he begins his dream visualization project after her death. Both departures—of the wife through death and of the aborigines by choice—become challenges to the view that science is more important than the end of the world. When the aborigines return to cure the son, Sam Farber, they lie him down between two of the "old fellas," embodiments of the force of nature, who "take his dream" and thereby restore him to the "dance of life."

Black hand extended to white hand to raise the white man out of his nightmare, his technological dream. "Time to get that shit out of your system. You're my brother. Come." These words clash with the words spoken by the father, Henry Farber, when his own black brother begs him to leave his laboratory. "It's alright for you to leave. You're a black fellow. It's not alright for a white fellow to leave." Technology is the way the white man can deal with his burden and it is this dream that the "old fellas" will remove from his son's soul to save him.

The message is clear: Sam's personal salvation has little effect on the nuclear explosion of the Indian satellite in space. Science is more important than the end of the world because it has power to bring about the end of the world. It is, in fact, the view that science is more important than the world that shapes the very end of that world. In the end, the end of egalitarianism, the end of nature, the end of the world—all these are not costed in within the spin of free market-technology-needs creation-consumption-market growth-free market.

The lyrics sung at film's end—"we can go on"—do not mean we have discovered how to go on, or that we have even stopped doing what will ultimately stop the world from going on. "We can go on" after this nuclear blast in space. We have a green light to go until the end of the world. We have not been stopped so we must be still going. There is no redemptive message here, no new plan of reformation and renewal.

The blind Jeanne Moreau has already 'seen' with computer mediation the sad state of things and she decides not to go on. Her death is like a giving in to infinite sorrow and despair. The images brought to her eyes by the computer stand in stark contrast to the images of the world her own mind has created since she lost her sight at the age of twelve. As an elderly woman, her well-being is grounded in those youthful images of the world. Those shapes and colors are the building blocks with which she has continued to narrate the world to herself. Her blind self-spin had extended a motherly beneficence and benediction upon us all. Her wisdom turned out to be ill-grounded.

Her husband's gift to her—his world-capturing machine-readable goggles—does not fill her with the joy of actually seeing the faces and the world that she had for so long only imagined. That reality is not fact to her but only representations to be interpreted, to be assigned value out of the world of valuing she is already within. Where she had always construed promise, she sees now only hopelessness; joy is saddened, and the computer world of images only darkens the blind woman's life-world. The will to live sustained by her blind self-constructions finally gives way to this assault of worldly darkness. How much darker it all appears when after so many years the computer makes it reappear. How much darker than what her own mind had imagined.

Our hope finally is in Claire. At film's end she is out there in space now orbiting the earth, watching for pollution crimes, for the dire effects of technologies. She is no longer mesmerized by self-interest but now gazes outward at the whole planet. Well-being has been extended outward, laterally, crisscrossing the entire globe. She has broken out of the market narrative of market progress through deeper and deeper levels of self-absorption. Self-interest has been countered.

In response to her question after reading Sam Elliot's novel *Dance around the Planet* "But now? What happens now?" she is told "That's for you to invent." If there are bad dreams that come out of technology they are our dreams, our inventions. But first we must take the aborigine's advice: we must lie down flat on the earth itself and "get that shit out of our system." And then imagine, concoct, invent dreams that do not haunt us. Claire celebrates her thirtieth birthday out in space, using her discriminative visual abilities to scan the earth's surface below. She is born into a new dream, a dream of watchfulness, a dream of caring.

NOTES

PROLOGUE

1. Wolfgang Iser, *Prospecting: From Reader Response To Literary Anthropology* (Baltimore: Johns Hopkins University Press, 1989), p. 236.

2. I am here referring to Wolfgang Iser's notion of "the play of the text," which I shall say more about in the *Intermezzo* chapter. I discuss this at greater length in Chapter One—" 'The Argument': The Play of Disorder" in *Mots d'ordre* (Albany: SUNY Press, 1992), pp. 15–27.

BASIC AND POSTMODERN INSTINCTS

1. Jacques Derrida, "La mythologie blanche, " *Poetique* 5 (1971): 4.

2. See especially Paul de Man, *Blindness and Insight: Essays in the Rhetoric of Contemporary Criticism*, 2d ed. (Minnesota: University of Minnesota Press, 1983).

3. See my own *Mots d'Ordre: Disorder in Literary Worlds* (Albany: State University of New York Press, 1992) for an extended discussion of this, and the work of Wolfgang Iser, especially *Prospecting: From Reader Response to Literary Anthropology* (Baltimore: Johns Hopkins University Press, 1989), on which I base much of my own theorizing here.

4. Catherine Belsey in "Addressing the Subject" in her *Critical Practice* (New York: Methuen, 1980) likes the word "interpellate"—culture drives itself between our words, interrupts our self–constructions. Derrida also gives us the sense of this checkered constituting and consti-

tuted by sort of subject when he asserts that subjectivity is "absolutely indispensable" but "inscribed in a system of *differance*." See "Structure, Sign and Play in the Discourse of the Human Sciences," *Writing and Difference*, trans. Alan Bass (Chicago: University of Chicago Press, 1978), p. 271; *Positions*, trans. Alan Bass (Chicago: University of Chicago Press, 1981), pp. 28–29.

5. Jean–Francois Lyotard, *The Postmodern Condition* (Minneapolis: University of Minnesota Press, 1984).

6. Zygmunt Bauman, *Modernity and Ambivalence* (Ithaca: Cornell University Press, 1991), p.7.

7. Zygmunt Bauman, *Modernity and the Holocaust* (Ithaca: Cornell University Press, 1989).

8. I go into the problems of New Historicist 'retrieval' in Chapter 9 of *Mots d'Ordre*.

9. Jurgen Habermas, "Modernity versus Postmodernity," *New German Critique* 22 (Winter 1981).

HUNTING THE HAUNTED HEART

1. *The Oregonian*, May 20, 1992, p. C4.

2. From a flysheet opposing the conferment of an Honorary Degree of Doctor of Letters on M. Jacques Derrida, Regent House, Cambridge University, May 1992.

3. On rereading this I realize how much I owe to the work of Norman O. Brown, especially *Life Against Death: A Psychoanalytic Interpretation of History*, 2d ed. (Middletown, Conn.: Wesleyan University Press, 1985, © 1959).

4. To follow the bibliography of difference, identity, and Otherness is to follow work in postmodernist studies. The electronic journal, *Postmodern Culture*, provides the most comprehensive and up–to–date bibliography. For a recent discussion, see the summer 1992 issue of *October*, "The Identity in Question." The whole dilemma of modernity's design of identity is handled in Zygmunt Bauman's *Legislators and Interpreters* (Oxford: Polity Press, 1987). For an interesting discussion of the "stranger" see Bauman's "Strangers: The Social Construction of Universality and Particularity," *Telos* 78 (Winter 1988–1989): 7–42.

5. For views of classic realism, see Colin MacCabe, "Realism and the Cinema: Notes on Some Brechtian Theses" and "Theory and Film: Principles of Realism and Pleasure," in *Tracking the Signifier* (Minneapolis: University of Minnesota Press, 1985) as well as Catherine Belsey, "Addressing the Subject" and "Deconstructing the Text," in *Critical Practice* (London: Methuen, 1980).

6. Life-world or *Lebenswelt* encompasses the variety of interactions among consciousness of self, others, world, and time. See Edmund Husserl, *The Crisis of European Sciences and Transcendental Phenomenology* (Evanston: Northwestern University Press, 1970).

7. Zygmunt Bauman, *Modernity and the Holocaust* (Ithaca: Cornell University Press, 1989).

8. Arthur Kroker and David Cook, *The Postmodern Scene: Excremental Culture and Hyper–Aesthetics*, 2d ed. (New York: St. Martin's Press, 1986), p. 8.

MOVING LATERALLY ACROSS THE CAPES OF FEAR

1. I extend Benoit Mandelbrot's notion of fractal geometry to what I call a "fractal sense of reality," one that is disruptive, full of gaps and fissures, discontinuities and irregularities, in opposition to a Euclidean order of continuous lines, right angles, and perfect circles. See Benoit Mandelbrot, *The Fractal Geometry of Nature* (New York: Freeman, 1977).

2. I take the notion of an absent universal rule of judgment from Jean-Francois Lyotard, *The Differend; Phrases in Dispute*, trans. Georges Van Den Abbeele (Minneapolis: University of Minnesota Press, 1988).

3. Michel Foucault, "Panopticism," in *Discipline and Punish: The Birth of the Prison* (New York: Vintage Books, 1979).

4. As I reread this piece the headlines are registering our cultural shock at Woody Allen's desire taking him into the arms of the adopted daughter of Mia Farrow, his long-time girlfriend. Has Woody been 'evil' all this time? Must we revisit all his films and reconnect the signs? Was desire always more important in Woody's films than personal responsibility, family values, and the social order?

HOME ALONE . . .

1. It is hardly surprising that in our present attempt to make cultural difference primary we are entranced with the topic of Otherness. I am not concerned here with political representation of the Other and the notion of "recognition" that Charles Taylor, for instance, discusses in *Multiculturalism and the Politics of Recognition* (Princeton: Princeton University Press, 1992), or sexual difference as presented in Craig Owen's classic essay, "The Discourse of Others" in *The Anti–Aesthetic: Essays on Postmodern Culture*, ed. Hal Foster (Port Townsend: Bay Press, 1983). The question I raise here is the accessibility of Otherness, a psychological matter, still most clearly pursued by phenomenological psychology. See for instance, Jan van den Berg's *A Different Existence* (Pittsburgh: DuQuesne University Press, 1972).

FREE MARKET OR FREE PLAY?

1. Julian Dibbell, "Reality Used to Be a Friend of Mine," *Voice Film Special*, June 2, 1992, p. 3.

2. B. Ray Horn and David Ellis, "Chaos in Communication: Reductio ad absurdum," unpublished paper, p. 4.

3. Ibid., p. 4.

4. Ibid.

5. Gilles Deleuze, "Postscript on the Societies of Control," *October* 59 (Winter 1992): 4.

6. Ibid., p. 6.

7. Ibid.

8. Zygmunt Bauman, "Is There a Postmodern Sociology?" *Theory, Culture, and Society* 5 (1988): 219.

9. Ibid., pp. 220–21.

10. Ibid., p. 222.

11. Ibid., p. 220.

12. David L. Hall, "Modern China and the Postmodern West," pp. 40–41.

13. Jurgen Habermas, "Modernity versus Postmodernity," *New German Critique* 22 (Winter 1981): 7.

14. Ibid., p. 8.

INTERMEZZO

1. "To consume/respond . . . is to engage what heretofore had no existence for us." Such engagement is not a matter of representation, not a matter yet of bringing something to a sayable level. See *Mots d'Ordre: Disorder in Literary Worlds* (Albany: State University of New York Press, 1992), *passim* for ways in which I try to work this into our dealings with disorder, or what 'haunts' us.

2. Wolfgang Iser, "The Play of the Text," in *Languages of the Unsayable* (New York: Columbia University Press, 1989), p. 327.

3. Roland Barthes, "Inaugural Lecture, College de France," in *A Barthes Reader*, ed. Susan Sontag (New York: Hill and Wang, 1982), pp. 457–478.

4. In discussing Alasdair MacIntyre's view that we indeed have lost this sense of security, R. W. Sleeper writes: "What MacIntyre misses in modernism is the sense of an authoritative tradition of agreed–upon canons of rationality that can be counted upon to be of use in resolving new problems and controversies as they arise in the everchanging circumstances of this postmodern world." ("Whose Reason? What Canon? Critical Reasoning and Conflicting Ideas of Rationality," in *Critical Reasoning in Contemporary Culture* [Albany: State University of New York Press, 1992], pp. 208–9).

5. This sort of Enlightenment 'functionalism' is what Christopher Newfield calls "managerial democracy," a cultural top–down authority. See "What Was Political Correctness? Race, the Right, and Managerial Democracy in the Humanities," *Critical Inquiry* 19 (Winter 1993): 308–36.

6. George F. Will, "Literary Politics," *Newsweek*, April 22, 1991, p. 72.

7. Francisco Varela, "Living Ways of Sense–Making: A Middle Path," in *Disorder and Order*, ed. Paisley Livingston (Saratoga, Calif.: Anma Libri, 1984), p. 219.

8. Thomas Bridges, *The Primacy of Cultural Difference: The Postmodern Reconstruction of Civil Society and Personal Life*. Forthcoming in *The Postmodern Culture* Series, State University of New York Press.

9. Jacques Derrida, *Of Grammatology*, trans. Gayatri Chakravorty Spivak (Baltimore: Johns Hopkins University Press, 1976), p. 62.

10. I owe this line of thought to the work of Thomas Bridges, especially *The Primacy of Cultural Difference: The Postmodern Reconstruction of Civil Society and Personal Life*, forthcoming, State University of New York Press.

11. See Roland Barthes, *The Rustle of Language*, trans. Richard Howard (New York: Hill and Wang, 1986), p. 160.

12. Colin MacCabe,"Preface" to *Fredric Jameson, The Geopolitical Aesthetic: Cinema and Space in the World System* (Bloomington: Indiana University Press, 1992), p. xii.

13. See Gilles Deleuze and Felix Guattari, *Anti–Oedipus: Capitalism and Schizophrenia*, trans. Robert Hurley, Mark Seem, and Helen R. Lane (New York: Viking, 1977, © 1972).

14. I owe this notion of seduction and repression of the market to Zygmunt Bauman, "Is There a Postmodern Sociology?" *Theory, Culture, and Society* 5 (1988): 217–37.

15. Angela McRobbie, "Post–Marxism and Cultural Studies: A Post–script," in *Cultural Studies*, ed. Lawrence Grossberg et al. (New York: Routledge, 1992), p. 730.

16. Thomas Bridges, "Postmodernism and the Primacy of Cultural Difference," *Inquiry* (March 1992): 23.

17. A contradictory 'serious' postmodernism is like metafiction that is really late modernist/formalist navel–gazing, always trying to equate its own narrating with the conditions of the 'real world.' See my discussion of metafiction in *Mots d'Ordre*, pp. 198–205. See also Linda Hutcheon, *A Politics of Postmodernism* (London: Routledge, 1989) for distinction between metafiction's modernist formalism and postmodern historiographic fiction or inscribing the prevailing order and also scribing against it.

18. G. Douglas Atkinsin in *Estranging the Familiar: Toward a Revitalized Critical Writing* (Athens: University of Georgia Press, 1992) takes a step that a move toward postmodernity asks us to take: writing not only modernity's *article*, a form of writing that presumes to be done from some Archimedean point of critical observation, but the *essay*, a crisscrossing of personal lives and impersonal discourse.

19. Bridges, "Postmodernism and the Primacy of Cultural Difference."

20. Gilles Deleuze and Felix Guattari, "Rhizome," in *On The Line*, trans. John Johnston (New York: Semiotext(e), 1983).

21. David Bohm, "Postmodern Science and a Postmodern World," in *The Reenchantment of Science: Postmodern Proposals*, ed. David Ray Griffin (Albany: State University of New York Press, 1988).

22. Zygmunt Bauman, *Modernity and Ambivalence* (Ithaca: Cornell University Press, 1991).

23. Henry Giroux, "Postmodernism as Border Pedagogy: Redefining the Boundaries of Race and Ethnicity," in *Postmodernism, Feminism, and Cultural Politics*, ed. Henry Giroux (Albany: State University of New York Press, 1991). Reprinted and quoted from *A Postmodern Reader*, ed. Joseph Natoli and Linda Hutcheon (Albany: State University of New York Press, 1993), p. 472.

24. Leslie Fiedler, *What Was Literature? Class Culture and Mass Society* (New York: Simon and Schuster, 1982).

25. bell hooks, *Yearning: Race, Gender, and Cultural Politics* (Boston: South End Press, 1990), p. 31.

26. Ian Angus, "Learning to Stop: A Critique of General Rhetoric," in *The Critical Turn: Rhetoric and Philosophy in Postmodern Discourse* (Carbondale: Southern Illinois University Press, 1993), p. 183.

27. John Keane, quoted in ibid., p. 188.

28. Ibid. p. 197.

29. Ibid., p. 202.

30. Ibid., p. 203.

31. Ibid., p. 198.

32. Ibid.

33. Ibid.

34. Ian Angus and Lenore Langsdorf, "Unsettled Borders: Envisioning Critique at the Postmodern Site," in *The Critical Turn* (Carbondale: Southern Illinois University Press, 1993) p. 14.

THE FREE PLAY OF POPULAR FILM

1. Gilles Deleuze and Felix Guattari discuss this "rhizome" ordering in *A Thousand Plateaus: Capitalism and Schizophrenia,* trans. Brian Massumi (Minneapolis: University of Minnesota Press, 1987). See also John W. Murphy and Jung Min Choi, "Theoretical Justification for a Politics of Difference," *New Orleans Review* 19 (Summer 1992).

2. Jurgen Habermas, "Modernity versus Postmodernity," *New German Critique,* 22 (Winter 1981): 9.

3. Zygmunt Bauman, "Is There a Postmodern Sociology?" *Theory, Culture, and Society* 5 (1988): 234.

4. "New York lost its traditional garment trade and turned to the production of debt and fictitious capital instead. . . . The trade is as vigorous as that which once dominated the harbour. But 'today, the telephone lines deliver the world's cash to be remixed as if in a bottling plant, squirted into different containers, capped and shipped back out' "(David Harvey, *The Condition of Postmodernity: An Enquiry into the Origins of Social Change* [Oxford: Basil Blackwell, 1989], pp. 327–35, 356–59).

GECKOID DEMOCRACY AND THE GARFIELDIAN AMERICAN DREAM

1. James W. Michaels and Phyllis Berman, "My Story—Michael Milken," *Forbes,* March 16, 1992, p. 78.

2. William Greider, "The Mess, the Scandal of the S&Ls" *Dissent,* Summer 1990, p. 297.

3. Larry Reibstein, "Hail Felons Well Met," *Newsweek,* October 7, 1991, p. 44.

4. Ibid.

THE UNFORGIVEN

1. William Gibson, *Neuromancer* (New York: Ace Books, 1984), p. 51.

2. Arthur Schlesinger Jr., "Was America a Mistake: Reflections on the Long History of Efforts to Debunk Columbus and His Discovery," *Atlantic* 270:3 (September 1992): 16–30.

3. Thomas Bridges, "Postmodernism and the Primacy of Cultural Difference," *Inquiry* (March 1992): 3.

4. Schlesinger, "Was America a Mistake," p. 27.

5. Ibid., pp. 27–28.

6. Ibid., p. 22.

7. Ibid., p. 30.

8. See Mary Lefkowitz, "Not out of Africa," *The New Republic,* February 10, 1992, pp. 29–36. She reviews Martin Bernal, *Black Athena* and *Cadmean Letters,* Cheikh Anta Diop, *The African Origin of Civilization,* George G. M. James, *Stolen Legacy,* Yosef ben-Jochanan, *Africa, Mother of Western Civilization,* and John G. Jackson, *Introduction to African Civilization.*

ROBBIN' N' THE HOOD N' THE NABE

1. "Like the historical Arthur . . . the real Robin Hood eludes the historian's grasp. The further back one traces his story, the less one succeeds in finding out." (Maurice Keen, "Robin Hood: A Peasant Hero," *History Today* 41 [October 1991]: 20).

2. Andrew Kopkind and Alexander Cockburn, "The Democrats, Perot and the Left," *The Nation,* July 20–27, 1992, p. 85.

3. Ibid.

4. bell hooks, "Postmodern Blackness," in *Yearnings: Race, Gender, and Cultural Politics* (Boston: South End Press, 1990), p. 29.

5. David Breskin, "Spike Lee: The *Rolling Stone* Interview," *Rolling Stone,* July 11, 1991, pp. 63–70.

GUNS AND PROVOLONE

1. American Survey Column, "John Gotti and the American Dream of Crime," *Economist,* December 7, 1991, p. 32.

2. James Cook, "But Where Are the Don's Yachts?" *Forbes 400,* October 21, 1991, p. 126.

3. Marshall Blonsky, "A (Post)Modern (Alleged) Mobster," *Harper's,* October 1990, p. 45.

4. *Forbes,* April 13, 1992, p. 66.

5. Thomas Byrne Edsall, *The New Politics of Inequality* (New York: W. W. Norton, 1984), p. 222.

6. Anthony DeCurtis, "What the Streets Mean: An Interview with Martin Scorcese," *South Atlantic Quarterly* 91:2 (Spring 199): 434, 439.

7. Victor Turner, *The Ritual Process: Structure and Anti–Structure* (Chicago: Aldine, 1969), p. 95.

AFTER *BOB ROBERTS*

1. It is the absence of such a critique that Christopher Norris, for instance, says is what's wrong with postmodernism. See *What's Wrong with Postmodernism* (Baltimore: Johns Hopkins University Press, 1991).

2. Terrence Rafferty, "This Land Is His Land," *The New Yorker* September 7, 1992, pp. 84–86.

3. See David Bohm, "Postmodern Science and a Postmodern World," in *The Reenchantment of Science, Postmodern Proposals*, ed. David Ray Griffin (Albany: State University of New York Press, 1988).

4. See Jacques Derrida, *Speech and Phenomena*, trans. David B. Allison (Evanston: Northwestern University Press, 1973).

5. John W. Murphy and Jung Min Choi, "Theoretical Justification for a Politics of Difference," *New Orleans Review* 19 (Summer 1992): 62–68.

THE FINAL DANCE AROUND THE PLANET

1. Gerald K. Kreyche, "Has Environmentalism Gone Too Far?" *USA Today*, January 1992, p. 98.

2. Lewis Thomas, "Crickets, Bats, Cats and Chaos," *Audubon,* March–April 1992, p. 99.

3. Marc Cooper, "Blame It on Rio," *Voice,* June 16, 1992, p. 27.

4. Kreyche, "Has Environmentalism Gone Too Far?" p. 98.

5. Martin W. Lewis, *Green Delusions: An Environmentalist Critique of Radical Environmentalism* (Durham: Duke University Press, 1992).

6. Zygmunt Bauman, *Modernity and Ambivalence* (Ithaca: Cornell University Press, 1991), p. 13.

7. It is physicist–philosopher David Bohm's view that this de–coupling is no longer possible within our postmechanistic or quantum physics: "It is a mistake to think that the world has a totally defined existence separate from our own and that there is merely an external 'interaction' between us and the world" ("Postmodern Science and a Postmodern World," p. 67).

8. I am endebted to Thomas, "Crickets, Bats, Cats and Chaos," for this thought.

9. David Bohm, *Wholeness and the Implicate Order* (London: Routledge and Kegan Paul, 1980). See also a very brief but informative essay, "Postmodern Science and a Postmodern World," in *The Reenchantment of Science: Postmodern Proposals*, ed. David Ray Griffin (Albany: State University of New York Press, 1988).

10. John Terborgh, "A Matter of Life and Death," *New York Review of Books,* November 5, 1992, p. 6.

11. See Jacques Derrida, "La mythologie blanche," *Poetique* 5 (1971) for links among white men, Western culture, its *mythos*, and reason.

12. Gilles Deleuze, "Postscript on the Societies of Control," 59 *October* (Winter 1992), p. 5.

13. Ibid., p. 6.

14. I follow the link that Stephen Toulmin has made between the Renaissance and postmodernity in *The Cosmopolis* and *The Return To Cosmology.*

15. Terborgh, "Matter of Life and Death," p. 6.

16. Thomas Bridges, "Postmodernism and the Primacy of Cultural Difference," *Inquiry* (March 1992): 23.

17. Mark Dery, "Cyberculture," *South Atlantic Quarterly* 91:3 (Summer 1992): 513.

18. Ibid., p. 501.

19. Donna Haraway, *Simians, Scyborgs and Women: The Reinvention of Nature* (London: Free Association, 1991).

20. Dery, "Cyberculture," p. 520.

21. For a succinct discussion of "fact" and "value" from a postmodern perspective, see John W. Murphy and Jung Min Choi, "Theoretical Justification for a Politics of Difference," *New Orleans Review* (1992), p. 63.

22. I take the term "technolopoly" and its meaning from Neil Postman's *Technopoly: The Surrender of Culture to Technology* (New York: Knopf, 1992). It involves "a grand reduction in which human life must find its meaning in machinery and technique."